FILM AND TELEVISION MAKEUP

FILM AND TELEVISION MAKEUP

By Herman Buchman

WITH DEMONSTRATION PHOTOGRAPHS
BY SUSAN E. MEYER

BACK STAGE BOOKS
An imprint of Watson-Guptill Publications / New York

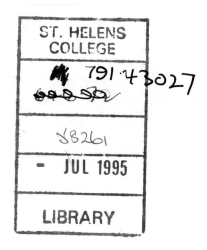
Paperback Edition 1990
A Back Stage Book

Copyright © 1990 by Watson-Guptill Publications

First published 1973 in the United States and Canada by Watson-Guptill Publications,
a division of BPI Communications, Inc.
1515 Broadway, New York, N.Y. 10036

Library of Congress Cataloging-in-Publication Data
Buchman, Herman.
  Film and television makeup / by Herman Buchman ; with
demonstration photographs by Susan E. Meyer.—Pbk. ed.
     p.   cm.
  Reprint. Originally published: New York : Watson-Guptill
Publications, 1973.
  Includes index.
  ISBN 0-8230-7560-5
  1. Film make-up. I. Title.
[PN2068.879   1990]
791.43′027—dc20   90–39107
                                              CIP

Manufactured in Japan.

1 2 3 4 5 6 7 8 9 / 95 94 93 92 91 90

ACKNOWLEDGMENTS

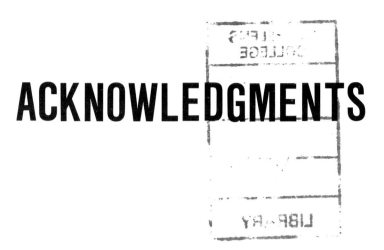

It is only after all the work has been put into a book such as this that I realize how many marvelous people participated in its creation.

I am grateful to Donald Holden and Jules Perel of Watson-Guptill Publications for their vision in recognizing the need for a work of this size and scope. Once again, Susan E. Meyer performed in a double capacity as photographer of all the work segments in the book and just as brilliantly as the editor, a difficult double undertaking indeed.

Another remarkable doubling of talents was performed by Jim Craig who, in addition to the designing of the cover and the layout of the book, also volunteered as the male model for a series of long and arduous sessions.

Two other models, Heather Meredith and Margit Malmstrom, also of Watson-Guptill, volunteered to sit as the female models and added enormously to the final appearance of the book.

I was indeed fortunate to have worked with Jay Fletcher on the film *Born to Win,* and he very kindly agreed to sit for the black actor sequence. Julie Woodson, a professional model, was equally kind in volunteering as model for the black female segment and she was a pleasure to work with.

Stan Lang Production Services were of particular help in my acquiring the two work sequences used in the chapter on television makeup. Ogilvy & Mather as the creative force behind the commercials on great book characters and Mike Cuesta as the director were delightful colleagues. For the aging sequence in television, VanSant Dugdale conceived the idea and Ray Baker's direction brought it to life. Together these commercials constituted the chapter on television makeup.

The chapter on special effects owes a great debt to Segal-Takofsky Productions and to George Segal—the star of *Born to Win*—in particular, for their help in providing the tattoo scenes and the photographs showing the application of tracks. Dominick Dunne, the producer of *Panic in Needle Park,* was of great help in my getting the photographs of Al Pacino and Kitty Wynn as we worked on making that film. It took considerable effort from all of these very considerate people to obtain these photographs while the films were in progress.

Robert Kushner of Ira Senz wigmakers was again enormously helpful in supplying all the wigs and hairpieces used in the demonstrations, and I am indebted to his fine company for its great assistance.

John Chambers, a superb makeup artist from Hollywood, supplied me with his excellent bald caps and his foam latex pieces for the aging chapters.

Without the help of all these generous and gifted people this work would not have been possible.

Finally, as any married author knows, no book is possible without the patience and dedication of his family. My dear wife Dian and my daughter Caitlin had to put up with a great deal of inconvenience and interruptions.

It is over at long last, and I thank you one and all.

CONTENTS

PROFESSIONAL APPLICATIONS OF THIS BOOK

Interested readers will of course study this book for a variety of reasons. Although this book is obviously most appropriate for the student preparing to become a makeup artist, I recognize that this is not the only function this book was meant to perform. Here are some of the other readers I have anticipated when I wrote the book:

TEACHERS OF FILM TECHNIQUES

The entire scope of the book should provide a solid base of discussion and illustration of any problems relating to makeup or hairpieces that can arise in theory or in practice when making a film. I have put forward sound principles and guides so that the film-maker will avoid many of the most common errors that, once filmed, cannot be rectified. The student of film production can, of course, use any of the related chapters as an aid in solving his makeup problems in the actual shooting of his projects.

TEACHERS OF THEATER

My earlier book. *Stage Makeup,* deals with all the problems and techniques arising in that work. It is also important for acting students to understand the different techniques and approaches to makeup used in film and television. Using the basic chapters on makeup for black and white and color film and relating this information to young performers should provide a strong basis for their preparation for professional work.

ACTORS

Major film studios or TV companies usually relieve the actor of any anxiety regarding his or her makeup, since they generally provide the services of a competent professional makeup artist. When, however, the actor or actress is required to work under conditions that do *not* provide this important service, it is absolutely necessary for the performer to be prepared to fill this gap. Using the pertinent chapters on techniques for black and white or color film or, if necessary, the chapters on aging, wigs, and beards can in most instances provide the performer with the additional information needed to adequately solve his problems.

TV STATIONS

If the TV station has a professional makeup artist on staff, the need for information on makeup would be minimal. In many instances, however, TV stations lack personnel for making up local announcers, news broadcasters, weather forecasters, and for programs of regional interest. This situation can be kept under control by assigning a member of the station to study the individual problems, using the techniques illustrated in the chapters on black and white and color.

INDEPENDENT FILM COMPANIES

Without the services of a professional makeup artist, independent film companies can usefully follow the techniques illustrated as a means of resolving most problems concerning skin color, tonal balance, and corrective makeup.

STILL PHOTOGRAPHERS

All of the principles of makeup for motion pictures are directly applicable to still photography. Modification of skin colors, balance of skin tones, and all aspects of corrective makeup can be utilized by the still photographer.

In addition to using all the techniques applicable to motion picture makeup, the still photographer has another advantage, particularly when the subject is to be photographed in a fixed position: he can carry corrective makeup techniques even *farther* than those illustrated in this book. The still photographer may use shadows and highlights on the subject's face so effectively that he can avoid retouching the negative at a later stage. The opportunity to use more extreme shadows and highlights is present as long as the subject is still. If the subject is moving, the still photographer must restrict himself to the degree of corrective work illustrated in these chapters.

BEAUTICIANS AND COSMETICIANS

Cosmetic manufacturers continually inundate the beautician and cosmetician with products, rarely providing adequate information on the proper techniques of application that will furnish the serious student of cosmetology with the skills necessary for the most perfect end product. With this in mind I included a *Course of Study* which, if applied diligently, will assist any student of the art of makeup in realizing these professional goals. This knowledge should provide an invaluable tool for the beautician or cosmetician dedicated to enlarging and satisfying his or her clientele.

THE LIBERATED WOMAN

No matter how free a woman becomes in mind, body, or heart, her ability to alter and/or improve her own appearance to her own taste will always be a source of intense personal gratification. I suggest, therefore, that any woman can, if she wishes, acquire the skills necessary to perform these changes with cosmetics, if this is what she is seeking. Knowing that skill is not achieved overnight, you will need patience. Skill, not magic, produces results.

OVERSEAS FILM INDUSTRIES

Not all nations have established major professional film industries, since these industries require high capital outlays and many years of investment in the training of qualified technicians. To those lacking makeup artists of sufficient skill, I suggest that the diligent and patient use of this book and, in particular, the full utilization of the *Course of Study* will go a long way in helping to establish the skills necessary for producing high quality work.

INTRODUCTION

Organizing my career as a makeup artist into book form seemed very simple at first. But in thinking back I realize that what I learned never progressed in an orderly fashion. Work consisted of many frustrations, challenges, new ideas, imitations of old ones, and very slowly, by taking work seriously, progress came about. Drawing upon these experiences to form a book of instruction in an orderly progression was an entirely different experience for me and, although enjoyable, was extremely difficult.

As I developed this book I had to consider the expectations of the reader at all times, anticipating the variety of needs the book would meet. I tried to visualize a design which would serve all the divergent needs of the readers.

The same problem occurs in all crafts, particularly ones that call for tactile ability: only through slow progression can skills be developed. Hopefully, this book will allow for the progressive development of painting skills and, at the same time, introduce the fundamental principles of the skill in areas of makeup that have the greatest practical usage for the largest number of readers.

The initial chapters on basic techniques and the application of makeup for black and white film and color film for the young male or female performer should be of fundamental service to teachers, students, actors, actresses, still photographers, cosmeticians, and men and women who care to improve their appearance. Only a few practice work sessions should be sufficient to see progress in these areas.

How much additional skill you want to develop and how much time you are prepared to invest in the growth of these skills will determine how much more of the book you will use. For those readers who desire more extensive training, I advise the use of the *Course of Study* section as a guide for developing your skills as far as you need them. I also suggest that you refer to the gallery. You will profit enormously by studying how some of the greatest stars of our time created personalities and characterizations that were unique and memorable.

1 TOOLS AND MATERIALS

A knowledge of the tools and materials is fundamental to every craft. All of the materials you will need as a makeup artist are broken down into appropriate categories and listed below. Although the tools and materials listed here may be produced by a large number of manufacturers, I recommend manufacturers whose products I consider best. At the back of the book you will find a list of suppliers from whom these materials are available.

The following materials represent everything you will need for applying film or television makeup properly and creatively. They constitute the components of the makeup artist's kit.

MAKEUP BASES

The makeup base is a cosmetic that creates the desired skin color. There are many kinds of bases manufactured in a variety of consistencies: hard grease sticks, soft grease paint, modified grease, liquid, pancake, and rubber grease.

Hard Grease Paint: These paints are available in a complete range of colors and come in stick form approximately 5″ long and 1″ thick. Hard grease paint is a long-wearing base, but is difficult to make thin enough for film use. Primarily a stage base, hard grease paint is very rarely used in films.

Soft .Grease Base: These are available in a complete range of colors. Manufactured in a toothpaste type tube, soft grease paint has a creamy texture and is quickly and easily spread. Soft grease paint tends to shine excessively because of its cream content. It must be powdered frequently, but can be used as a body paint. It is rarely used as a base in films.

Liquid Base Paints: These come in a wide range of colors and are bottled. Their primary use is as a body—as opposed to a face—base. Liquid base dries quickly and streaks, which makes it impractical for use as a facial base.

Modified Grease Paints: These are available in a vast range of colors and are manufactured by many companies. Modified grease is packaged as a stick, or in a jar, or in a flat dish container. Its texture is somewhere between a hard stick and soft grease. Its consistency spreads evenly and easily, and when applied thinly, it provides a soft, natural skin texture very practical for films.

Pancakes: Pancake is available in a vast range of colors. It is manufactured in a flat, round container. Pancakes dry quickly and have a matte finish. They can be applied quickly and the colors blend well. This base does not stand up well, but can be touched up easily, which makes it very usable for films.

Rubber Grease: These are available in most colors, but must be ordered directly from the manufacturers. Rubber grease is used for application onto rubber facial pieces, since rubber facial pieces will not take ordinary makeup bases. In an emergency you can make your own rubber grease by adding a small amount of castor oil to a modified grease base color. Rubber grease has a limited but vital use in film makeup.

LINING COLORS AND ROUGES

Lining colors are paints frequently used for shadowing and highlighting effects, and are usually applied over the base color. Lining colors come in all shades, manufactured in the form of grease paint or compressed powder.

EYE MAKEUP

Eyebrow pencils are colored, soft wax pencils used to outline the eye and to sketch in eyebrows. Although many colors are available for this purpose, black and brown are the most useful. In addition, a soft graphite artist pencil can be used in the same areas for a softer eyeline and eyebrow when such an effect is desired.

To darken the lashes, *mascara* is applied. Mascara can be purchased in blocks, rollers, or tubes. The hard block is best for accenting the eyeline; rollers are best for all-around use; tubes contain waterproof mascara which is most appropriate for a performer in a rain or water sequence. Black and brown are usual colors and should be adequate for your needs.

False eyelashes are now almost part of every contemporary woman's wardrobe. Modestly priced lashes are frequently better than the expensive ones, so do some comparison shopping before you buy.

CLEANSERS

Cleansers are various oils or greases available most commonly in cream form. They are used to cleanse and prepare the face for makeup and for removing makeup. There are few true differences between cleansers in liquid or cream state. I find liquids rather messy to use; they tend to splatter and can soil clothing. Cold cream cleansers differ little in substance except for the amount of perfume and air whipped into them. Perfume in a cream acts as a drying agent, and only adds to the cost. Cold creams containing hormones are extremely dangerous and should be avoided completely. Unscented albolene is my own preferred choice.

Acetone is a strong solvent designed to dissolve and remove gums or adhesives used in makeup. Acetone is also used to remove hairpieces glued to the head or face and to clean the hairpieces upon removal. Acetone is excellent for cleaning hairpieces, but is too harsh and abrasive to use directly on the skin. Cinema Secrets Adhesive Remover and Mehrons Spirit Gum Remover are liquid cleansers that are effective in removing spirit gum from the face, and will do so without irritation. After cleansing apply a mild astringent, such as Sea Breeze.

APPLICATORS

To apply makeup you'll need a number of applicators designed for specific tasks.

Flat Red Sable Brushes: These will be your most useful tool for basic shading work on the face. These brushes can be purchased in any art supply store. You'll need a number of brushes in different sizes: two each of no. 2, no. 4, and no. 6 are a good start. Since most brushes come with 18″ wooden handles, I suggest you cut down the handle to a convenient pencil length for easier manipulation.

Japanese Writing Brushes: These provide the finest painting possible, ideal for areas where fine detail is required. Japanese writing brushes are available at art supply stores or Japanese shops. Two or more of these brushes will serve your needs; buy brushes with long bristles ¼″ thick at the widest point.

Foam Rubber Sponge: Used for applying moderate grease base, the foam rubber sponge is available at upholstery shops or variety stores. Buy an inexpensive sponge in any convenient size sheet at least 1″ thick, and cut the sponge into rectangles 1″ by 2″ for convenient handling. Use a separate piece for each performer. Since you should discard the sponge at the end of each day's use, prepare a plentiful stock of sponges in advance.

Natural Sponges: These are best for applying pancake makeup. Natural sponges are available in a variety of qualities, the best for your use being the *silk sponge*. Most cosmetic departments and drug stores carry silk sponges, and I advise you to purchase a half dozen. Get the largest size possible.

POWDER AND POWDER PUFFS

Powdering is used to set grease bases and to maintain a matte finish on pancake bases. Transparent, colorless powders are best. Baby powder, although white, is transparent and excellent for makeup. Buy large size powder puffs from any drug or variety store.

MATERIALS FOR BUILDING UP FEATURES

There will be times when you will want to build up features on the face. When time does not permit the casting and molding necessary for latex prosthetic pieces (Chapter Nine), you can use nose putty and mortician's wax for this purpose. These are available through manufacturers, makeup suppliers, or drug stores that carry theatrical makeup. Mortician's wax may be obtained from a funeral parlor if such a drug store is not available in your area. If the work requires repetition over a period of successive days, putty or mortician's wax will not be adequate, since matching each day requires excessive time. Furthermore, these materials are soft in their original state and tend to soften even more from body heat, which means that constant maintenance is required.

For building up scars, plastic scar material is available in a tube. (Check the list of suppliers in the back of the book for this item.) The scar material is easily modeled into the desired shape.

ADHESIVES

Adhesives are used for particular makeup effects and for attaching face hair and hairpieces. There are two basic adhesives you will use: surgical adhesive and spirit gum.

Surgical adhesive is a natural liquid rubber (latex), available in small tubes at most drug stores. It is an essential item for adhering false eyelashes and for creating disfiguring scars and burns.

Spirit gum is a fast-drying bottled adhesive, used to glue hairpieces, false hair, rubber pieces, and bald caps to the head or face. Spirit gum is available in the traditional theatrical form (an adhesive with the strongest bond, yet dries shiny), in a plastic solution (less shiny, but has less adhesion), and in the newest form called *Undetectable* (see Suppliers List), which has the least adhesive strength but is absolutely invisible. Spirit gum can be purchased at theatrical drug stores, directly from the manufacturer, or from a wig shop. You should purchase both the traditional spirit gum and Undetectable.

Spirit gum is quickly removed with acetone, or with the oil base cleanser.

LOOSE FACE HAIR

You will probably need to create additional facial hair in some of your work. Here are the varieties available:

Crepe wool: This is a wool-like material that comes in an assortment of colors. Crepe wool is inexpensive, can be applied quickly, and gives satisfactory results for a background or mob scene player. For more detailed realistic work, yak hair or human hair must be used.

Yak hair: This is a coarse-textured animal hair and provides reasonable results. It is more expensive than crepe wool and less expensive than human hair.

Human hair: This is the most expensive of the available hairs and requires the most skillful application technique. Human hair produces the best results. Because of the cost and detailed labor involved, human hair application should be used for one-day shooting. For repeated use on successive days, facial hairpieces are much more practical.

FACIAL HAIRPIECES

Facial hairpieces are ready-made pieces to be used as mustaches, beards, sideburns, or eyebrows, and are more practical for repeated use than loose facial hair. These pieces consist of a fine lace netting to which the hairs are tied and knotted by hand. There are many different qualities of the lace netting used. All of these pieces must be handled with extreme care because the lace net cannot tolerate abuse. A well-made piece applied carefully will achieve a truly realistic look.

WIGS

Like the facial hairpiece, the wig is very suitable for repeated use to create unique effects. Sewn on cloth bases for strength, full wigs may consist of a silk body and lace net fronts. *Toupees* may have a partial silk body and lace net front. Additional hairpieces, such as falls, curls, wiglets, may have some lace net depending on their design.

BALD CAPS AND RUBBER PIECES

Made of plastic or latex rubber, a bald cap fits over the head like a bathing cap. These can be obtained from special suppliers. (See Suppliers List.)

For building up features, rubber pieces are ideal. Rubber pieces can be made (see Chapter Nine) or purchased ready-made.

THEATRICAL BLOOD

For special effects, you may want to have a supply of theatrical blood. This is available ready-made in panchromatic colors for black and white films (a very deep red, totally unsuitable for color), and technicolor blood is available for color film. To make your own theatrical blood, see Chapter Twelve.

BASIC MAKEUP KIT

For storing and carrying your materials you will need a suitable box. To obtain a kit locally, check your classified phone directory under *Sample Case Suppliers.* These companies provide a large selection of fiber sample cases with accordion trays that are an excellent feature. One word of advice in selecting a box suitable to carry your tools: avoid the largest sizes. When filled they are unwieldy and heavy. It may be more practical to have two cases. A small one such as a camera case or attache case to carry tools for everyday use, and a large one to carry materials to cover all other situations should keep you prepared for any unexpected emergencies that might arise.

Here is a check list of materials I suggest you gather for inclusion in your makeup kit:

One makeup cape

Two towels

One large square of white silk (for gluing on hair)

One pair of barber's shears

One pair of thinning shears

Box of cleansing tissues

Cleansing cream

Bottle of astringent (Sea Breeze or witch hazel)

Bottle of acetone

Can of colorless powder

Four powder puffs

Six silk sponges

Foam rubber sponges

One red rubber sponge

Six flat sable brushes

Two Japanese writing brushes

Two black eyebrow pencils

Two brown eyebrow pencils

Two soft graphite artist's pencils

One eyebrow tweezer

Two eyebrow brushes

Six lipsticks ranging from light to dark red

Mascara in black and brown blocks

Mascara in black and brown rollers

Mascara in black and brown waterproof tubes

Eyelashes: red, brown, black; thin, medium, and thick; short and long for both top and bottom of eye

Hair in all colors for laying-on beards (crepe, yak, or human)

One Johnson & Johnson Duo Adhesive

One Blistex (for chapped lips)

Blood: panchromatic and technicolor

Bald caps and latex pieces

Grease lining colors in tins: white, gray, black, brown, maroon, light blue

Dry lining colors: white, gray, brown, brown-gray, blue

One bottle liquid latex

One can of face putty wax

One bottle of old age stipple

One bottle of Visene eye drops

One bottle of glycerin

One bottle of castor oil

One Vicks inhalator

One box of cotton swabs

One hand spray atomizer

One barber comb

One regular comb

One hand mirror

Hair clips, hair pins, bobby-pins

Pancake (most commonly used colors)

MEHRON	BEN NYE	MAX FACTOR
White	White	N.A.
Fair Tan	PC1 Natural	Natural
6.5B Medium Male	PC7 Rose Beige	Olive
True Tan	PC9 Tan #1	Deep Olive
26A Tan Glow	PC11 Tan #2	Tan Rose
TV2 Ivory Bisque	PC13 Old Age	Tan #2
TV6 Light Tan	PC15 Suntone	Suntan
8B Light Egyptian	PC17 Light Egyptian	N.A.
12B Dark Egyptian	PC19 Dark Egyptian	N.A.
LE Light Ebony	PC21 Golden Ebony	N.A.
ME Medium Ebony		
Black	PC23 Black	N.A.

Moist Rouge

MEHRON	BEN NYE
#15 Tech Orange	CR3 Sandy Rose
#11 Pink Coral	CR2 Dusty Rose

Highlights

MEHRON	BEN NYE
17 Creamy Beige	CH0 Ultralite
18 Honey Tan	CH4 Medium

Dry Rouge

MEHRON	BEN NYE
#RC10 Terra Cotta	DR6 Coral
#RC14 Grayed Mocha	DR3 Dark Technicolor

Shadows

MEHRON	BEN NYE
Sable Brown	CS1 Subtle Brown
Chestnut Brown	CS2 Medium Brown

Modified Grease Base (most commonly used colors)

MEHRON	BEN NYE	MAX FACTOR
White	P1 White	Not Available
22A Soft Peach	N1 Fair	Fair
6.5B Medium Male	N3 Subtle Beige	Olive
True Tan	N4 Deep Olive	Deep Olive
TV2 Ivory Bisque	FT5 Bronze Beige	Twilight Blush
TV4 Soft Beige	FT2 Subtle Tan	N.A.
TV6 Light Tan	M1 Lite Bronze	Medium Beige
TV8 Medium Tan	M2 Suntone	Cool Bronze
TV10 Bronzed Tan	T2 Bronze Tan	Sun Tone
8B Light Egyptian	FT9 Olive Amber	N.A.
12B Dark Egyptian	Y5 Olive Tan	N.A.
LE Light Ebony	FT11 Olive Sable	N.A.
ME Medium Ebony	FT13 Golden Ebony	N.A.
10C Ebony	Black	N.A.

Sealer

MEHRON	BEN NYE	CINEMA SECRETS
Fixative A	Castor Sealer	Liquid Cap & Scar Material

Scar Material (liquid)

MEHRON	BEN NYE	CINEMA SECRETS
Collodion	Wrinkle Stipple	Scar Material

Scar Material (wax and plastic)

MEHRON	BEN NYE
Modeling/Putty Wax	Nose and Scar Wax

Hair Whitener

MEHRON	BEN NYE
Hair White	Silver Grey Hair Color

Cleansers

MEHRON	BEN NYE
Remover Lotion	Makeup Remover
Makeup Remover	
Cold Cream	

Spirit Gums and Adhesives

MEHRON	BEN NYE
Spirit Gum	Spirit Gum
Medical Adhesive	
IRA SENZ WIGS	CINEMA SECRETS
Spirit Gum	Spirit Gum

Spirit Gum Removers

MEHRON	BEN NYE
IRA SENZ WIGS	CINEMA SECRETS

Blood and Special Effects

MEHRON	BEN NYE	CINEMA SECRETS

Bald Caps

MEHRON	CINEMA SECRETS

Crepe Wool

MEHRON	BEN NYE	IRA SENZ WIGS

The tools and materials on this list are all the tools of an artist. The techniques you need to develop combine the arts of painting and sculpture. Increasing your tactile sense will be of great advantage to you. You must learn to sketch, using soft pencil, charcoal, and pastel, since these art forms require blending with the fingers. In addition, a modeling sense can be developed by using soft modeling clay to sculpt faces and figures.

These implements listed here, combined with the required skill of painter and sculptor, will prepare you for the work to follow.

WORKING AREA

Ideally you should work at a makeup table. The seated performer should be high enough so that you do not have to bend over excessively. Bending creates strain and interferes with the efficient progress of your work. A hydraulic barber's chair is most practical because it permits easy adjustment of the performer's height—with its convenient headrest—and is also more comfortable for the performer.

On your makeup table you should have a good-sized clean mirror with light bulbs attached around its perimeter so that the performer will be evenly lit. There have been many arguments about the advantages of incandescent light bulbs over fluorescent lighting. In some instances I know of makeup artists who have insisted on lighting of the same color temperature as those of the lights used on the set. I find this unnecessary; a clean, well-ventilated, well-lit room with a good mirror and comfortable chair are really all you need. If these are unavailable, simply do the best you can with what is available.

Set a clean towel on the shelf in front of the mirror, and place your tools neatly on the towel. Check to make sure your pencils are sharp, your rubber sponge is fresh, and your silk sponges are washed and clean. Your brushes should also be clean and sanitized. Wash your hands, seat the performer, insert cleansing tissues around the collar of the garment worn by the performer, and drape a towel or makeup cape around his neck and shoulders, and you are ready to start work.

TOOLS ON LOCATION

Permanent studio working facilities are usually adequate. Once you leave the studio, however, to work on location, you must be prepared to improvise. It is possible, of course, to have the crew carpenter make portable tables, including built-in mirrors and lights. (Naturally, the lights require a source of electric power, which is not always readily available.) Mobile dressing rooms or trailers—with their own generators—are ideal, if available, and they eliminate the problems of space, mirrors, lights, and sanitation. If you are working outdoors you can move to an open shade area, and you will not need any artificial lighting.

If you are working in a house, any well-lit room can be adequate, and if the bathroom is well-illuminated and has a mirror, even better. You must think ahead and anticipate what might be available and what you bring along. Don t be afraid to ask: you will be saving the company money and time if there is no unnecessary delay.

There are small portable mirrors with built-in lights which are light in weight and very practical for location work if you cannot arrange for the larger professional sized units. I personally prefer the mirror manufactured by Clairol.

Make sure you have a supply of clean water (for washing sponges and pancake makeup applicators). Also be sure to provide as comfortable a seat as you can obtain for the performer. I've worked in the Sahara Desert, the Okeefenokee swamps, the Great Smokey Mountains, Lake Placid in the winter, and on a schooner in the Caribbean Sea. I have frequently been hot, cold, or wet, but there has always been an area that could be improvised for makeup work, so I'm sure—with a little ingenuity—you can succeed in finding an adequate place to work, too.

2
BASIC MAKEUP TECHNIQUES

Throughout this book we will be using basic makeup techniques. These techniques will be fundamental to all makeup problems you will be solving in the following chapters. Wherever possible I have described the techniques as part of a demonstration, but I have included in this chapter some fundamental techniques you will be encountering again and again.

First I will describe some of the aspects of makeup base and base color which you should know before you begin. Then I will discuss the specific techniques you will be using continually: blending and shading, highlights, shadows, wrinkles, and painting the eyes, eyebrows, and mouth.

CLEANSING THE FACE

In order to achieve good results in makeup work, it is most important to cleanse the model's face so that it is free of soot, face oils, and old makeup.

To cleanse the face thoroughly, dip your finger into the cleansing cream, removing a dab about ½″ in thickness, and apply this to the forehead, nose, cheeks, and chin. Spread the cream gently and evenly with the fingertips. After the entire face has been covered, cleanse your fingers with tissues and, with fresh cleansing tissues, carefully remove the excess cream from the face. Do not rub the face dry; avoid excess friction because this can be a frequent cause of irritation to the performer's skin. Gently remove all the cream and then remove the thin remaining film with cotton dipped in a mild astringent, such as witch hazel or Sea Breeze.

BASE COLORS FOR ALL SKIN TONES

Base or base color refers to the skin tone most suitable to the performer you are making up. As a general rule it is desirable to slightly darken pale Caucasians' skin tones and to slightly lighten dark Mediterranean and black skin tones for cinematic purposes, and in Chapter One I recommended a minimum number of base colors that should be included in your kit to account for the most common skin tones. However, the range of human skin tones is far more varied, extending from the palest Caucasian to the blue-black of the Austrialian aborigine. Through practical observation you must become aware of the vast range of hues in the Caucasian, Negroid, and Oriental skin tones. It is important to realize, however, that cosmetic manufacturers' colors are only approximations of skin tones. You may need to mix colors to arrive at the desired base color.

It is astonishing how few cosmetic colors are required to span the entire range of human skin tones. Although I dislike categorizing people in any way, I do think it helps clarify my point if I chart out some specific examples.
Reading the chart of skin tones on the opposite page, you may consider this information an oversimplification of your problems. Why, if what I claim is true, do cosmetic manufacturers continue to create and manufacture such an enormous range of base colors? My answer to this is simple: profit.

APPLYING MODIFIED GREASE PAINT

For base colors in film makeup you will be using modified grease and pancake most frequently, and it is important for you to know how to apply both of them correctly.

For modified grease paint a foam rubber sponge is used for application. This should be discarded after use. To make an applicator for moderate grease paint, cut up a piece of foam rubber sponge to a section of 1″ x 1″ x 2″ (Figs. 1 and 2). Using this piece of sponge, pick up a quantity of grease on one edge of the sponge (Figs. 3 and 4). Start on one of

BASE COLORS

	MEHRON	BEN NYE	MAX FACTOR
Pale Caucasian Women	1B Alabaster 2B Extra Fair 22A Soft Peach	N1 Fair FT4 Medium Beige N3 Subtle Beige	Natural Olive Tan Rose
Dark Caucasian Women	3B Juvenile 24A Lt. Beige Blush 26A Tan Glow	N4 Deep Olive FT5 Bronze Beige T1 Golden Tan	Deep Olive Tan #1 Tan #2
Pale Caucasian Men	6.5B Medium Male 26A Tan Glow 28A Light Cinnamon	FT1 Pale English FT2 Subtle Tan M1 Light Bronze	Deep Olive Tan #1 Tan #2
Dark Caucasian Men	30A Dark Cinnamon TV10 Bronzed Tan TV12 Extra Bronzed Tan	M2 Suntone Y3 Medium Olive T2 Bronze Tan	Tan Rose Tan #2
Black Men & Women	8B Light Egyptian 12B Dark Egyptian LE Light Ebony	FT9 Olive Amber FT11 Olive Sable FT13 Golden Brown	N.A. N.A. N.A.
Black Men & Women Lip Color	Special #5	LS9 Plum LS12 Natural Brown LS13 Magenta	N.A. N.A. N.A.
Asian Women	26 Dark Khaki TV6 Light Tan	P11 Chinese TW20 Rice Paper TW22 Golden Beige	Deep Olive Tan Rose Tan #2
Asian Men	28 Amber Tan TV8 Medium Tan	P12 Japanese P7 Bronzetone	Tan #2 Suntan
Latin Women	4C Light Cocoa	TW22 Fawn TW24 Honey P6 Natural Tan	Deep Olive Natural Tan Tan #2
Latin Men	7C Sable	Y1 Lite Olive Y5 Olive Tan	Tan #2 Suntan
Mexican Women	29A Medium Cinnamon	P7 Bronzetone	Tan #2
Mexican Men	31A Ruddy Bronze	Y3 Medium Olive	Suntan
American Indian Women	10B American Indian	TW27 Coco Tan	N.A.
American Indian Men	31A Ruddy Bronze	TW29 Blush Sable	N.A.

the areas of the face—like the forehead, for example—and spread the grease smoothly and thinly across as much of the forehead as the amount picked up will permit. (See Fig. 5.) Do not allow the grease to clump or streak; spread it evenly and, I repeat, thinly. When you have used up that initial amount of grease that you picked up on the sponge, repeat the process, continuing down the face. Do not rub hard or press the sponge onto the face with uncomfortable pressure. While you are applying makeup, remember the physical comfort of the performer, since you can easily cause him discomfort. Bear this in mind at all times.

When you have applied the grease to the entire face, examine your work for excess grease. Be sure there are no lumps of paint, streakiness, or excessive shine (an evidence of too much paint). If there is an overall consistency of application, an even skin tone, your base has been correctly applied.

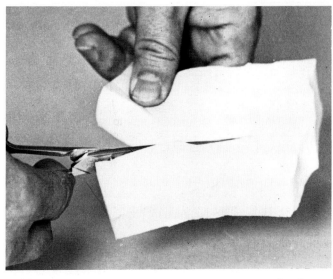

1. Take a section of foam rubber and cut it down to 1″ x 2″ thickness.

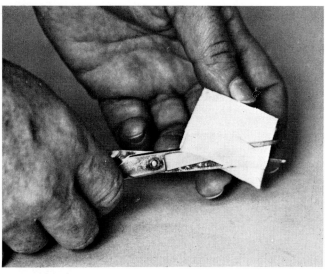

2. Trim the sponge even further to 1″ x 1″ x 2″, to complete the applicator necessary for modified grease paint.

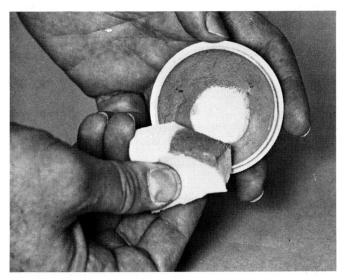

3. With foam rubber sponge pick up a quantity of grease in a round container.

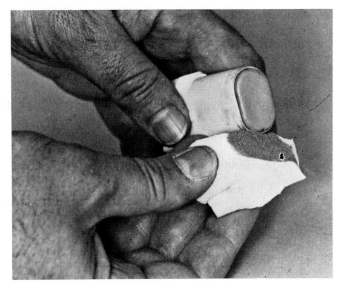

4. Or do the same using a stick container.

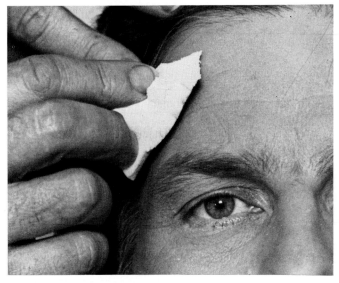

5. Apply this small amount of base to the face and repeat until the entire face is covered with a thin layer of base.

APPLYING PANCAKE BASE

For pancake, a silk sponge is used for application. This can be washed and reused. Pick up a silk sponge, moisten it thoroughly, and squeeze out most of the water so that the sponge is still moist. (See Figs. 6 and 7.) Rub a corner of the sponge across the pancake until you pick up a small quantity of the makeup on the sponge. (See Figs. 8 and 9.) Now begin to apply the pancake to one area of the face, using a smooth back-and-forth motion (Fig. 10). The amount you will have picked up will cover only a portion of the face, so repeat the process until the entire face is covered. As in applying the grease, check carefully for an even, thin application. If there are streaks, add more pancake or go over the area with a clean moist sponge to reduce areas with excessive amounts.

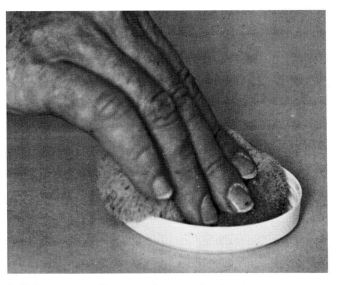

6. Saturate your silk sponge in water that has been poured into the lid of your base container.

7. Squeeze out most of the water. The sponge should be wet, but not soaked.

8. Rub the sponge firmly onto the pancake.

9. Pick up a quantity of makeup on the sponge.

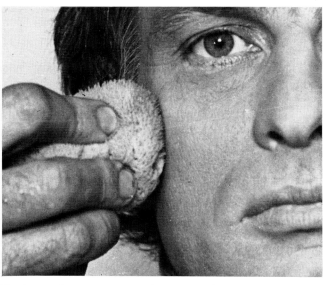

10. Stroke the sponge on the face to transfer the pancake. Then repeat the process until the base is applied as desired.

HOLDING THE MAKEUP BRUSH

To blend or to paint specific effects you will use a brush. The most important factor in painting is being able to control the brush, and the way in which you hold the brush will facilitate better control. Hold the brush as you would a pen or pencil, close to its tip. Use the little finger of your hand as a fulcrum, resting it lightly on the face—carefully, to avoid smearing the makeup—and use the edge or flat of the brush as if you were writing or painting. (See Figs. 11 and 12.)

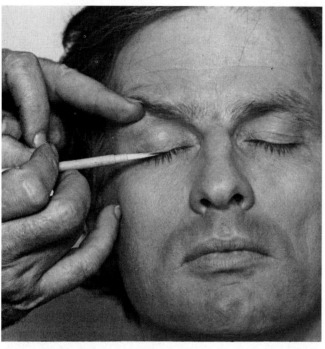

11. To hold the Japanese writing brush, use your little finger to steady your hand.

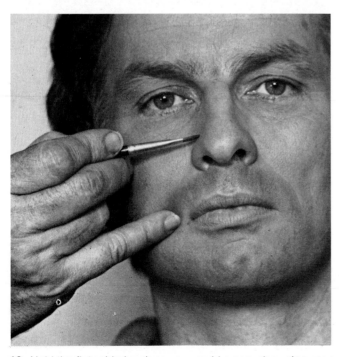

12. Hold the flat sable brush as you would a pen, also using your little finger, resting against the face, to steady your hand.

FINISHING THE SKIN COLOR

When you have completed the facial makeup, always look at it critically and reexamine the skin color. Since no skin has a single even color throughout, and since most roles call for a healthy skin tone, you can kill two birds with one stone by heightening the healthy effect of your base with the addition of rouge on the cheeks, nose, chin, and forehead.

An application of rouge breaks up the evenness of the makeup and produces a more natural effect at the same time. Rouge *must* be used for color film, but it is also desirable for makeup in black and white photography as well. Actually, rouge should be used in black and white primarily as a morale factor for the performer. A bit of rouge will look better to the performer and will not, if applied properly, harm the makeup. In applying rouge for black and white, bear in mind that it should not register on the film. For this reason, I suggest you use a color similar to Light Technicolor, manufactured by Max Factor. This will not register on black and white film, but will improve the look of the performer.

Beard tone in the male performer is another element to be considered when finishing the skin color. Without any beard tone, the makeup work will seem artificial. Every man, even when clean shaven, has a darker skin tone in the beard area than in the rest of the face. If the beard tone is too heavy and you wish to minimize it, apply a thin coating of moderate grease paint to the beard area (Fig. 13). If you can match the actor's own skin tone with the grease paint, you may need no further makeup. Powder this base lightly (Fig. 14) and remove excess powder with a damp sponge. If more makeup is called for, continue to apply base over the entire face.

If the beard tone does not appear to be dark enough, create a darker beard tone by using a dark blue-gray base for Caucasians and Orientals, and a dark or brown lining color for black performers. With a small amount of the paint on the fingertip, gently dab the color on through the beard and mustache areas. Dab only enough color to create a slight beard tone to the skin tone. (See Figs. 15 to 17.) Don't forget to carry this tone down onto the neck and be careful to avoid smudges or clumps of paint. The end result should appear to be no more than a clean-shaven effect. If you desire more growth you will have to add hair to the face, a technique that will be discussed in Chapter Eleven.

POWDERING

Powdering is a method of setting the modified grease base you have already applied. Once the face is powdered the base will not shine or spread easily. This seemingly simple process, if done carelessly or incorrectly, may damage or destroy what you have worked so hard to achieve.

Be sure that you use only a transparent or very lightly colored powder. The purpose of powdering is to set your makeup, not to discolor it, which is exactly what a colored powder will do. Pick up a quantity of powder on your powder puff. Fold over the puff and roll the powder into it. Then open the puff and lightly shake off any excess powder (Figs. 18 and 19). Starting at the neck, use a slight slapping action to pat a layer of powder onto the base. Move the puff up to an unpowdered area and repeat the patting until all the powder in the puff is used. Now reload

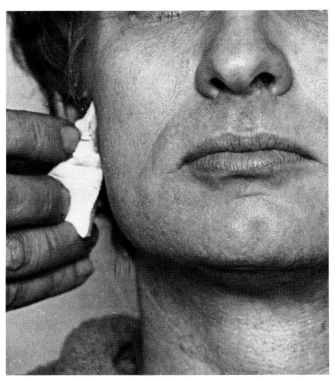

13. To eliminate excessive natural beard tone, apply a thin coat of base color over the beard area.

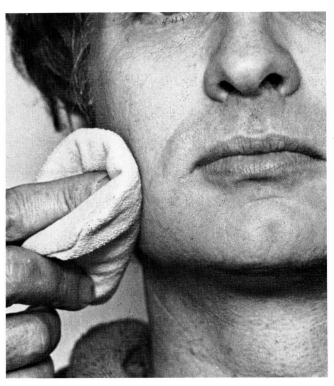

14. If the base is grease, powder it lightly to remove shine.

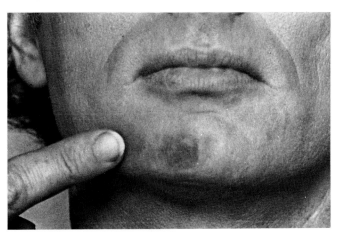

15. To create the effect of a heavy beard tone, add blue-gray lining color to the beard area.

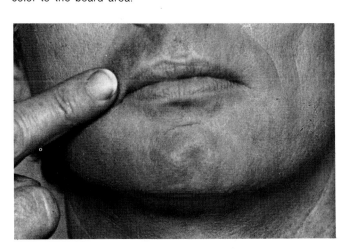

16. Carry this tone over the entire face that would normally have some hair growth.

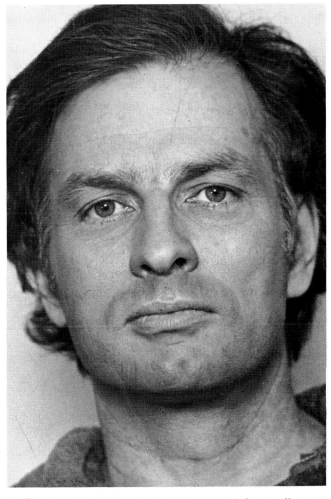

17. The tone should be uneven, strong enough for an effect, yet not so strong that it looks like paint.

18. Shake powder onto the puff.

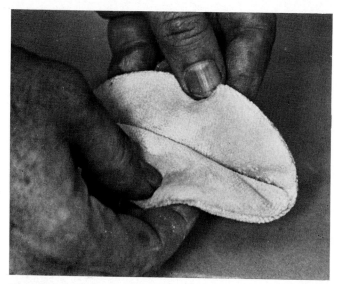

19. Roll the powder into the puff, then shake off excess. The puff is ready to be used.

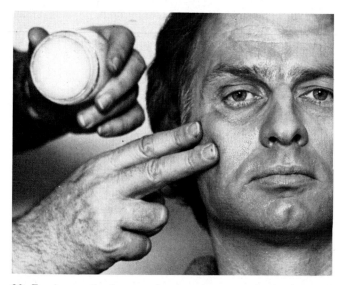

20. To cleanse the face, apply cleansing cream to the face and gently work it in. Clean this with tissues and repeat until the face is entirely clean. Avoid excessive rubbing.

the puff with more powder and repeat the patting until the entire makeup area of the face has been covered with a layer of powder.

Now shake the excess powder from the puff, then fold the puff around your index finger. With a rolling motion, press and roll the excess powder from the face onto the puff. Shake the puff clean as it becomes filled with powder and repeat the process until nothing but a very thin film of powder remains on the face. Remember, always *roll* the puff across the face. Avoid streaking the makeup.

The remaining film of powder is easily removed. Using a moist silk sponge, pat off the powder film, blot the face dry, and your modified grease base is powdered and set.

REMOVING MAKEUP

At the end of the day's filming, you will be doing the performer a great service if you help him remove the makeup properly. There is nothing more harmful to the skin than excessive rubbing, leaving grease on the face, and then going out into cold weather, so that anything you might do to avoid this situation will help the performer.

To remove makeup correctly, apply cleansing cream to the face, working it into the skin gently with your fingertips (Fig. 20). Using soft cleansing tissues, remove as much of the cream as you can without irritating the performer's skin. Then apply more cream to the face and remove this, again as carefully and gently as possible. When all the makeup has been removed, have the performer wash with a gentle soap and warm water. Close the pores of the skin with cold water or with a mild astringent, such as witch hazel or Sea Breeze.

BLENDING AND SHADING

In all makeup work you will constantly be creating illusions, techniques demanding that you master the art of blending (or shading). Blending is the most important technique in makeup application. Blending means graduating the intensity of a color—whether it is dark (shadow) or light (highlight)—from its strongest color to its lightest tone, until it disappears into the base. So important is this technique, in itself, that you should practice blending before you go on to creating the illusions to come.

Start by applying a quantity of paint (it doesn't matter how much) with the fingertips to the skin (it doesn't matter what color) and, by gently patting it with the fingertips, gradually reduce the amount of paint from the darkest point of application to where you can make it fade onto the skin. Pat until all spots or blotches are shaded. This technique is the key to all makeup and should be practiced constantly.

Once you are familiar with the basic concept of blending, try to create some abstract illusions. Study the illusions illustrated in Figs. 21, 22, 23, 24 to see what you achieve with blending. In Figs. 21 and 22 the shading is darkest at the edge, blending light at the outer, to give the illusion of a round cylinder. We use this type of blending in makeup whenever an edge is permissible, such as wrinkles and skin folds, or jaw and eyeline shading. In Figs. 23 and 24 we get the effect of roundness or of a tube by paint application darkest at the center and blending out to disappear at the outer edges. We use this type of blending whenever we cannot have any edges showing at all, in dark rouge and highlighting, for example.

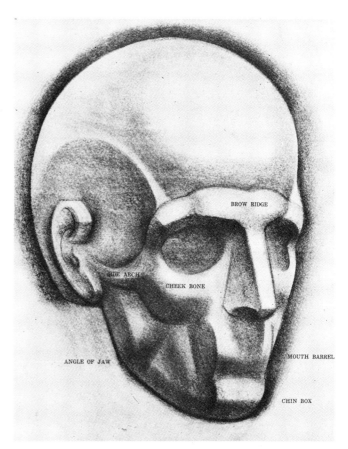

STRUCTURE OF THE HEAD

All makeup is directly related to the actual structure of the head and face. It is necessary to know and understand that structure in order to effect any alterations with makeup. (See Fig. 25.) The bone structure of the head includes the prominent high points of the bone masses—the forehead, cheekbones, jawbone—as well as the cartilage of the nose, the eyeball of the eyesocket, and the teeth. The face has two major sinkings: the cheeks sinking between the prominences of the cheekbone and the jawbone, and the depression behind the region of the temple bone. These prominences and depressions are used to create the illusions we are after in makeup work.

The illusion of sinking can be created with painted shadows running from one prominence into the hollow, and then out to another prominence. We use this technique to sink the cheekbone, for example. Let's actually begin to create the illusion of the sinking cheekbone.

25. Study the structure of the head, making note of the areas of depression and the prominent areas in the face. You will use these for effect in your makeup work. From *Drawing The Human Head* by Burne Hogarth, Watson-Guptill.

SINKING THE CHEEKBONE

If you are working in modified grease, use a lining color and apply it with a fingertip. If you are using pancake, use a dark pancake as the shadow color and apply it with a brush, blending with the fingertip or with a moist silk sponge.

Apply a small quantity of the shadow color (in its deepest intensity) at a point equidistant between, and parallel to, the cheekbone and jawbone, about 1″ to 1½″ in length.

21. (Left) Try blending this form in makeup: shade darkest at the edge and blend to the lightest tone in the center. This creates the effect of a round ball. 22. (Right) This blending uses the same idea, but the shape is elongated, much the way you would shade a wrinkle.

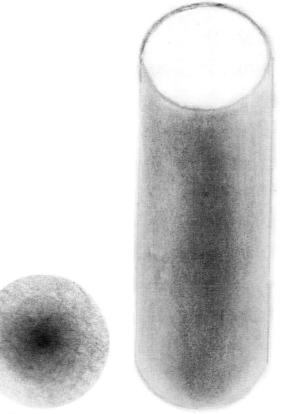

23. (Left) This illusion also creates the impression of roundness, but the shading is darkest at the center, grading to light at the edges. 24. (Right) Blending in the same way as Fig. 23, the illusion is one of a cylinder or tube, a technique used in painting the cheek rouge.

This shadow does not extend back to where the jawbone and cheekbone join, and is not to extend forward to where it would intrude into any of the fleshy folds around the mouth. (See Figs. 26 and 27.)

With a patting technique of the finger, or a gently brushing stroke of the brush, blend the shadow up to, but not on to, the cheekbone, down but not to the jawbone, back but not to the cheek and jawbone junction, and forward but not into the fleshy folds around the mouth. (See Fig. 28.)

This blending must graduate the paint so that its greatest darkness and intensity is in the center, graduating until it fades into the skin color (Fig. 29).

When the entire shadow has been blended, the total size should be no more than about 2″ in length and 1″ in width. To achieve this properly demands a great degree of practice and slowly acquired skill.

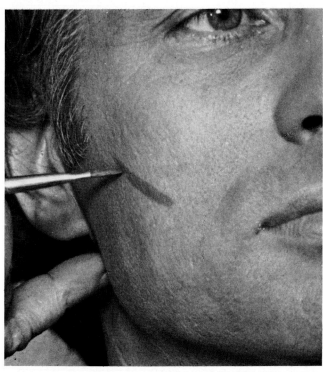

26. To sink the cheek, first place the shadow between the heights of the cheekbone and the jawbone.

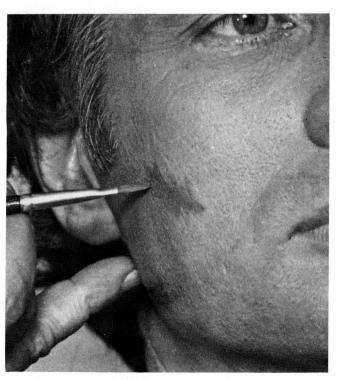

27. Blend the shadow up and down, back and forth.

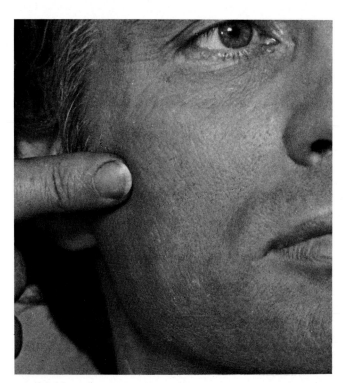

28. With the fingertip, blend the shadow so that it disappears into the base color.

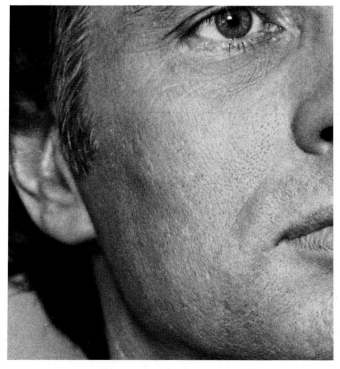

29. The effect of sinking should be soft and natural.

SINKING THE TEMPLE

To give the illusion of the temple sinking requires a technique that varies from the above. Unlike any of the other facial bones, the temple line is the only one with a specific edge. Therefore, apply your shadow directly behind the temple bone. (See Fig. 30.) The illusion is somewhat sharp, but avoid a straight line, since the temple bone arcs from the outer edge of the brow, back and into the hairline. Blend the paint back toward the hairline and ear, carrying the graduations about ½" in width at the hairline and widening to about 1" at the brow. (Figs. 31 and 32.)

The grading of the shadow must be perfect, so that from the front you have the illusion of an indention, and from the profile, the suggestion of a shadow. (See Fig. 33.)

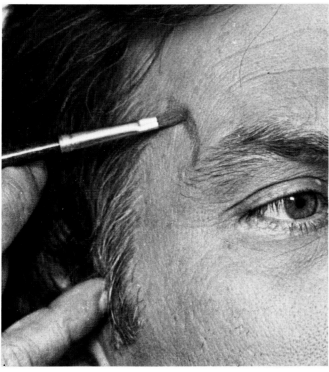

30. To sink the temple, apply shadow just below the ridge of the temple bone.

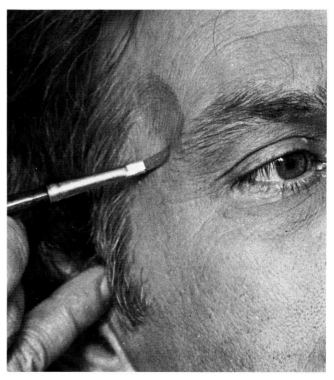

31. Blend this shadow tone back toward the hairline.

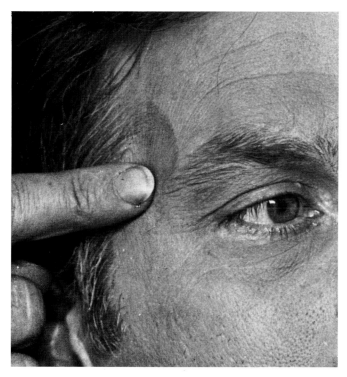

32. Blend the edges off to disappear into the base color.

33. The sinking should appear natural, yet retain its effect.

PAINTING SKIN FOLDS

Painting a wrinkle involves a specific technique that includes all of the variations of skin folds denoting age. These are called wrinkles, folds, jowls, bags, or pouches. Since the camera is so accurate in recording the image, and the projector increases the size of the created work, we can at best only *suggest* skin folds with paint. Advanced evidence of aging requires the addition of artificial pieces, which we will discuss in a later chapter. Painting folds and wrinkles is of great value in creating changes of age that are not extreme.

In all painting the sinking is deepest, therefore heaviest, along a specific delineation. In addition, each fold has a beginning point and an end point, starting small, widening to its widest point, and diminishing to where the fold disappears in the base.

In painting these structures, the shadow is applied darkest along the line of the fold. Let's examine the painting of the nose wrinkle, for example. Starting on the nose at the beginning of the nostril, the paint is applied with a brush and carried down alongside the lip to where it disappears, usually a bit below the mouth. This paint is then blended up and away from the mouth. This application of paint is then blended so that the color grades from its darkest (at the initial line of application) to where it disappears into the base. (See Figs. 34 and 35.) Refer to the optical illusions (Figs. 23 and 24) so that you can see the ultimate effect of this kind of blending.

All effects must be subtle. Spots of paint, sharp edges, and careless blending are not tolerated by the camera. If there is ever any question in your mind concerning the reality of the work you have painted, and it appears too strong, soften it. But don't carry this advice to the extreme. Work so soft that it does not create any effects is of no value either. You must question, and judge, and learn by practice and experience.

PAINTING THE MOUTH

The two most expressive features of the face are the mouth and eyebrows. These features are in constant motion, and they can be defined and reshaped to suggest a variety of expressions.

The mouth consists of an upper and a lower lip, each of which can be dealt with as a separate expressive entity. By considering each lip a three dimensional area, you can obtain the greatest potential from this expressive feature. Take a look at the mouths around you. Notice that lips are composed of various round areas. It helps to sketch out the mouth you want on a sheet of paper and to experiment before you finally select the one you consider suitable.

In film the mouth can be altered far more readily for women than for men, since women can be expected to alter the size and shapes of their lips with lipsticks. Unfortunately, men can make little use of this technique.

The natural coloring of the mouth varies from a soft pink to a rose color and sometimes almost to brown. For a natural effect in black and white, touching the lips lightly with a coral brown lip rouge will work equally well for men and for women. Avoid using too much; all you want is a tint. The same colors will frequently work well in color film, but may require the addition of a light touch of a rose tone.

34. To paint a nose wrinkle, first start at the beginning of the nostril and carry the line down alongside the lip to where it disappears, usually a bit below the mouth.

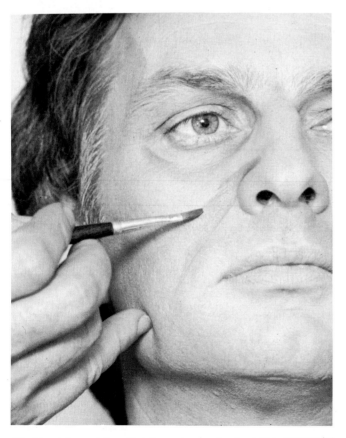

35. Blend the paint so that the color grades from the darkest (at the initial line of application) to where it disappears into the base.

To paint a woman's mouth, use your flat sable brush and very carefully outline the shape you want. Avoid large shapes at the beginning. It's easier to add and slowly build up the shape than it is to remove the lip coloring and correct the base color where the lipstick has stained it. When the shape suits you and both sides balance, fill in the color, blot carefully with a cleansing tissue and, if necessary, touch up the edges with your lipstick brush. If you must cut down the lips, use your flat sable and carefully etch in the base color to correct any flaws in the lip shape.

PAINTING EYEBROWS

As with the mouth, the eyebrows can be more readily altered and used expressively for women than for men.

Even here, however, in most instances the amount of change you can realistically effect is slight. But this slight alteration can still be vital to the character.

The technique of drawing the eyebrow on the head is very close to that of sketching with a pencil on paper. Develop a short light rhythmic stroke to produce a realistic effect, lifting the pencil away from the skin at the end of each stroke to achieve the feathered effect of hairs. Use light strokes and add more as needed, avoiding solid heavy lines. Add only as much penciling as is needed to effect the slight change of eyebrow line possible for camera. I suggest using a soft graphite drawing pencil. Black or brown eyebrow pencils may be used if you wish, but they tend to get too dark too quickly. Their results are not as natural.

3 BASIC MAKEUP FOR BLACK AND WHITE FILM

During the infant days of motion pictures, film makeup was unknown. Stage actors condescended to play in the new medium and brought to films their own limited knowledge of stage makeup. Film and its techniques were primitive and called for exaggeration in acting, and for strong visual projection of emotions through body and facial expression. A pale face, with strongly accented eyes, eyebrows, and mouth became the standard for film makeup.

Slowly, the dramatic content, styles of acting, and technical improvements evolved into contemporary standards. These standards demand natural yet attractive looking performers.

BASIC PRINCIPLES OF BLACK AND WHITE

To begin this process, let us examine black and white film, some of its problems and some of the necessary solutions. Black and white film converts all colors into varying shades of gray, starting with pure white at the lightest extreme and progressing through the light grays, medium grays, dark grays, into black at the darkest extreme. (The gray scale manufactured by Kodak—Fig. 36—will show this gradation.) Obtain a panchromatic conversion glass, which, when you view your subject through the lens, will help you in translating colors into the gray scale.

Most Caucasian skin tones, when translated into black and white, will register between the extremes of white and black in the gray scale. The difference between the skin tones of actors playing together is frequently great enough to create problems. The basic purpose of black and white makeup is to create a harmonious balance between the various skin tones. A practiced rule requires the male performer's skin tones to be two or three shades darker than that of the female performer. Furthermore, all of the actors' skin tones must be considered in regard to the tone of the background, as well. Obviously you can't change skin tones to suit all backgrounds, but a suitable skin color may require considerable darkening when played against a black background or, conversely, heightened a great deal when played in front of white. You must bear in mind, then, that a satisfactory balance will usually have the female a few shades lighter than the male, and all performers' skin tones contrasting only moderately with their backgrounds.

Not only does makeup for black and white serve the function of producing a variety of values—both in relation of one performer to another and in relation to the background—but makeup is also used to alter, or improve, the appearance of the performers. We will deal with this in detail later.

Either pancake or modified grease paint, or both, can be used satisfactorily as a makeup base for film. Flesh tones (in modified grease or pancake) ranging from light to dark and designed for use in black and white films are called *panchromatic*. When you determine a satisfactory skin base for male or female, select as a shadow color (pancake or modified grease) a tone about three shades darker, and for a highlight a tone about three shades lighter than the base color. If stronger effects are called for, it may require going lighter or darker than the usual three or four shades.

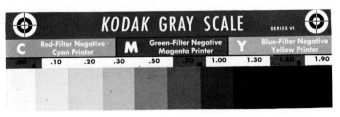

36. The Kodak Gray Scale illustrates gradation from white to black.

28

ANALYZING THE FACE

Now that you have a base color, shadow, and highlight, how do you proceed? The actual application will depend upon the face you're intending to make up. This demands that you analyze the proportions of the face.

Contemporary concepts of beauty are derived from the classic Greeks. This embodiment of male and female beauty, heroic yet serene in its dehumanized regularity of features, has been the standard of beauty for the Western world for thousands of years. Greek artists created a perfect model, a face that was an oval, wider at the cheeks and narrowing slightly at the chin. This oval face was divided into three equal areas: the distance between the hairline and the brows equalled the distance of the brows to the tip of the nose, and equalled the distance of the tip of the nose to the bottom of the chin.

This oval face was also divided equally into five eye widths: the distance of one eye width from the hairline to the corner of the eye, the eye itself, an eye width in the space between the eyes, the other eye, and a fifth eye width from the corner of that eye to the hairline. In addition, the mouth was of a particular size as well: if an imaginary line were drawn up the face vertically from the corners of the mouth, these lines would bisect the pupils of the eyes.

This, then, is the standard of beauty we accept when we attempt to modify all performers whose appearance we want to improve. Most faces will be at some variance from the Grecian, and although we cannot begin to deal with the infinite variety of face shapes, there are a few basic shapes that cover most variations: the round, square, diamond, and long faces.

Obviously, having a face shape at variance with the classic Greek does not classify anyone as ugly or unattractive. In fact, many faces at variance with the classic form can be even more beautiful than the ideal oval. I use the Greek standards because they provide a solid and useful guide toward which we attempt to moderate the face. At best, these changes can only be moderate, since, in films especially, we are very limited in the amount of shading that can be used if we want to retain a natural effect. To effect greater changes, the makeup artist is obliged to turn toward hairstyling and wigs, if necessary.

Before we consider these variations, let us consider a model with a relatively oval shape.

MAKEUP FOR THE FEMALE PERFORMER

Makeup should always be purposeful. If the purpose of your work is corrective, determine beforehand what needs correcting. Is the desired effect a natural one, or should the performer actually look made up? These are questions you should pose before beginning to work.

In this demonstration we will show a number of things. Freckles will be covered and small corrective work will be shaded into the features. First we will try for a natural effect, then develop the same makeup into one more theatrical. Undershading will be applied first, then a modified grease base—which will cover some of the freckles. (Frequently this is all the base that is needed.) Next a light pancake base will be added, and some final rouges and shading.

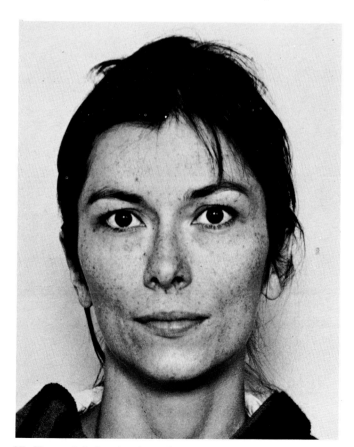

37. The model's face has been thoroughly cleansed. Refer back to this photo at intervals to note the stages of progress.

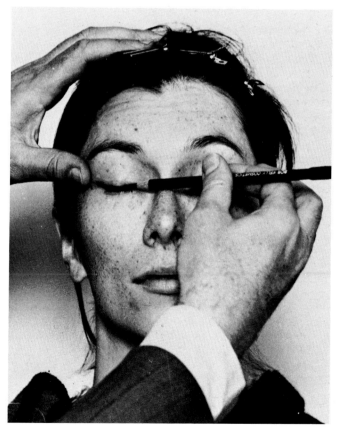

38. Holding the eyebrow pencil horizontally, start the eyeline ¼″ to ½″ beyond the outside corner of the eye and carry it midway onto the lid.

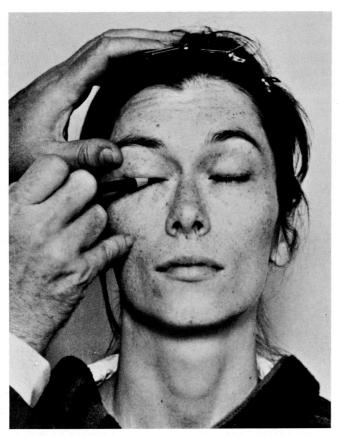

39. Take the pencil to the inside corner of the eye and carry it along the lid of the eye to meet the first half of the line.

40. On the opposite eye, start at the inner corner and carry the line midway onto the lid.

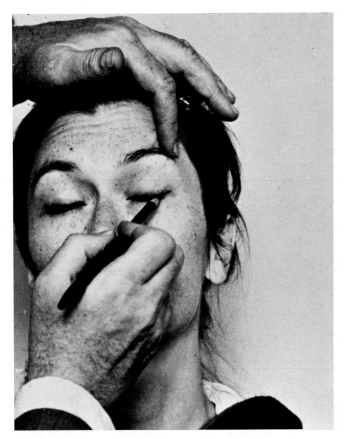

41. Take the pencil to the outside corner and carry it onto the lid to complete the line.

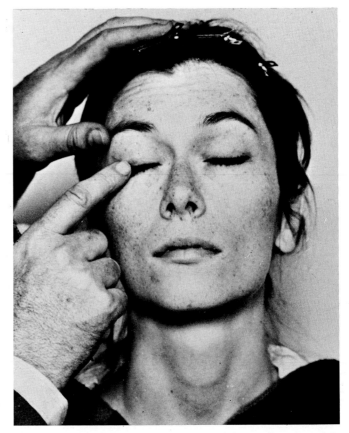

42. With the fingertips, blend the edge of the eyeline down into the lashes so that top of line is softened and is invisible.

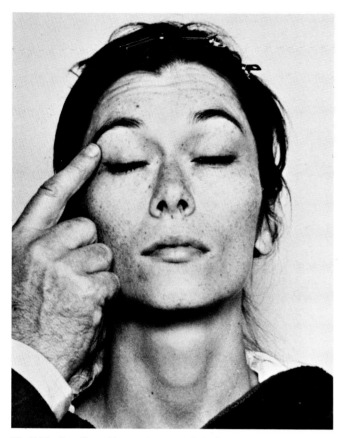

43. With the fingertip, apply some light blue eye shadow to the lid, along the lash line, blending it up toward the brows.

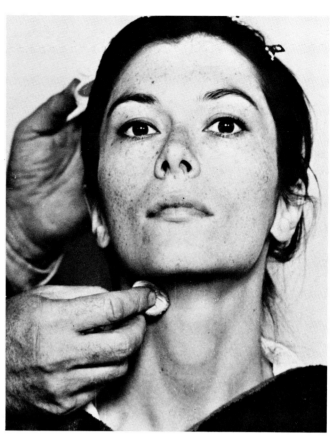

44. Apply shadow—in this case dark, dry rouge has been used—underneath the chin and jaw line and blend it down on to the neck. Separating the jaw and neck is helpful in all beautifying makeup.

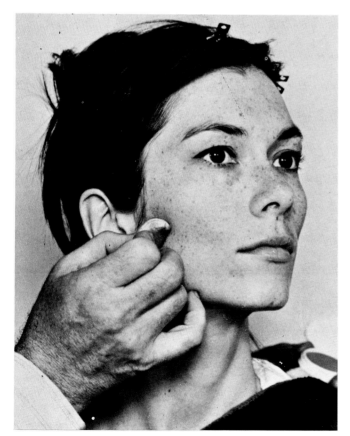

45. Using the same dry rouge shadow, sink the cheekbones, blending up toward the cheekbone and down toward the jawbone.

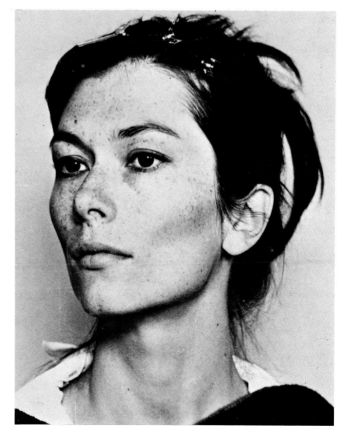

46. Rouge has been applied to the opposite cheek.

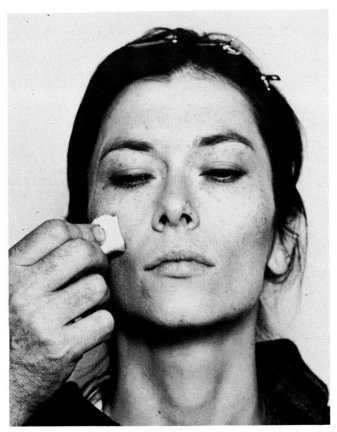

47. Using a section of foam rubber sponge, begin to apply the modified grease base evenly. Avoid lumps, pockets of excessive grease, or streakiness.

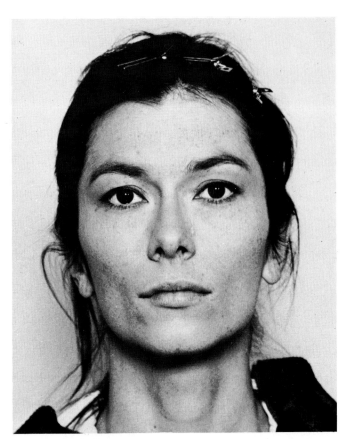

48. Base has been applied over the entire face. Note that thin application of base evens the skin tone, yet is not so thick that it covers freckles.

49. When you are satisfied that you have a thin, natural application of the base, powder it lightly. Roll off powder with puff.

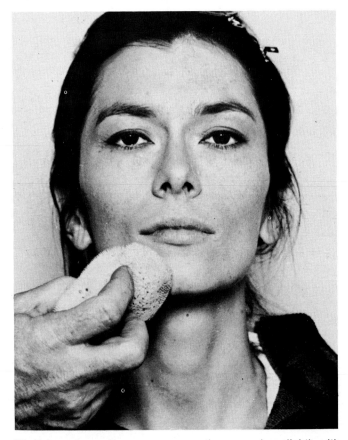

50. Using a damp silk sponge, go over the grease base lightly with a pancake wash.

51. Check your base for natural skin quality and an even, natural tone.

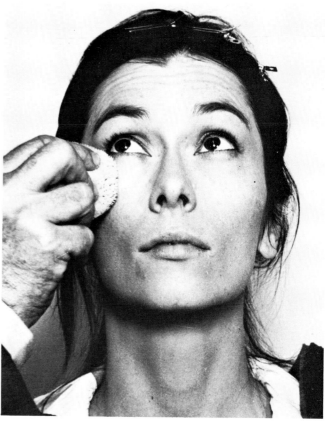

52. With a corner of the silk sponge, pick up a quantity of highlight and apply it to below the eye from the inner corner out.

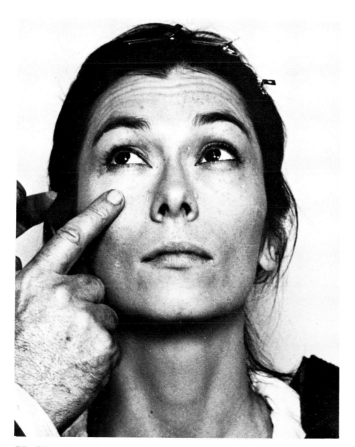

53. Blend the edges of the highlight so that they fade into the base color.

54. We want to achieve enough light under the eyes to combat discoloration or bagginess, not to be evident as paint.

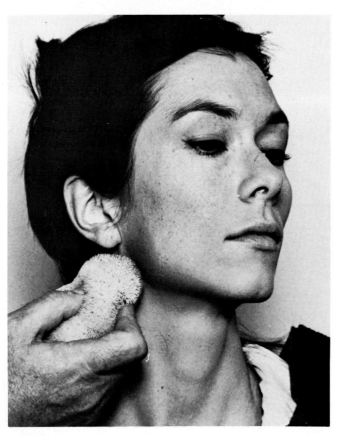

55. With the silk sponge, apply shadow (three shades darker than base) along jaw, starting at hairline and blending up onto the cheek.

56. Apply shadow along the nose, blending both jaw and nose shadows into the base color.

57. With the silk sponge, apply rouge to the cheeks, chin, nose, and forehead, and blend this into the base color.

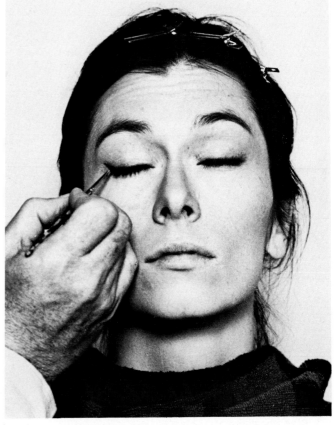

58. Go over the eyeline with a small, pointed sable brush, painting the lash line with black eyeliner, and blending off top edge.

59. Blend the edge of this line with a clean, slightly damp brush. Apply shadow along the blended line with a flat sable brush and blend this shadow up toward the brow and in toward the eye.

60. Note the development of the eyes thus far.

61. Using the small pointed sable brush, apply a faint suggestion of a mascara line to the line of the bottom eyelash.

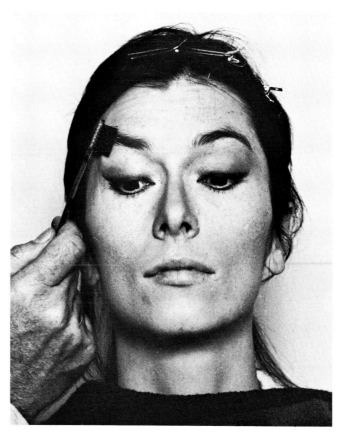

62. Brush the eyebrows out into a soft arch shape.

63. Gently sketch in the new eyebrow line.

64. Note how much of the natural eyebrow was used in shaping the new brow.

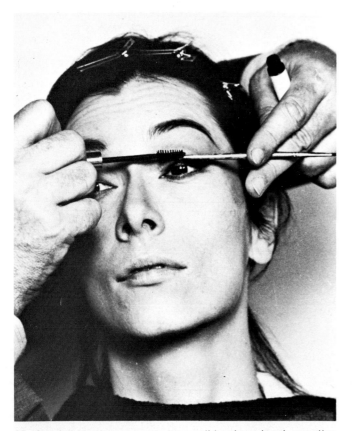

65. Carefully apply mascara to top eyelid, using a brush or cotton swab behind the lashes to catch any excess mascara.

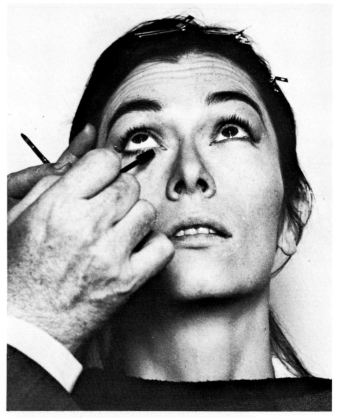

66. Now apply a touch of mascara to the bottom lids.

67. For a natural mouth, pick up a dab of moist rouge or lipstick and apply it to the lower and upper lips.

68. The basic makeup for black and white is now complete.

69. A wig is placed on the model for a finishing touch.

70. For character roles, a more shaped lip line may be called for. For this purpose, I personally like to give the corners of the mouth a slight lift. Use a flat red sable brush (no. 4 or 5) to paint on the lipstick. Adding false eyelashes is also in keeping with the exaggerated mouth and wig.

MAKEUP FOR THE MALE PERFORMER

Makeup for the male performer differs from that used for the female in essentially one respect: it is frequently possible to photograph the male performer who is wearing no makeup at all, or very slight amounts of makeup. This does not, of course, apply to all or even most instances. Makeup should *not* be used: (1) if the skin color and quality make the use of makeup unnecessary; (2) if the appearance of his wearing even the slightest bit of makeup diminishes the effect of his performance.

In view of this, makeup should be used for the male performer in the following circumstances: (1) when an excessively heavy beard tone is unattractive; (2) when the performer's skin tone is too light, or too dark, for proper skin tone balance; (3) when the use of makeup is required to improve the actor's features and appearance.

How much makeup will be determined by these factors? We might successfully tone a dark beard area only, or we might add additional base color, or add corrective makeup. This varies with each circumstance.

In this demonstration modified grease will be used— though pancake would have been just as effective. The hair will also be altered slightly to create a more youthful effect: the hairline will be brought forward with a small hairpiece and all traces of gray will be removed. Moderate use of the pencil and shading will also enhance the youthful appearance.

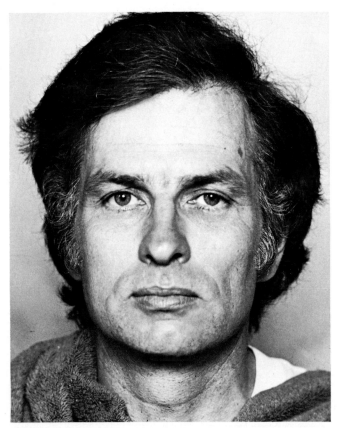

71. The male performer without makeup. (In some instances this may be suitable for photography.)

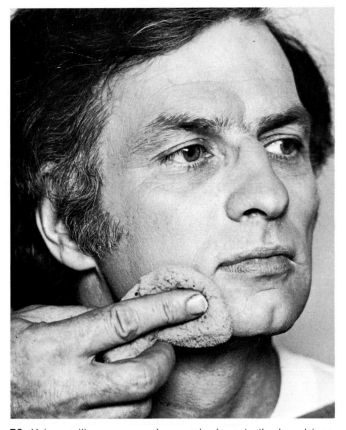

72. Using a silk sponge, apply pancake base to the beard tone. Modified grease may also be used, and frequently this may be all the makeup needed.

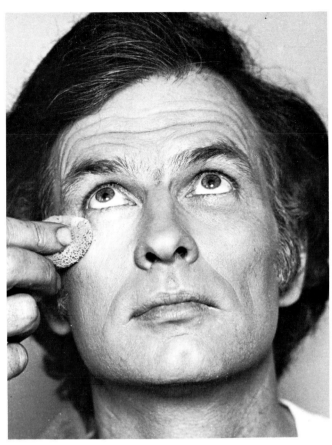

73. Using a corner of the sponge, apply a highlight from the inside corner of the eye·outward and blend.

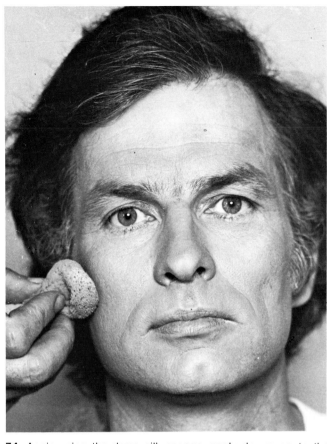

74. Again using the damp silk sponge, apply dry rouge to the cheeks, chin, nose, and forehead.

75. I have decided to alter the performer's slightly receding hairline. Ordinarily, I attach a hairpiece before applying any makeup, but since the piece will be so small, I add it now.

76. The hairpiece is positioned carefully.

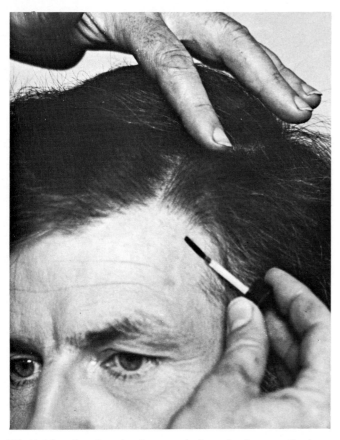

77. Holding the piece in place, apply the adhesive over the lace.

78. The hair of the piece is carefully combed onto the model's own hair.

79. Since the temple and sideburns contain some gray hairs, creating a younger effect means eliminating the gray hairs.

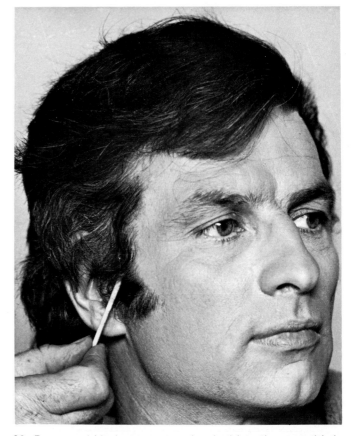

80. Brown and black mascara are brushed into the grayed hair area. This coloring is applied slowly and is combed into the natural hair color for a realistic color blend.

81. Note the effect achieved by darkening the gray areas and adding hairpiece.

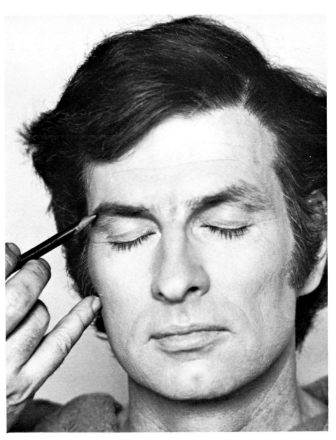

82. Sketching softly with a soft graphite pencil, arch and shape the eyebrow.

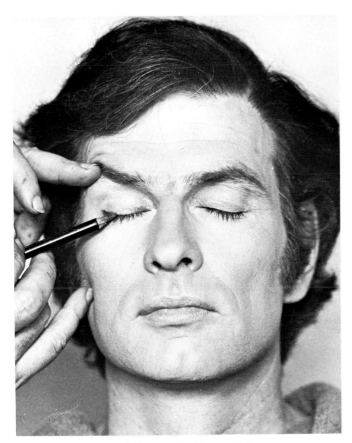

83. The top of the eyelid is accented by a soft line.

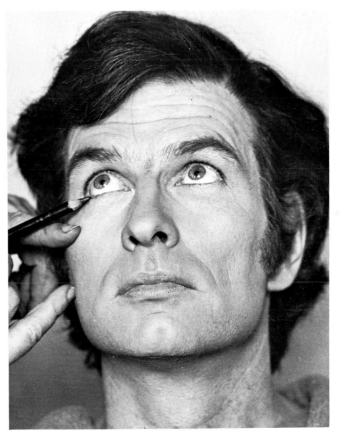

84. Now accent the bottom with the pencil.

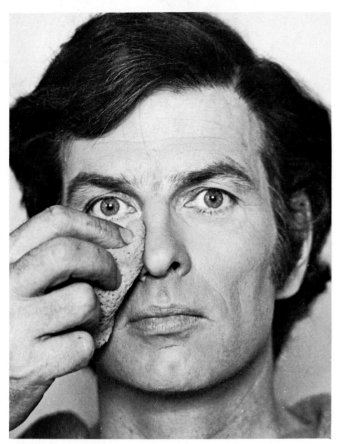

85. A darker tone—two or three shades darker than the base—is applied with the damp silk sponge down the sides of the nose.

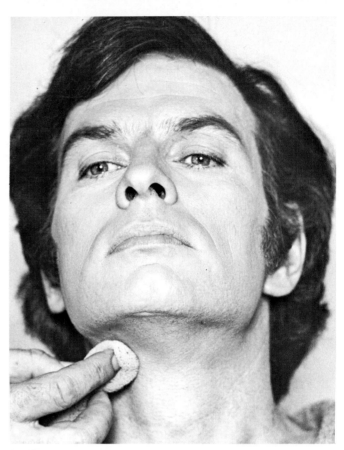

86. The same shadow color is applied to underneath the chin and jaw, and blended down on the neck.

87. With the fingertip, a faint touch of moist rouge is dabbed onto the lips.

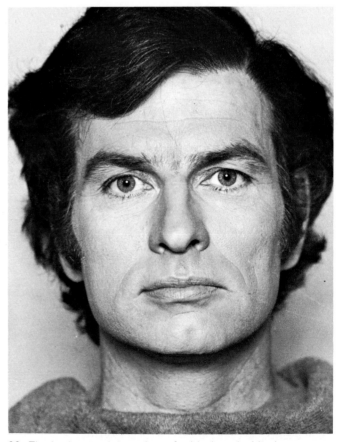

88. The basic complete makeup for black and white is now complete.

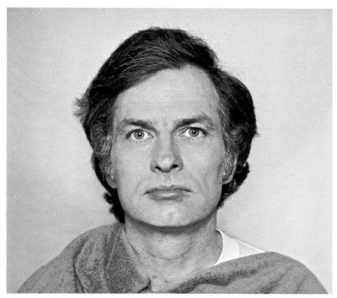

A. Model's face has been cleansed in preparation for makeup.

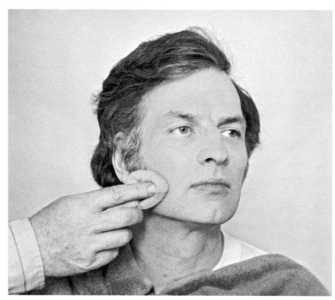

B. Pancake makeup base is applied with a damp silk sponge.

C. Highlight is applied under the eyes.

D. Rouge highlights are added to cheeks, forehead, nose, and chin.

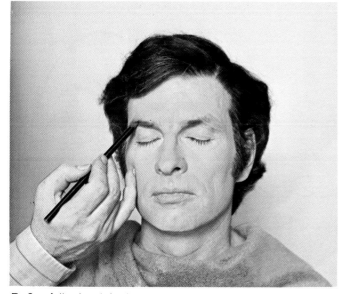

E. Carefully sketch in the eyebrow shape.

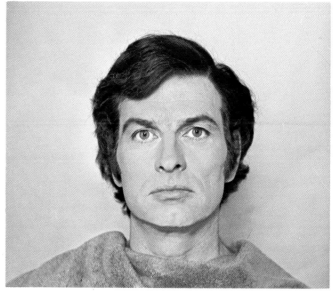

F. Sideburns are darkened to match hair color and a tiny touch of color is added to the lips.

VARIATIONS

Now that we have studied two rather oval faces, let's examine some of the methods that could be used when a face may vary from this norm—the round, square, diamond, and lean faces discussed earlier.

ROUND FACE

The round face, obviously, will require slimming. In your mind, transpose an oval shape onto the existing round face. Carry the jaw shading up to the imaginary oval line, and blend it into the base. The eyebrows should be arched a bit, to counteract any horizontal line, and the eyes should shade up toward the new brows.

The cheek rouge requires a vertical placement, rather than horizontal. Starting at the outer corner of the eye and running down vertically past the mouth should help to slim the face. In addition, a soft sinking of the cheeks following this same direction is also a help.

The mouth should arch to overcome the horizontal line. Also try to use up a bit of the upper and lower lip space.

Neck shading is useful in black and white, but must be used with great discretion in color. This removes weight from the chin.

Hair can be used to add height to the face, and women may even carry some hair onto each jaw to minimize the roundness.

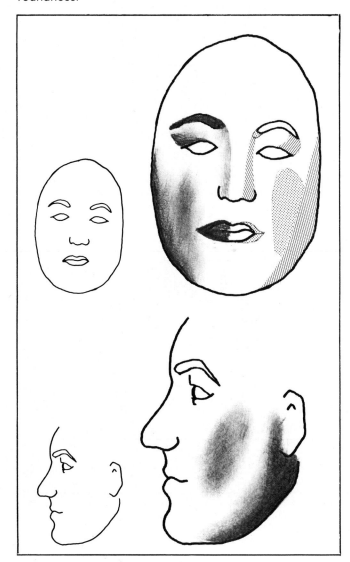

SQUARE FACE

Corrective work for a square face is similar to work done on the round, except it is important to minimize the jaw area. Again, effective shading is possible in black and white, and color demands discretion.

DIAMOND FACE

This face structure, with its dominant width across the cheekbones, can be changed by adding vertical lines. Shading in the cheek area must be modest. Apply cheek rouge in a vertical direction rather than at an angle. Lift the eyebrow and eye a bit into the forehead area. Lift the hair for height, and use it to cover the breadth of the face at the cheekbones.

LEAN OR LONG FACE

The lean face requires effects quite different from those described above. Here, all illusions are designed to create width. Eyes, eyebrows, and mouth should be shaped as horizontally as is reasonable. Rouge also should follow this horizontal direction and the hair used to shorten the brow a bit to fill in the sides as a means of countering the vertical line of the face.

The inherent principle is a very simple one: round, broad faces require slimming and elongation, and excessively long faces require widening and shortening. Although this inherent principle is a simple one, effecting these changes requires careful application and subtle change. The camera will not tolerate broad, obvious effects.

While the sequence demonstrating makeup for the male performer has shown the progression of a basic black and white makeup, I repeat—and this fact cannot be stated too emphatically—what I said earlier: it does not constitute stages of makeup to be used in all instances. The model's face may very well have been satisfactory without any makeup applied at all, or simply softening the beard tone might have been sufficient, or perhaps merely evening out the skin tone with an application of base may have sufficed perfectly well.

The most important thing to determine in advance is how much change is demanded by the situation. Find out what the director requires first, then determine from the cameraman how much skin color balance is called for, if any. Finally, try to ascertain how much work the performer wants done, and if these three separate needs can be reconciled, go ahead and apply the makeup required. If, however, there is a conflict between the expressed wishes of these associates, look for a diplomatic way in which to reconcile divergent interests. Once these are reconciled, you may safely proceed, and using your acquired skill, create the changes needed to satisfy everyone.

MAINTAINING THE MAKEUP

When the makeup is completed and the performer is costumed and on the set, your responsibility has not ended. It is now necessary to *maintain* the makeup you have applied so that it remains constant throughout the course of the day's filming. Since the performer will be working frequently under a hot sun or under studio lights, the heat will frequently create discomfort and perspiration. Beads of sweat must be blotted from the performer's face gently with a cleansing tissue. Minor patching may also be necessary. You may have to apply an additional bit of base color with a slightly damp sponge, or add lipstick—which some nervous performers constantly eat off—or remove a particle of soot, or you may have to see that the hair remains combed as it should be.

It may be necessary to call the performer away from the set. For these circumstances, you should have all your makeup materials set up on a table, with mirror and lights if possible, as close to the set as you can. Seat the performer, and make the needed repairs quickly. After each meal break a complete touch-up is usually required. To allow time for this work, notify the performers in advance. Ask the director or assistant director the sequence in which the performers will be needed on set, so that you can have those needed first ready to start, and, if necessary, you can continue with the other repairs without holding up production.

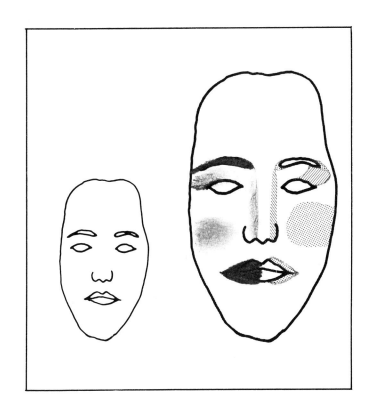

4
BASIC MAKEUP FOR COLOR FILM

The degree of subtlety in blending, the softness in shading, and the base application for natural skin that is required for black and white makeup is permissive and heavy-handed when compared to the standards required for color photography. Sharp, bright screens, strong projectors, and true color renditions of film emulsions create a degree of technical excellence that makes any skin flaw discernible. The makeup required to correct these flaws—or any other alterations necessary in makeup, for that matter—must be subtle and perfect.

Except in some particular instances, your goal should be to avoid any appearance of makeup in your work. If makeup looks greasy, chalky, or artificial in any aspect, you, as makeup artist, are obliged to *get rid of that look!* Except in those instances that call for the obvious appearance of cosmetics, or other manifestations of aging, or ill health—which will be dealt with in later chapters—your goal is to achieve a natural, healthy, fresh look.

GENERAL PRINCIPLES OF MAKEUP FOR COLOR

The modified grease or pancake base should be applied thin. This is very important. Moreover, you will have to be constantly aware of the degree of lightening or darkening you intend to use. A very dark skin tone is particularly difficult to apply in a thin coat, and streaking is a common error, a danger to be avoided at all cost. Conversely, if necessity demands that you lighten an excessively dark tan, for example, a carelessly thin application can easily produce a chalky and unattractive tone. It is practically impossible to illustrate these minor excesses photographically in this book. To demonstrate these faults in small color plates would require exaggerated phony effects which I prefer not to use. I can only alert you to these dangers and urge you to look constantly at all work with

care and intensity. This awareness, plus experience, will slowly improve your capacity for solving all problems that arise.

ESTABLISHING THE MAKEUP FOR THE FILM

As in all your work in any makeup job, first determine from your director, cameraman, and performer the desired end results. Whenever you can, try to select a base color that is as close as possible to the performer's own skin tone. Highlights should be a few shades lighter than the base color, and shadow colors a few shades darker.

Whenever possible try to arrange for a test shooting, a method of recording on film necessary details to be established before the actual filming takes place. At this time you can explore the ranges of skin colors you consider appropriate to the film. With test shooting you can confirm your initial judgments. Always film a range of skin tones for test shooting so that your final selection can be based on visual evidence. Once these choices are made, you have the basis for the entire film.

During the tests, keep a complete written list of all makeup materials used: the base, highlight, and shadow colors, and the intensity of the application. If it helps you, make a sketch of the face, a guide showing the placement of makeup and directions and extent of the blending. This is especially handy if the film calls for changes in the performer's appearance, and the scenes are filmed out of sequence. These charts are invaluable as reference points, in case questions arise regarding the accuracy of your makeup matching another sequence.

Another precaution is equally important: as soon as a makeup or hair style is approved, make arrangements for a still photographer to take photos that will act as your permanent record. Arrange for these photographs to be taken against a neutral background and with flat lighting. You don't want a beautiful photo; you want an accurate record, a full front shot, a profile, and the back of the head. See to it that these are developed as soon as possible and blown up to 8″ x 10″. If having a photographer is too costly, or if time does not allow it, settle on Polaroid shots, if necessary as many as will give you an accurate record of all phases of your work.

These photos will be your permanent guide to the accuracy of all future work in the film. This form of recording is also necessary for male performers whose haircut must be maintained at a determined length for the duration of a segment, or for the entire film. Of course, any significant changes in the appearance of the performers, male or female, face or hair, should be recorded in this fashion as well.

Assuming you've decided on a moderate makeup for a female performer in color, let's proceed with the stages involved in making her up. These stages have been illustrated in color only.

A. Seat the model, cleanse her face in preparation for makeup. Drop a protective cloth around her shoulders.

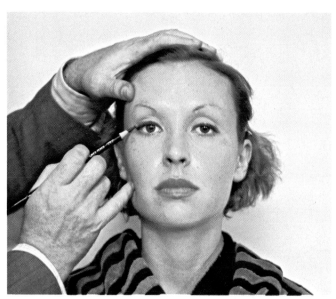

B. The eyeline is applied with a black eyebrow pencil and is extended beyond the outer corners and lifted a bit toward the brows.

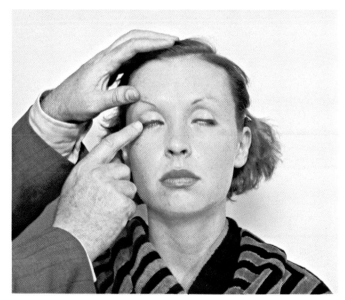

C. With the fingertip, blend the top part of the black eyeline down into the lashes.

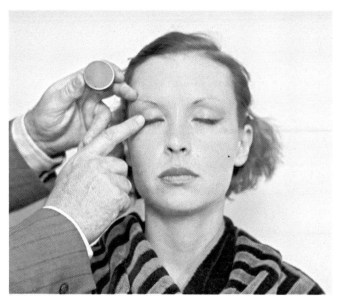

D. Apply a thin layer of shadow along the lash line and blend up toward the brow and in a bit toward, but not onto, the nose.

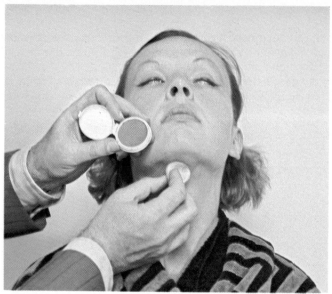

E. Apply shadow (here a dark, dry rouge) under the chin, along the jaw, and blend onto the neck.

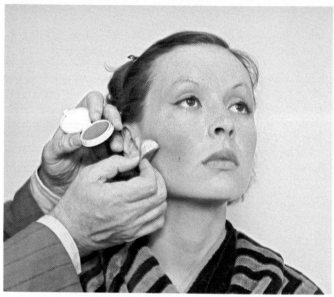

F. Here, using the same dark, dry rouge as shadow, sink the area between the cheekbone and the jawbone.

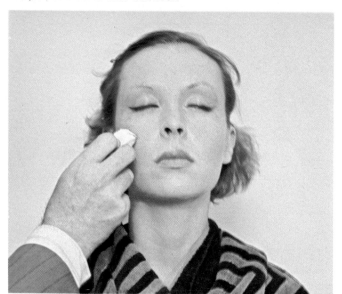

G. Using a section of foam rubber, apply the modified grease base evenly and thinly. Cover the entire face and shadow area.

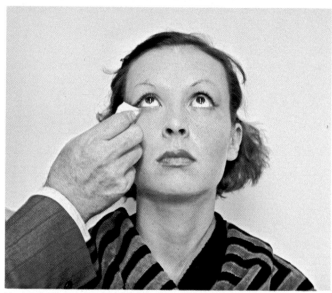

H. A highlight (two or three shades lighter than the base) is applied under the eyes with a corner of the foam rubber sponge.

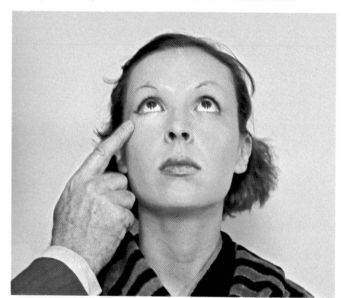

I. This highlight is carefully blended into the base color.

J. Shading (two or three shades darker than the base) is applied along the jaw and blended up toward the cheek into the base color. Use a clean piece of foam rubber sponge.

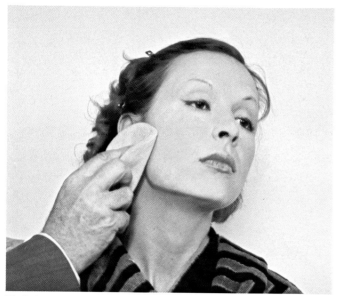

K. Colorless powder is puffed on to set the makeup, and a damp sponge is then used to remove the excess powder film.

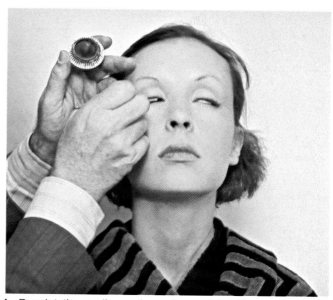

L. Repaint the eyeline, using a fine pointed Japanese writing brush and black mascara.

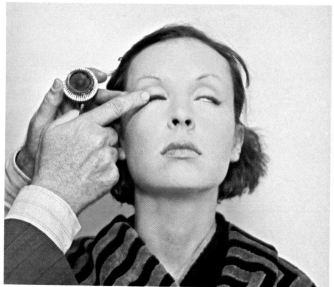

M. The edge of this line is blended off to soften into the base color.

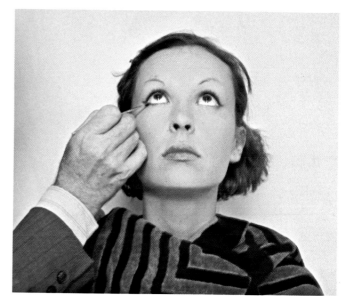

N. Using the same brush, paint the faintest suggestion of a line under the eyes at the lashes.

O. Sketch in the eyebrows very carefully, a hair at a time, with a soft graphite sketching pencil.

P. The new brows, carefully shaped and arched. Compare this to previous plate.

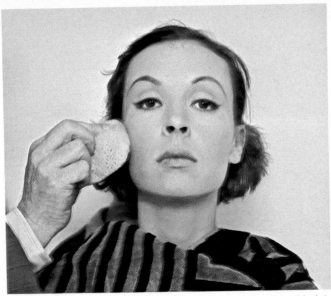

Q. Dry rouge, here applied with a damp sponge, is added to cheeks, chin, nose, and forehead.

R. A light lip coloring is added with the fingertip to the original mouth shape.

S. Mascara is applied to the lashes by a roller: a brush or cotton swab is held behind the lashes to pick up excess mascara.

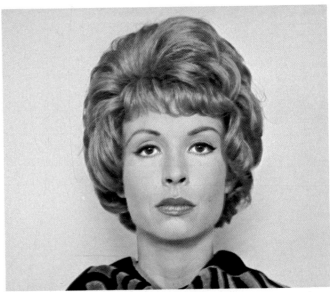

T. Dressing the hair will complete the makeup. Here we have used an auburn wig.

U. To apply a painted mouth use a flat sable brush. I like to lift the outer corners slightly beyond the mouth line.

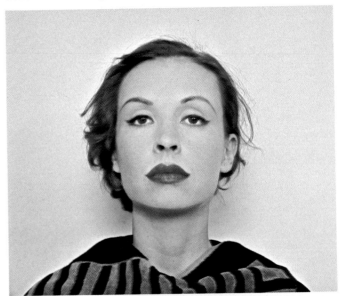

V. Roundness in the lips has been created by painting darker at the outside and blending in toward the centers.

W. Lip gloss has been added to the mouth and false eyelashes to the lids.

X. A new hairdo, here a frosted wig, completes the makeup.

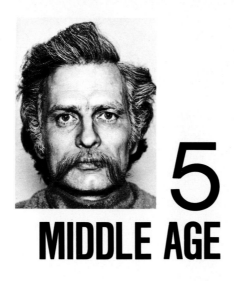

5
MIDDLE AGE

Age or aging is a state that is difficult to define, since it has very different meanings for different people. For a child, a person who is twenty years of age is old. To a teen-ager, thirty years is decrepit, while someone who is fifty considers fifty to be young. We must, then, *arbitrarily* define certain age approximations into specific terms to which we can refer in the following chapters.

CATEGORIES OF AGE

Today we can safely merge the period from eighteen to thirty into a category called *youth*. There are changes in the face from eighteen to thirty, but they are so subtle that they defy accurate re-creation by a makeup artist. He may make some small alterations, like placing very soft shadows about the eyes to indicate slight sinking, but apart from this, hairdressing and costume are more significant in effecting change in this age category.

We can call the period from thirty to fifty *middle age*. Obviously, this term is not totally accurate, since some fifty-year-olds appear very youthful, while some thirty-year-olds appear positively middle-aged. Nevertheless, this time span—thirty to fifty—is one in which the face does begin to reveal the process of aging.

Aging is actually a progressive decline of that extraordinary machine, the human body. This decline manifests itself in the face in a number of ways: because of a loss in elasticity, the skin stretches and begins to fall into the hollows of the face. Where there are no hollows, the skin sags into jowls, eye bags, pouches, and wrinkles. At the same time, the body experiences a number of losses. Vision frequently declines, making eyeglasses necessary. Of primary visual effect is the gradual loss of hair. One of the more amusing travesties out of Hollywood's past was the way in which a leading man "aged" by adding a white

wig with even more hair than his own. At that time, no leading man would allow wrinkles, let alone something as obscene as baldness, to mar his handsome looks! It took the imagination and courage of Orson Welles in *Citizen Kane* to age himself progressively to the point of total baldness.

We call old age the period from fifty to almost seventy. During this period aging is usually indicated by a further loss of hair and an increase in the size of eye bags, pouches, jowls, and wrinkles.

TECHNIQUES FOR AGE MAKEUP

Since aging is a gradual, progressive process we must use different techniques and materials in trying to simulate each of the various phases. In this chapter I will discuss aging when only moderate alteration is necessary in middle age. In the next chapters more extreme effects will be described to create older characters.

The first signs of age become apparent by a slight sinking of the area around the eyeball, and a suggestion of pouches and jowls. This suggestion of age can be successfully created by painting in the proper shadows, but the painting must be extremely subtle and skillful.

During the next stage of age (demonstrated in Chapter Seven), the pouches and jowls are fully formed. This stage can only be projected by adding artificial pieces molded to fit specific areas of the face. These pieces, made out of liquid latex or rubber foam, are usually sufficient to indicate age into the fifties, providing accurate loss of hair is also created.

For our purposes, after seventy the signs of age become most acute, with the face resembling the wrinkles of a dried prune. This stage is obviously extreme old age and is demonstrated in Chapter Eight.

Before we begin to study the various techniques of aging, I must reiterate: what you will see demonstrated here can be successfully used only after a considerable period of practice. Because you see results accomplished easily here does not minimize the fact that skill and knowledge can only be realized after you have expended a great amount of effort. Skill in painting, modeling, and application will develop slowly. Don't be disappointed if your first efforts turn out less successfully than those in the following demonstrations. It took me many years to acquire my skills. You have the advantage of having this experience presented in an explicit step-by-step manner that should eliminate many years of trial and error that I was unable to escape. Practice continuously, examine your work for flaws, and look for progress; then practice again and again.

Do not attempt to paint age on a performer until you have fully explored the techniques described in Chapter Two. You must develop these skills to a high degree in order to avoid smearing, blotches, and obvious lines.

For middle age, your goal is to create a minimal effect, yet this will require great skill, a skill that you will call upon frequently in your makeup work. (The demonstration in this chapter and all the ones to come have shown work made deliberately heavy for instructional purposes, so that you can *see* in the photographs the changes taking place. Ordinarily this would be too heavy for use in film.) Simply because these effects are infinitesimal, do not fall into the trap of depreciating them. More scripts will call for a slight change in an actor's appearance than will call for a large dramatic effect.

PAINTING THE EYE

After you have selected and applied the proper base color, choose a shadow tone four or five shades darker than the base. Obviously, this may vary more or less, depending on the intensity of the effect desired.

Using a flat sable brush, pick up a bit of the shadow and apply it to the inner point of the eyelid. Carry this along the top of the eyesocket to the outside of the eye. Then clean your brush and blend the paint up into the corner of the eye and blend it around the shape of the bone below the eyebrow. This will create the effect of sinking the flesh above the eyeball. If you wish to accentuate this sinking effect even more, repeat the application of shadow on the same area, and this time blend it down onto the eyeball. The intensity of the shadow plus the distance you blend it onto the eyeball itself will determine the degree of sinking into the eye socket. Repeat the above on the other eye. (See Figs. 90 to 93.)

To sink the bottom part of the eyeball, follow the same basic technique: pick up some shadow, apply it to the inner corner of the bottom of the eye. Then carry the paint along the shape of the eyeball to the outer corner. Once again clean your brush and then blend this shadow up onto the eyeball. Blend and graduate the shadow so that it blends into and disappears into the base color. (See Fig. 94.)

The eye pouch beneath the eyeball can only be created partially with paint. Again, start the shadow at the inner corner of the eye and carry this down and around below the bottom of the eye about half or three quarters of the way to the outer corner. Clean the brush and blend this shadow *down,* grading it no more than ¼", and disappear-

ing into the base. The outer corner must diminish completely in width at that point where the pouch is to end. (See Fig. 95.)

SINKING THE CHEEK

Find that point on the face midway between the cheekbone and jawbone, and imagine a sinking (or shadow) along this line that will stop before it gets to the point where the cheekbone and jawbone meet in front of the ear, and will also stop where you feel the rear molars of the mouth. Apply the shadow along this line, and blend it up toward but not onto the cheekbone, down toward but not on the jawbone, back but stopping about 1" before the ear, and toward the mouth but stopping at the molars. This shadow should be no more than 1" or 1½" in length and not more than ½" in width. (See Figs. 96 to 98.)

SINKING THE TEMPLE

To sink the temple, the shadow is applied with a brush, or with the finger just below the edge of the temple bone. (See Chapter Two.) The shadow is most intense at this point. It then is blended back toward the hairline and ear to disappear into the base color. At its widest, this shadow is to be no more than ½" in width. You are only looking for the effect of a *slight* sinking, no more than a suggestion. If your eye sees a more obvious effect, the effect will most likely look painted and false when magnified and projected on the screen. (See Figs. 99 to 101.)

NOSE WRINKLES

The nose wrinkle can only be suggested, since any attempt to create it with paint would be very obvious on the screen. Carry a small amount of shadow through the area of the nose wrinkle. Start at the beginning of the nostril and around and down, ending at, or more usually below, the mouth. Blend this shadow up away from the direction of the mouth; at its widest—opposite the bottom of the nose—it should be less than ½". Start at the nostril, taper out to this widest point, and then taper its width down to disappear at its end. The wrinkle line should graduate in intensity from darkest at its initial line of placement, getting gradually lighter and disappearing into the base color along its breadth. (See Figs. 102 to 103.)

FOREHEAD

The rest of the face contains only slight sinkings and therefore calls for very subtle shading. Apply shadow in the depressions of the forehead, around each prominent bone of the eyebrows, and blend this shadow up toward the brows and into the base. Then blend around the large frontal bone of the forehead and blend up toward the hair and into the base. (See Figs. 104 to 107.)

CHIN WRINKLE

To locate the chin wrinkle have the performer pull his chin into his neck and grin. The wrinkle that starts mid-cheek and runs under the chin and around to the other side is the chin wrinkle. After locating this wrinkle, softly paint it in. Blend toward the mouth and into the base, softening the starting and the finishing points of the line in particular.

The corners of the mouth can be pulled down slightly to create a sag in the mouth. This can be intensified by shading under the bottom lip and carrying the shading around the contours in that area. (See Figs. 108 to 111.)

CORRECTIVE MEASURES

After you have created the basic shadings and sinkings of early age, look over your work carefully. If any painting is really obvious, the makeup is either too dark or too clumsily applied. If this is the case, you must then soften or blend the makeup so that the final effect is absolutely natural and real. If it is necessary to heighten your work, you can very lightly sketch over the area with a soft graphite lead pencil to accent softly your shadows, yet still avoiding any painted, false quality.

Sketching is obviously at the heart of this phase of work, and you can never practice this skill too much. To improve your dexterity, try to sketch in soft graphite, charcoal, or pastels, since each of these media is very close to the type of skill needed for painting with grease paint or pancake. Become as familiar as possible with the human face and always carry your sketchpad with you so that you can make note of interesting facial characteristics.

GRAYING THE HAIR AND COLOR CHANGE

As has been stated earlier, loss of hair is one of the most obvious ways to create the effect of aging. Because most aging described in screenplays generally does not span many years, the most common evidence of moderate aging is gray hair.

For a performer who is to work only one or a few days, only a temporary application of gray is necessary. Temporary colors can be obtained with silver hair spray, white grease paint, gray grease paint, or sometimes even white cream shoe polish, each with reasonable effects. These are used separately, or combined, depending on the effects you want to achieve. Gray hair includes a wide spectrum of colors and densities: there may be only occasional gray hairs, patches of gray hairs, pepper and salt, gray temples, streaks, or any variations of these. At the greatest extreme is the solid head of pure white hair.

Graying the hair for temporary use is not too difficult. Dip a toothbrush, a hair-dyeing brush, or an eyebrow brush into the graying material. (In Fig. 113 I have used white grease paint, but any of the other materials would perform relatively the same way.) Pick up a little material on the brush, and lightly stroke the gray onto the surface of the combed hair. Use a light touch, and don't apply a great amount of gray at a time; rather, put on a very small amount and add a bit more each time until you begin to obtain the appropriate color. At intervals, very carefully comb through the grayed area to avoid the formation of any clots or clumps.

Another method of temporarily graying the hair is with spray. "SpectraSpray," manufactured by Mehron, is a product designed for just this purpose. You can buy several different shades which can be used to make a quick color change. Since the aerosol spray coats the hair, the hair will not dress or handle easily once the spray has been applied. Do not spray the hair until the hair is in the position you desire. This spray is ideal for emergencies when you don't have time for more professional application.

What I have described are methods of applying gray for a one-day or brief appearance. If the performer's hair must be gray or changed in color for a considerable period of time, it is most practical to have his hair bleached and dyed to the proper shade. Only a highly skilled professional hairdresser should perform this operation. If such a skilled person is unavailable, it is possible to work with prepared packaged hair dyes, which are available in most drug stores. Dyes come in many brands, but Clairol is a manufacturer with a particularly long history of quality and experience in the field.

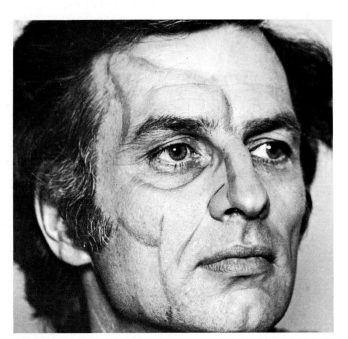

89. This is a diagrammatic drawing of the areas of the face to be painted for middle age.

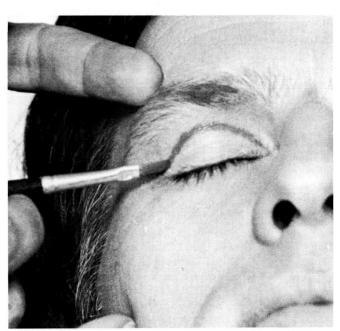

90. To sink the upper portion of the eye, first apply shadow around the deep hollow of the eyeball.

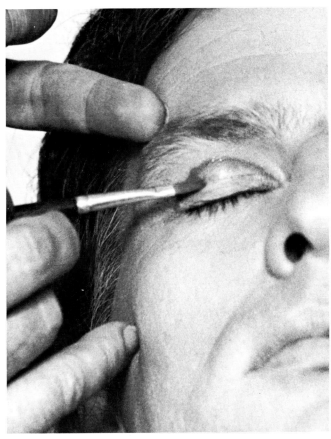

91. Blend this shadow color down onto the eyelid.

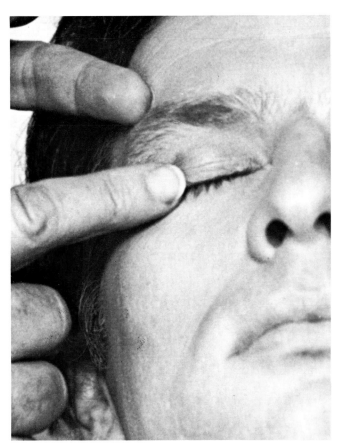

92. Blend the edges of the paint with your fingertips.

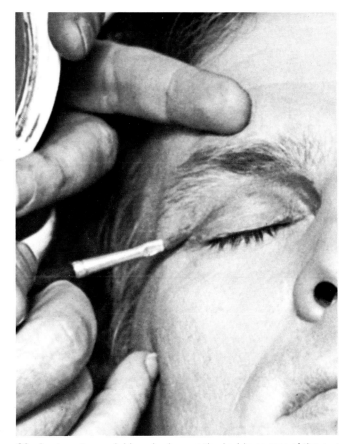

93. Apply a strong sinking shadow on the inside corner of the eye. Carry the shadow from the inner corner of the eye and bring it onto the eyeball sinking and around the bone under the eyebrow.

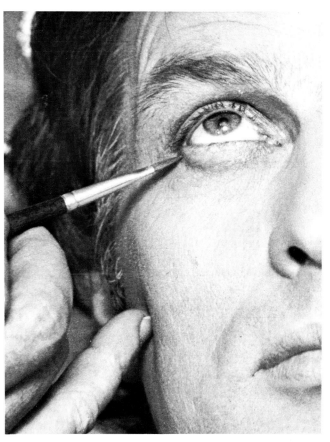

94. To sink the lower portion of the eye, apply a strong sinking shadow to the inside corner of the eye.

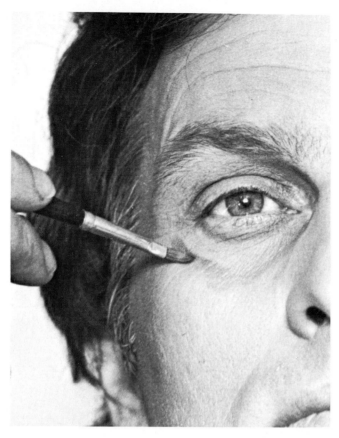

95. A slight pouch is created by bringing the shadow from the inside corner of the eye around under the eye. Blend this shadow toward the cheekbone.

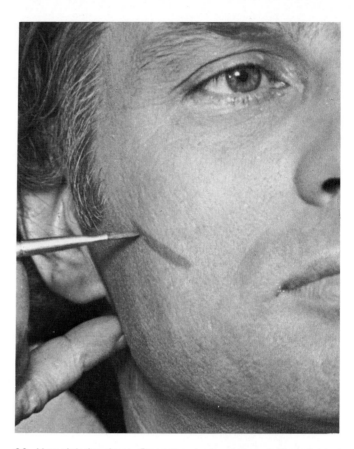

96. Now sink the cheek. Place the shadow between the height of the cheekbone and jawbone.

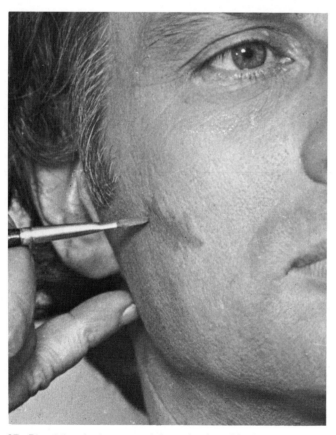

97. Blend the shadow up and down, back and forth.

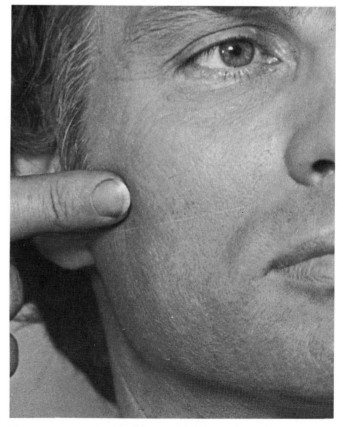

98. Blend the shadow with the fingertip.

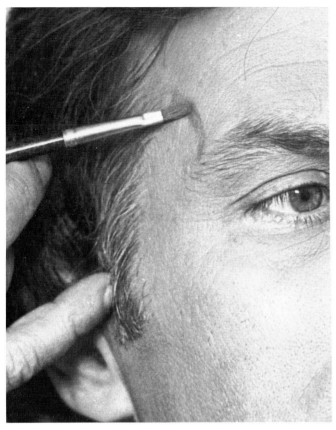

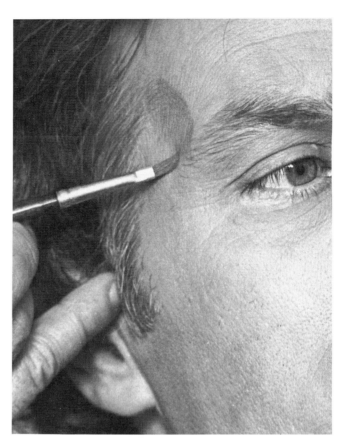

99. Now sink the temple. Apply shadow just below the ridge of the temple bone.

100. Blend the shadow back toward the hairline.

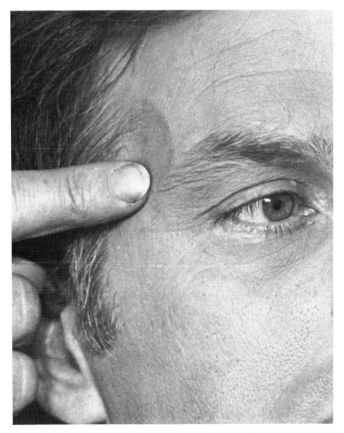

101. With the fingertip, blend the edges off to disappear into the base.

102. Now paint the nose wrinkle. Carry the line from the nostril to just below the mouth.

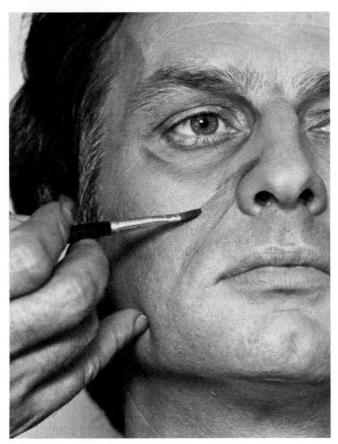

103. Blend the paint so that the color grades into the base.

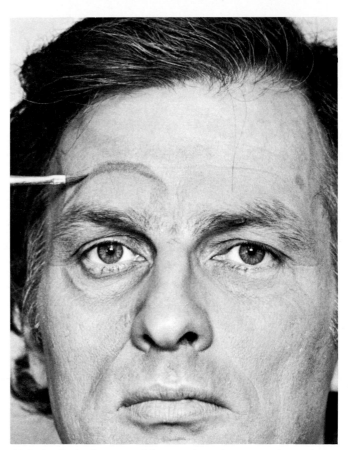

104. Apply shading around the prominent brow over the eyebrow.

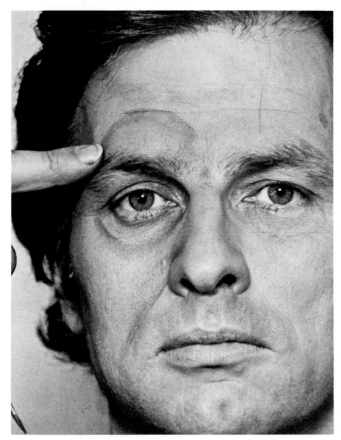

105. Blend this shading down toward the eyebrow and into the base color.

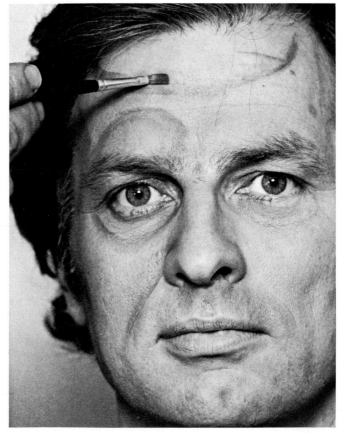

106. Apply shadow around the prominent forehead frontal bone.

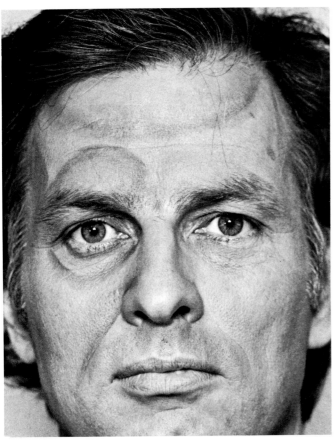

107. Blend this shading up toward the hairline and into the base color.

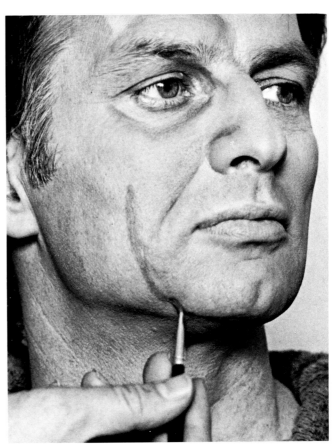

108. Now the chin wrinkle: start the shadow line in the cheek area and extend it down to and under the jaw and up the other side.

109. Blend this shadow toward the mouth and into the base color.

110. Pull the corners of the mouth down slightly.

111. Accent the natural sinking of the chin slightly with shadow.

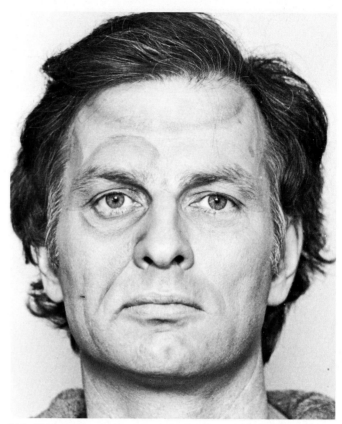

112. This demonstrates the basic sinkings and wrinkles that you can suggest with paint. Compare the right to the left side, which is unpainted. (Caution: all of this work has been deliberately accented for the demonstration. For real film work, this should be far more subtle.)

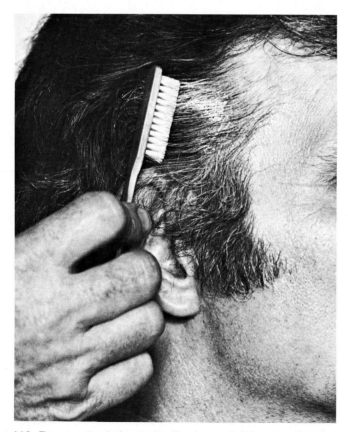

113. To gray the hair, stroke the brush lightly, repeating the process until the hair is the desired shade of gray.

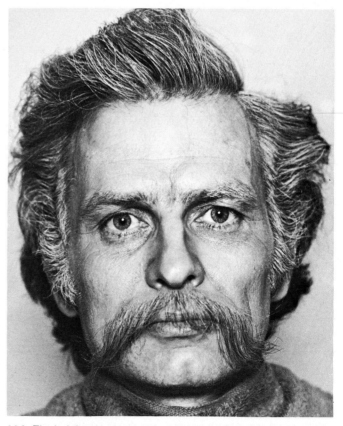

114. The hair has been grayed and a mustache added to complete the effect of middle age.

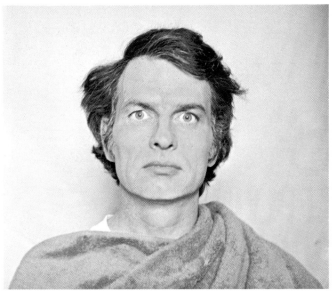

A. Model with thin base color applied.

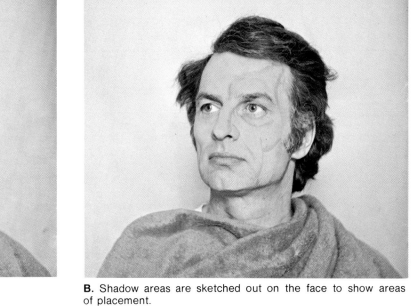

B. Shadow areas are sketched out on the face to show areas of placement.

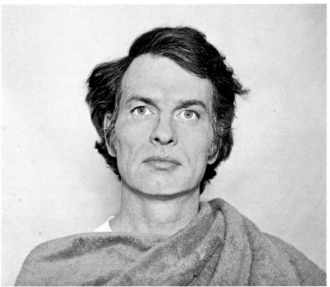

C. Aging has been very faintly suggested by the addition of shadows and blending.

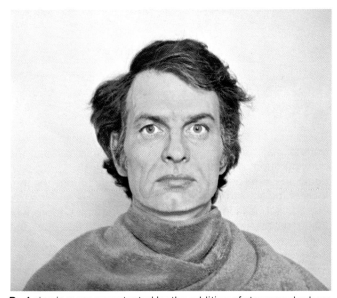

D. Aging is more accentuated by the addition of stronger shadows and blending.

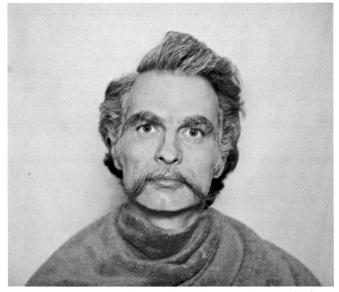

E. Hair has been grayed. Note that eyebrows and mustache have been added.

F. The only addition here is a lace beard.

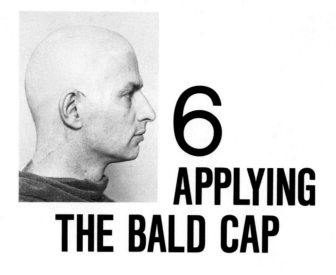

6
APPLYING
THE BALD CAP

It is almost impossible to do any degree of aging in makeup on the male performer without taking loss of hair into consideration. As has been stated, during the process of aging the skin generally stretches and falls into the hollows of the skull to create sinkings in the face, and the less elastic flesh falls into wrinkles, bags, and jowls. Moreover, aging usually includes some loss of faculties—hearing, sight, and occasionally teeth—but most frequently aging includes a loss of hair, particularly on the head.

This is not to say that balding necessarily becomes evident in an aging person or that a person need be particularly old to lose his hair. Nevertheless, in theater, films, or TV, loss of hair is usually associated with some advanced age, and while I think it realistic to avoid categorizing the loss of hair with any particular age, I do believe it should be considered when painting alone is not effective enough to denote age.

Since the performer would be extremely reluctant to shear his own head to create the effect of baldness, it becomes necessary to create this effect artificially. I do know of a number of instances where shearing was permitted by the performer, and of course the effect was excellent. (Two examples come to mind: Ernie Kovacs in *It Happened to Jane* and James Edwards in *The Joe Louis Story.*) Nevertheless, the length of time necessary for regrowing hair may interfere with a performer's other professional commitments, and he may simply be unwilling to go through the process of regrowing his hair. In most instances, therefore, baldness is created artificially. The bald cap is the most effective way to remove any trace of hair, and new hairpieces may be added to create whatever hairline or degree of baldness is desired. In this chapter, I will demonstrate the application of the bald cap, and in the next two chapters you will see how the cap is combined with the entire makeup effect.

THE BALD CAP

A bald cap is a paper-thin cap made of rubber or plastic, which is fitted and glued onto the performer's head. The best caps I have ever seen, and the one I use in this demonstration, are made by Cinema Secrets of Burbank, Calif. (See Suppliers List on p. 220.) The caps are extremely thin, yet strong enough to stretch without tearing, and they take makeup very well.

PAINTING THE BALD CAP

Once the bald cap is applied, you will incorporate the makeup on the cap with that applied to the face. The skin tone applied to the face should be carried onto the bald cap, reflecting the same variety of colors. First apply the base color, then tones of rouge, light and dark bases stippled on to accent the bone structure of the forehead. Since you will probably be using a fringe of hair around the temples and back of the head, your aging effect should be limited to sinking the shape of the bone structure of the head, in addition to the temples, frontal bony prominences, and frown bones over both eyes. The base and shading will aid in breaking up any last vestige of a line remaining from the bald cap.

PREPARING THE PERFORMER

Before applying the cap, comb the model's hair back and out of the way. Check the model's haircut to make sure that the hair around his temples and neck is cut short enough for you to glue around the sideburns, around and in back of the ear, and all along the nape of the neck. Hair in these areas will defy adhesion and may very well interfere with the proper fit and gluing of the cap.

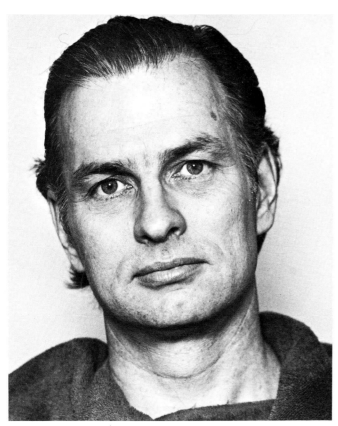

115. The model's hair has been trimmed satisfactorily around the temples and neck. If the hair is very wiry, flatten it as much as possible with water or setting lotion.

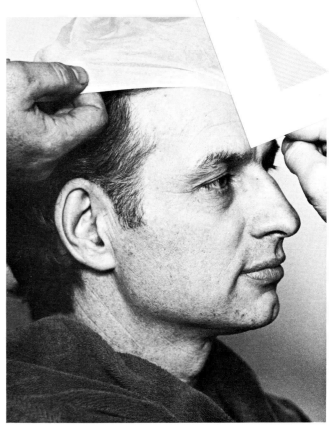

116. Open the cap wide and have the performer hold down the edge of the cap below his hairline as you slip it over his head.

117. The cap should cover his entire head. The cap should be large enough to cover his ears with a bit more to spare as well. The cap should fall about an inch beyond his hairline. Any more should be trimmed off.

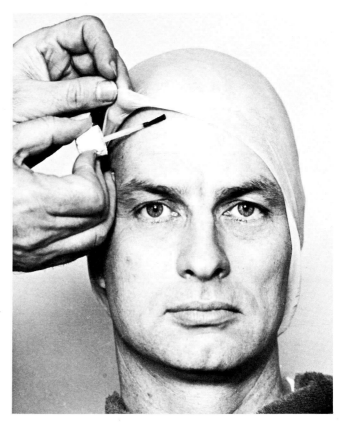

118. Lift the front of the cap away from the head and apply a layer of spirit gum beneath the center of the forehead area.

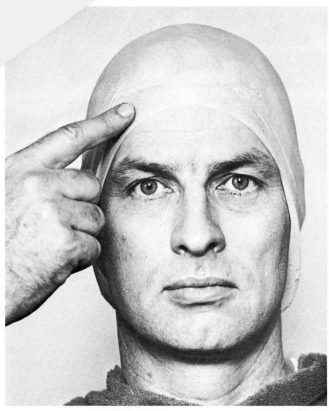

119. With a clean silk cloth or with a clean finger, press down the cap to check the fit and to hasten the drying.

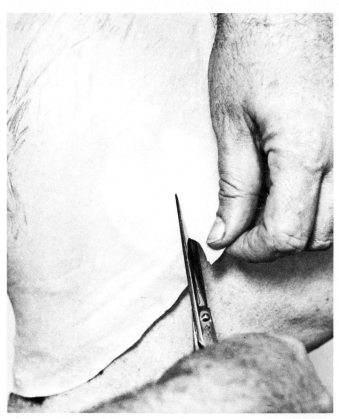

120. Once the upper portion has been glued, you are ready to trim the cap around the ears. Place the cap in position, and begin to trim. Don't make the cut too large, but rather cut less than you think necessary, because the cap can stretch.

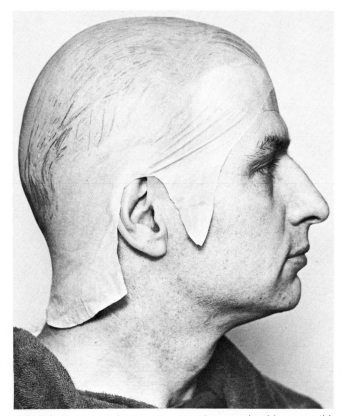

121. When trimmed around the ear, the cap should appear this way.

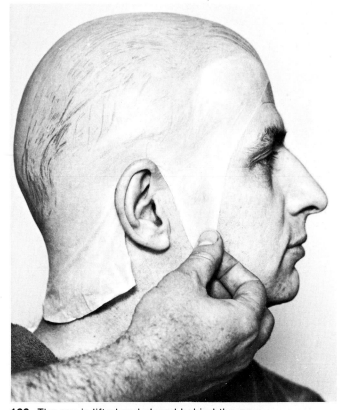

122. The cap is lifted and placed behind the ear.

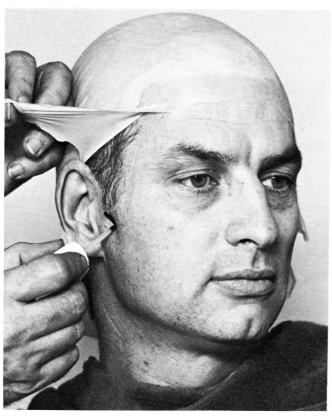

123. Carefully roll back the cap from the sideburns and apply spirit gum. Press the piece down to cover the sideburns. Be sure to avoid any wrinkles around the ear and smooth them away if they appear.

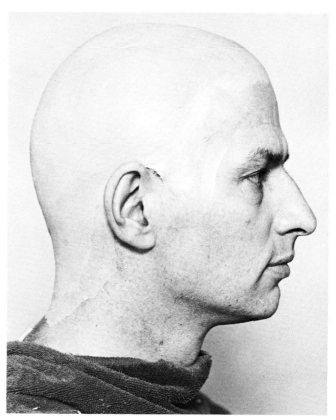

124. Fasten the cap behind the ear and down the neck in the same manner. Trim off excess cap material when necessary. Stretch the cap to avoid wrinkles. Be sure all edges are glued.

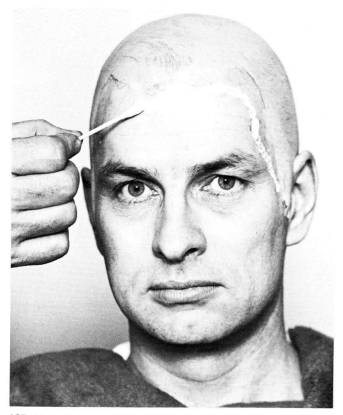

125. Using a brush or cotton swab, dab on a thin layer of liquid latex all along the edge of the cap. Overlap the edge only about ¼″. The milky color of the latex will dry transparent, covering the edge.

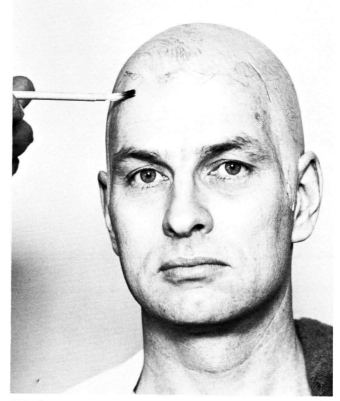

126. Over the dry latex film, brush on a layer of sealer, extending past the edge onto the skin slightly. This colorless sealer coats the latex so that makeup may be applied without discoloration. The cap is now ready for makeup application.

7
MODERATE OLD AGE

To create the early stages of aging, only shading can suggest the slight sinkings and minor wrinkling in the face. With increasing age, the loss of elasticity in the face produces wrinkles and bags that are too pronounced to be created by painting alone. Other methods must be employed to create illusions that will remain convincing even to the demanding eye of the camera.

A subtle and effective way of indicating wrinkles is with a substance known as *stipple.* This is a plastic or rubber substance applied to the face which will form natural and convincing wrinkles. Stipple can be used effectively around the eyes, for example. However, wrinkles do not tend to form on the face without other aspects of age occurring at the same time—jowls and bags tend to accompany the formation of wrinkles. In view of this, stipple by itself can only suggest modified age. Additional pieces must be added to the face to effect further evidences of age, pieces which will suggest the pouches, jowls, and bags of an aging face. In this chapter I will demonstrate the application of stipple and methods of aging the face with the addition of pieces. In the next chapter, even more extreme effects will be demonstrated.

AGE STIPPLE

Stipple is a rubber or plastic substance that you can make yourself or buy ready-made. In this demonstration I use Ben Nye's Old Age Stipple, an excellent product, although you can also use a homemade stipple by following the recipe given below.

Stipple is applied to the skin before the base. Stretch the skin in the area you intend to stipple, remembering that you can only apply the stipple to a small area at a time (Fig. 128). Each area must be stretched while stipple is applied. Using a coarse-textured red rubber sponge—the type used by cashiers to dampen their fingers—apply the stipple to the stretched skin area (Fig. 129). As soon as the stipple is dry—a matter of a few minutes—powder the area (Fig. 130), then pinch the area to aid the wrinkling. If the effect is not strong enough, stretch the skin again and repeat the process until you have achieved the desired degree of wrinkling.

127. Before applying stipple, cleanse the face thoroughly.

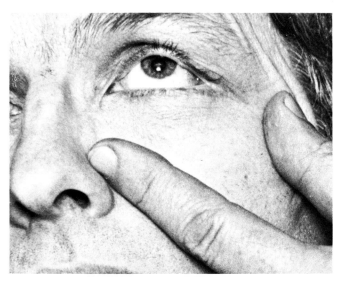

128. Using your thumb and forefinger, stretch the area of the skin to be stippled, holding this position as you apply the stipple material.

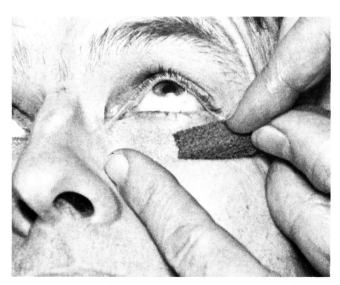

129. Using a coarse-textured red rubber sponge, dab on the stipple material. Let this dry, then dab on some more.

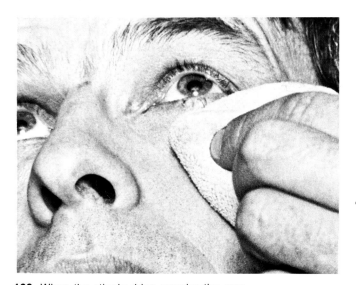

130. When the stipple dries, powder the area.

131. Press the skin together to induce wrinkling. If the effect is insufficient, stretch the skin again and repeat the process. Compare this effect to the first photograph.

HOMEMADE STIPPLE

To make your own stipple, follow this recipe:

(1) Mix together ¾ tablespoon face powder, ½ tablespoon pancake makeup (in the color closest to the base color you intend to use).

(2) Add ¾ teaspoon powdered gelatin and mix.

(3) Add 1 tablespoon hot water and mix into a paste.

(4) Add 2 oz. (60 cc.) liquid latex and mix.

You can use this stipple material immediately. If you prefer to mix it in advance, pour the mixture into a 2 oz. jar and refrigerate it until needed. When you are ready to use it, remove the jar from the refrigerator and warm it up, either under the hot water tap or in a double boiler. (Remember, simply warm it; do not overheat or boil it.) When the mixture is soft and liquid, apply it as described.

FACE PIECES

As you can see, the amount of wrinkling achieved with the stipple alone is convincing but limited. You can use it successfully for some effects, but it is insufficient for any great amount of aging when used alone. Stipple is used most effectively with the addition of face pieces which stimulate pouches, bags, and jowls on the face.

Face pieces can be made at home with rubber latex, a process that will be demonstrated in great detail in Chapter Nine. A face piece can also be made of foam rubber. Its shape is formed in a double mold of latex rubber which is first whipped to a froth with air, and then carefully baked until vulcanized in an oven. The foam latex piece will usually fit better than the homemade variety, but the process of producing it is much too complex to make yourself; it demands a permanent laboratory with a good deal of equipment. Foam pieces must be ordered from highly specialized laboratories or makeup artists.

It is useful to know about both rubber latex and foam pieces, so I will demonstrate the application of both. In this chapter foam pieces will be applied and in the next, rubber latex pieces.

In emergencies, when no pieces are available, you can improvise with Derma-Wax. I do not recommend this as a substitute, but I do feel that knowing how to use the wax could very well save the day in an emergency. For this reason, I also demonstrate the application of a wax nose.

FOAM PIECES

Ideally, foam pieces should be custom-made for the performer. This is not always expedient. For this demonstration I have used foam pieces from Cinema Secrets of Burbank which fit our model fairly well. Under ideal circumstances you should take the performer to Cinema Secrets and fit him or her from available stock, or you can send a face mask (see Chapter Nine) with sketches to Cinema Secrets for a custom-made fit.

PREPARING THE PERFORMER

Since this demonstration using foam latex pieces will be designed to age the performer significantly, baldness has also been taken into consideration. The bald cap should be applied first according to the methods described in Chapter Six. The performer's face should be cleansed.

THE DEMONSTRATION

Please keep in mind that all aspects of this demonstration have been somewhat exaggerated for instructional purposes. Makeup for film work should actually be even more subtle than shown here, but would not serve any function for the artist trying to learn. Also remember that these photographs are much smaller than life-size, whereas for film the image is magnified to many times life-size, demanding work that is extremely careful and subtle. Do not mistake these demonstration photos for the real standard of your work. They have been strengthened for you to perceive changes only.

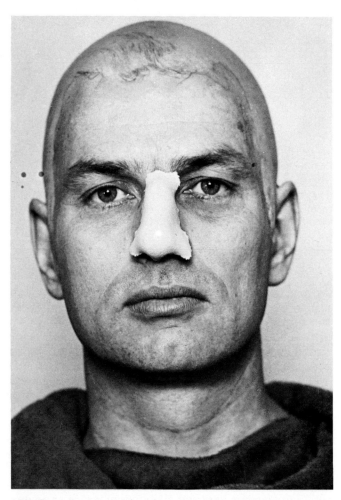

132. Fit the foam latex piece onto the nose to determine if the size and shape are suitable. Apply a thin coat of spirit gum along the bridge of the nose and adhere.

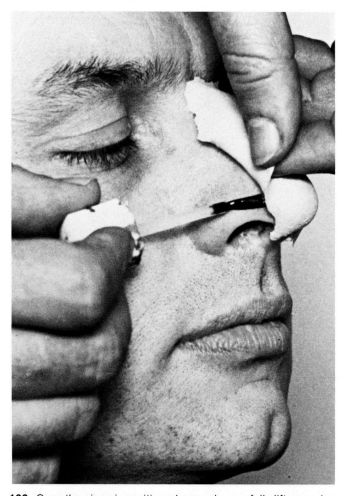

133. Once the piece is positioned properly, carefully lift one edge and apply spirit gum on the nose down the edge of the piece. Press down and repeat on other side.

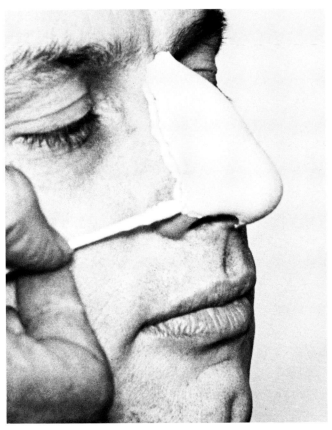

134. When the piece is on firmly, apply liquid latex thinly along the edge of the piece to blend off its edges.

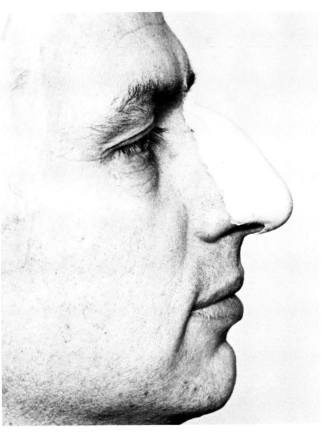

135. Profile view of nose glued and blended. The piece is secure.

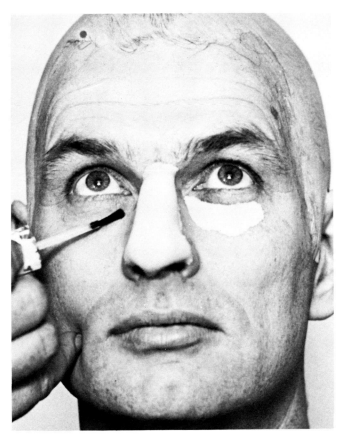

136. Pouches under the eyes are now applied. Brush spirit gum below the eyes and fit in the foam pieces. Apply liquid latex around the edges.

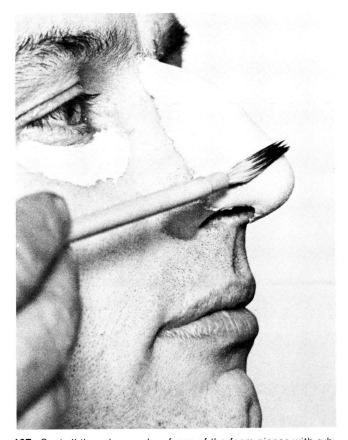

137. Coat all the edges and surfaces of the foam pieces with rubber sealer. This will enable the pieces to take makeup.

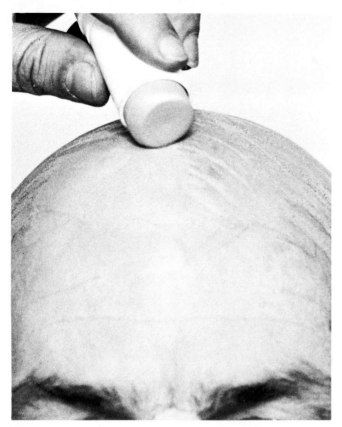

138. When the rubber sealer is dry, begin to apply makeup base, first on the bald cap.

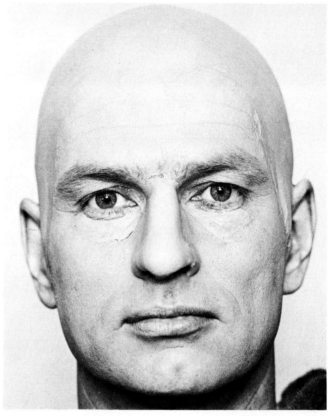

139. Carry the base onto the face, covering the foam pieces. Notice that the inner corner of pouch under right eye reveals that additional gluing is necessary.

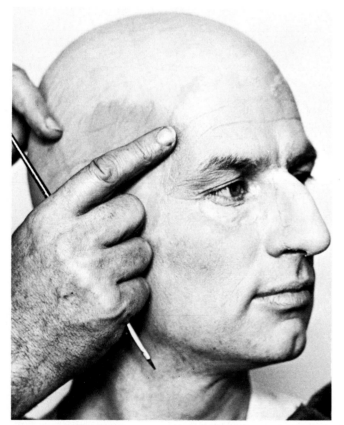

140. Begin to shape the temple structure, sinking the temple with shadow. Apply shadow along the temple bone, carrying the shadow onto the bald cap.

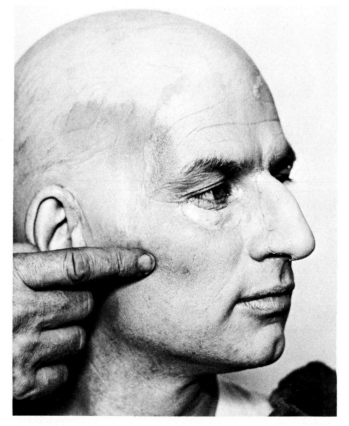

141. Carefully sink the cheekbone.

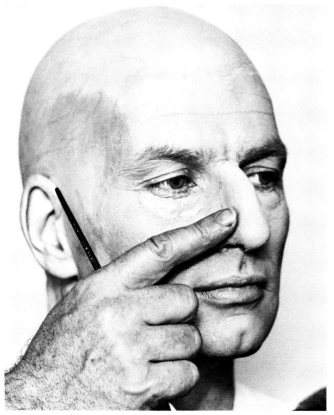

142. Apply shadow along the nose and blend it into the base.

143. With the brush, delicately shade and shape the nose wrinkle.

144. Accent the upper portion of the pouches beneath the eyes.

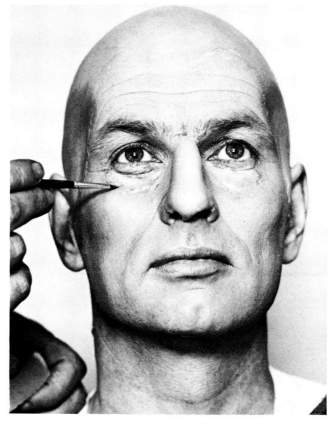

145. Now paint over the foam pouches to accent their entire shape.

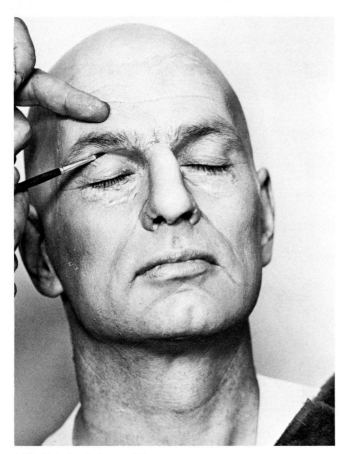

146. Sink the hollows of the upper eye.

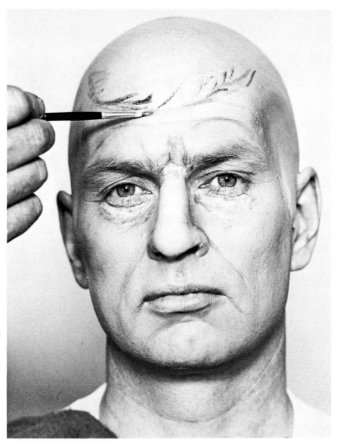

147. Shape and blend the bone structure of the forehead.

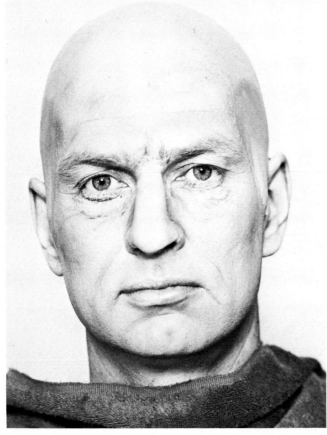

148. The painting is complete.

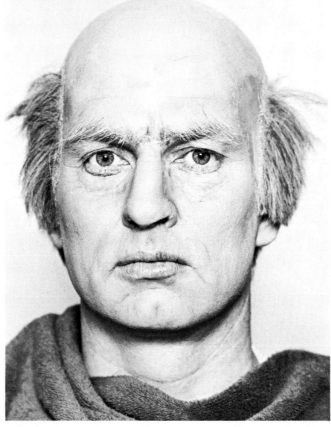

149. To complete the aging, add eyebrows and hair.

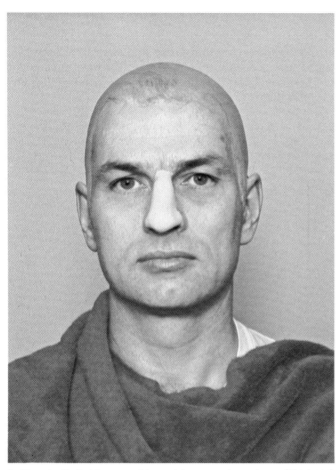

A. The plastic bald cap and foam latex nose have been fitted and glued into place.

B. Foam eye pouches have been glued on, and all edges have been blended.

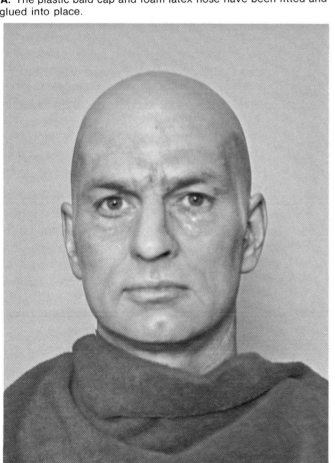

C. Base color has been added along with temple and cheek sinkings.

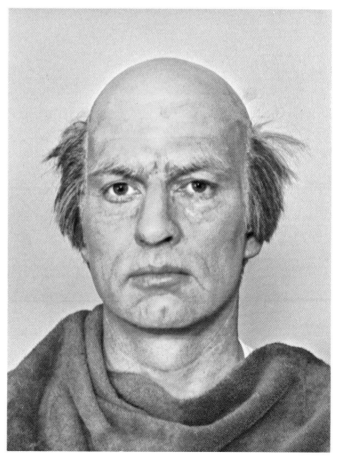

D. Lace eyebrows and a hair fringe complete this phase of aging.

USING WAX IN EMERGENCIES

As I have already stated, wax is not adequate for film work; it is not permanent. If the performer must appear for more than one day's shooting, you must repeat the entire application of wax the next day, and exact duplication is extremely difficult. Moreover, wax is fragile. Body temperature and the heat from lighting may cause the wax to form bubbles, making continual repairs necessary. But there are times when emergencies arise; when last-minute changes require you to build up features when pieces are simply not available. For this reason, I have included a brief demonstration on the use of wax, a technique that you may have to use as a last report.

Derma-Wax is the name for the soft wax used in this manner. It is available at various cosmetic houses or—also adequate—mortician's wax will suffice. The wax is very soft and malleable. Here is the method of applying it for a nose piece.

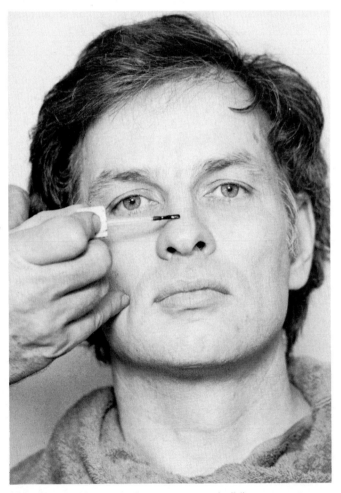

150. Apply spirit gum to the area you are building up.

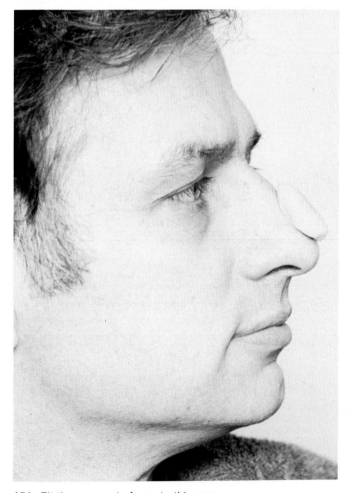

151. Fit the segment of wax to this area.

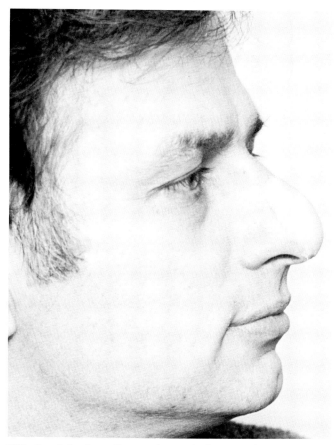

152. Carefully shape the wax to create the new shape.

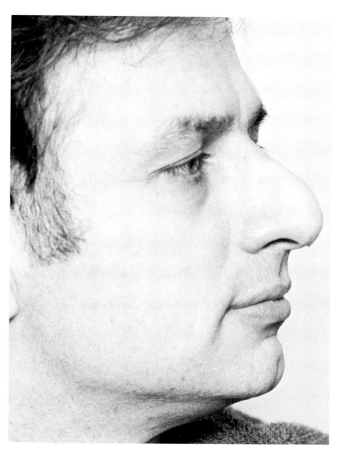

153. Blend off the edge of the wax into the face.

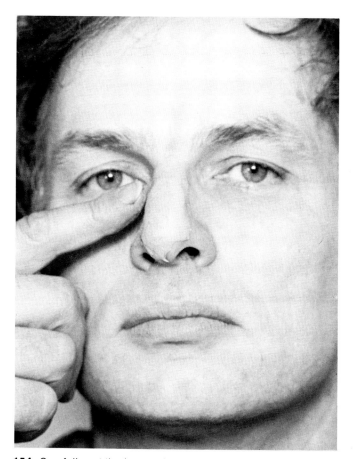

154. Carefully pat the base color onto the wax.

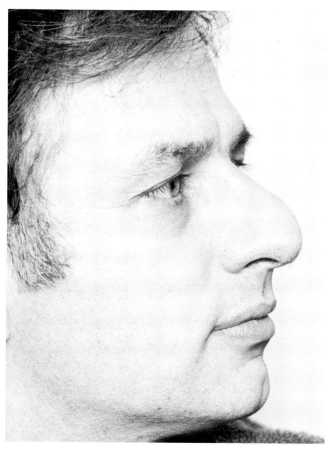

155. Blend the base color into the face and shadow the new nose carefully.

75

8
EXTREME OLD AGE WITH COTTON AND LATEX

Extreme old age, with its severe folds of flesh and a skin, is the next and final stage in aging. This advanced effect can be accomplished in two basic ways:

(1) A complete age mask made of foam rubber, consisting of a few or many pieces made specially for the performer. These pieces are designed to create the ultimate effect of very advanced age, but I find that using masks requires a prolonged period of preparation and ultimately ends up functioning with the limitations of a mask, partially or totally covering the actor's face and therefore limiting facial mobility and hampering the actor's performance.

(2) Stippled old age, as has been demonstrated in the previous chapter, is a rather simple technique in which a stipple material is dabbed directly onto the skin, dried, and powdered. This is covered with a modified grease or a rubber grease paint base.

This technique creates a wrinkled skin all over the entire face, and if it is done carefully the effect is quite good. There is a limitation in this technique: although the wrinkling of the skin is effective, it is not really sufficient in itself, and it fails to create full facial sags and folds denoting old age.

I use rubber pieces to create sags and folds, and I stipple latex over a layer of absorbent cotton. The combination of the rubber pieces and the additional ingredient of absorbent cotton creates an old age with sufficient facial sagging, extreme wrinkling, and, most importantly, provides total facial mobility for the actor.

BASIC PROCEDURE

Before demonstrating the actual stages of operation, I'd like to summarize the basic procedure involved in aging the performer with cotton and latex.

First, apply the bald cap as described in Chapter Six. Rubber pieces (see Chapter Nine) are then applied to the nose, over the eyes (to sink the eyeballs), under the eyes (to form pouches), and on the jaw (to create jowls). (See Figs. 156 to 161.)

After the pieces are applied, unroll a segment of sterile absorbent cotton and cut off a segment about 8″ across the width, separate as thin a cross-section of this cotton as possible, and continue to separate the cotton until it is practically transparent, yet still holds together. Cut up eight or ten such sections, each about 6″ x 8″. Put these aside until you are ready to use them. (See Figs. 162 to 164.) These will be glued over all areas of the face and head. Working in sections of the head, first apply spirit gum, then adhere the cotton. Once the cotton completely covers the face, comb it lightly until you have a thin, even film of cotton. Don't comb it all off, just enough to leave a soft fuzz over the entire face. (See Figs. 165 to 172.)

Now cover the fuzz with a coating of spirit gum. Use enough to saturate the cotton so that the cotton immediately flattens onto the face in a thin film. As you apply the spirit gum on sections of the face, use a hair dryer to hasten the drying process. Be careful around the eyes. When dry, apply some powder to the eyelids—top and bottom—so that the lids will not stick together. (See Figs. 173 and 174.)

After the spirit gum has dried, apply a liquid latex as a stipple, dabbing it firmly on the entire face, using a fresh piece of sponge rubber. Overlap the stippling to make sure the entire head is covered, and be particularly attentive to the back of the ears, the eyelids, and the lips. Powder the entire face, then go over the face with a damp sponge or a tissue to remove the excess powder. Now special base (see recipe below) can be applied, and hairpieces added. (See Figs. 175 to 180.)

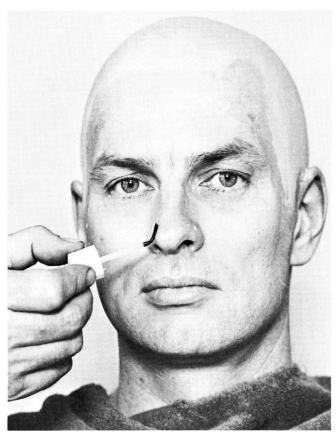

156. After applying the bald cap, brush spirit gum along the bridge of the nose, covering the area to be fitted with a nose piece.

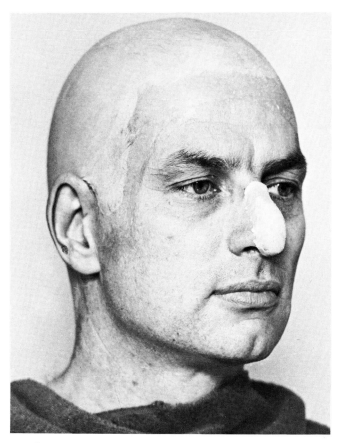

157. Seat the latex nose carefully, to make sure the fit is natural, with the edges of the piece thin and feathered.

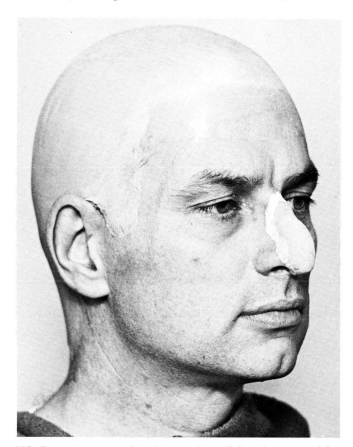

158. Paint a thin layer of liquid latex along all the edges around the nose to help the edge blend into the surrounding areas.

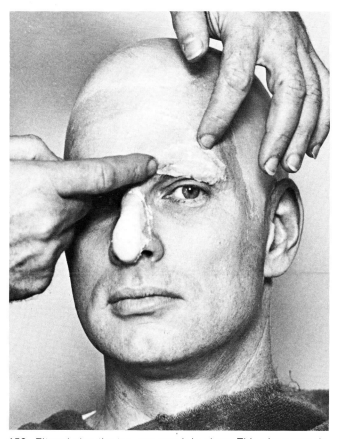

159. Fit and glue the top eye pouch in place. This piece was designed to cover the eyebrow as well. When it is glued, dab liquid latex over all the edges.

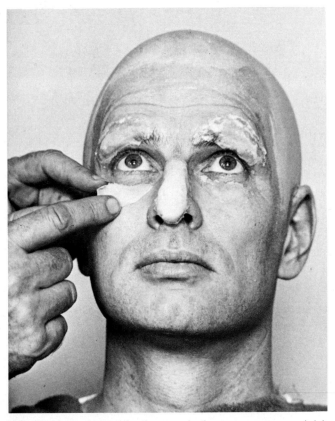

160. Apply pouches under the eyes in the same manner and dab liquid latex around these edges as well.

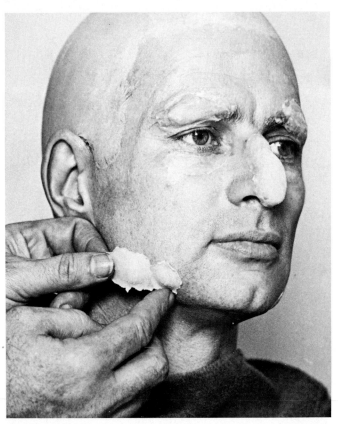

161. Follow the same procedure for the jowls, placing them with care, gluing them, and softening the edges with liquid latex.

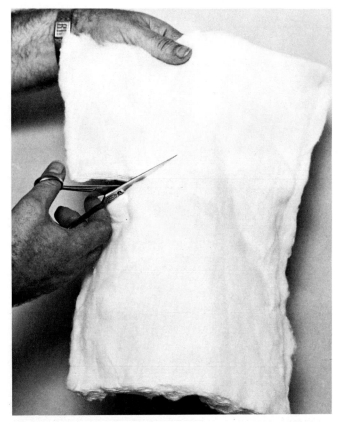

162. Unroll a segment of sterile absorbent cotton and cut off a segment about 8″ across the width.

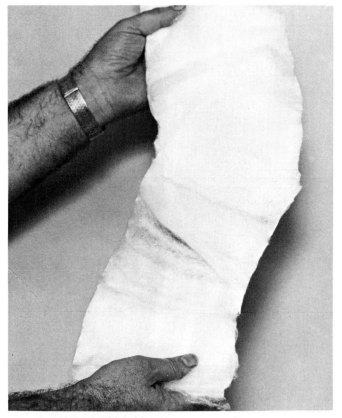

163. Separate a thin cross-section from this segment.

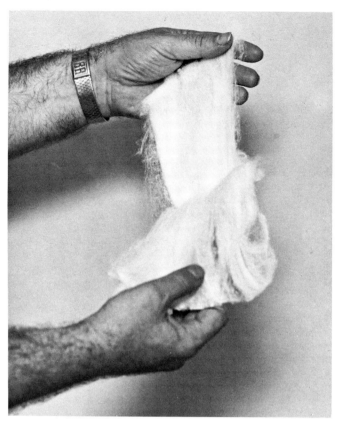

164. Further separate this layer into as thin and transparent a section as you can get. Continue this process until you have 8 or 10 sections, each about 6″ x 8″.

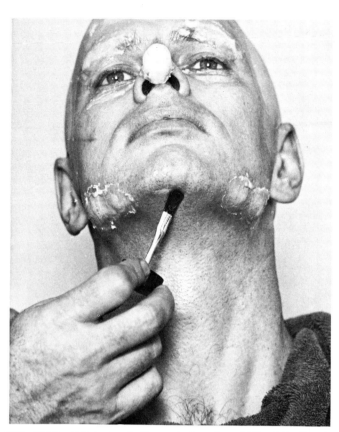

165. Brush spirit gum onto the neck, from the middle of the throat back along one side of the neck and all the way to under the ear. Do not overlook any spots, yet work swiftly and smoothly.

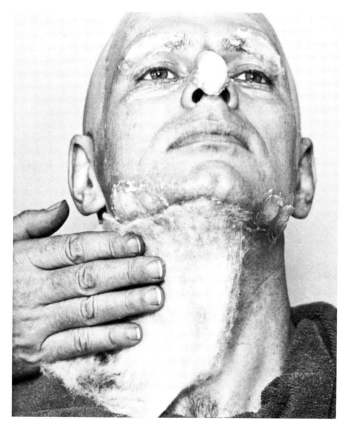

166. As soon as the gum is applied evenly, place a segment of cotton carefully onto the neck and press it lightly into place. Press over the entire section to be sure it is entirely adhered. Repeat this process on the other side of the neck.

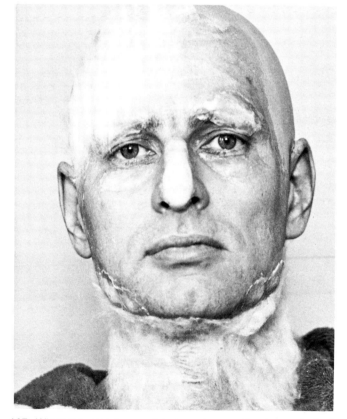

167. When the neck is completed, apply a section to one half of the forehead, extending over and onto the bald cap. Use the same technique.

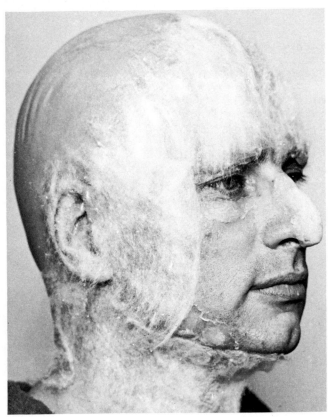

168. Apply the next segment over the ear and extending onto the cheek. Make sure the cotton aheres to the convolutions of the ear and to the area behind the ear.

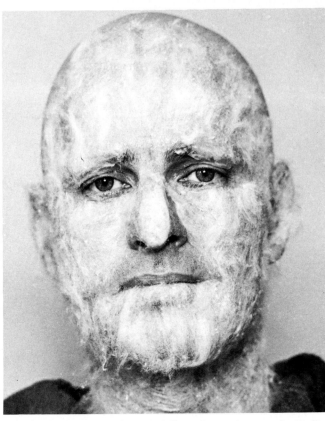

169. Now adhere a section carefully under each eye and onto the cheeks.

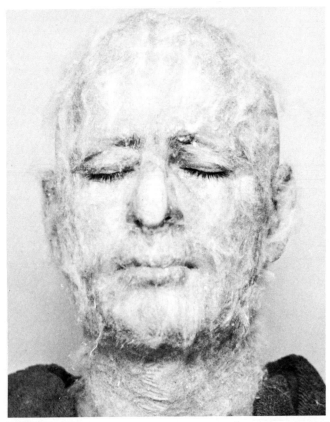

170. Even more carefully press the cotton on top of the eyes and over each of the lips and the balance of the face.

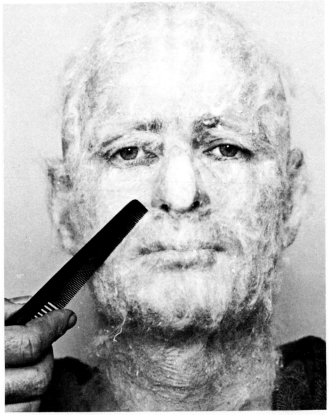

171. Lightly comb over the entire area covered with cotton until you have a thin, even film covering the face. Don't comb it all off.

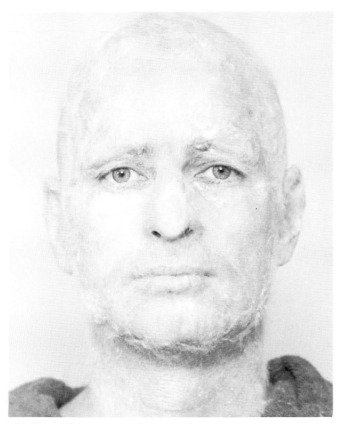

172. The soft fuzz covers the entire face.

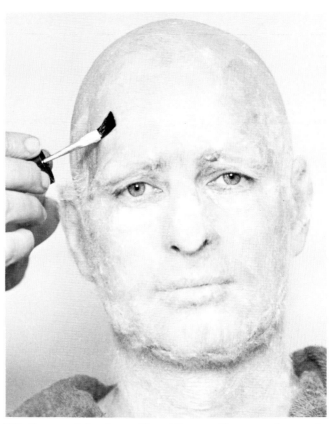

173. Now coat the fuzz with spirit gum. Use enough gum to saturate the cotton so that it will immediately flatten onto the face in a thin film.

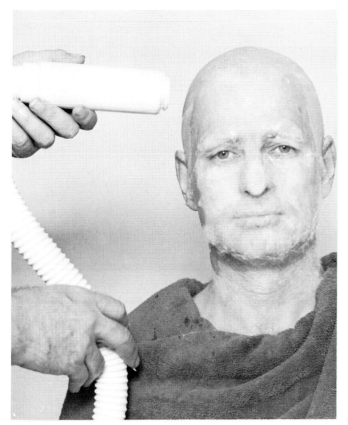

174. Work on one section of the face at a time, using an air blower, hair dryer, or the nozzle of a hair dryer to hasten the drying. Direct the flow of warm air over the layer of spirit gum until it is dry.

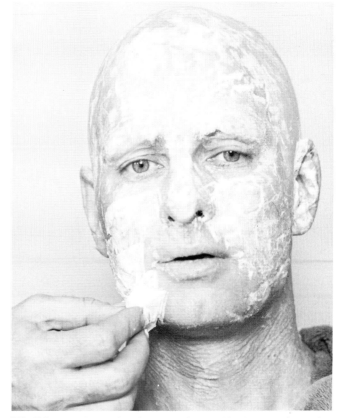

175. When spirit gum has been applied and is dry over the entire face, apply liquid latex over the gum, using a piece of sponge rubber. Use a stipple, patting technique. Overlap the stipple and be sure to cover the entire head.

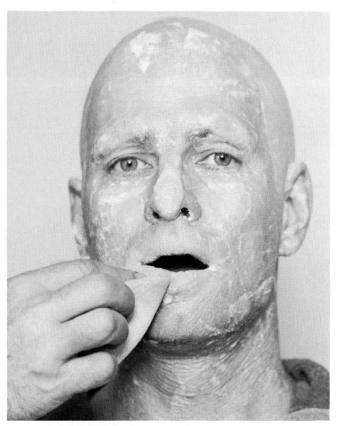

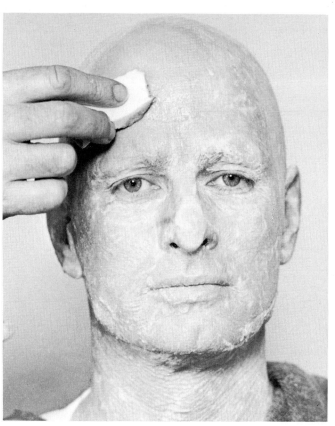

176. Be particularly careful in back of the ears, the top and bottom of the eyelids, and the lips. Have the actor open his mouth when you stipple in that area, and powder it as soon as it is dry. Do the same with the eyes and ears.

177. When the latex has dried, apply a rubber grease base with a rubber sponge, covering the entire face.

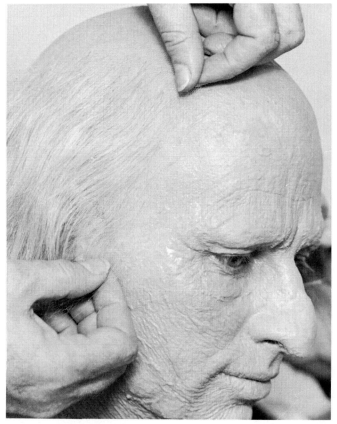

178. Once you have applied the rubber grease base, powder lightly to remove the shine.

179. Now fit a lace hairpiece onto the head. (See Chapter Ten for application directions.)

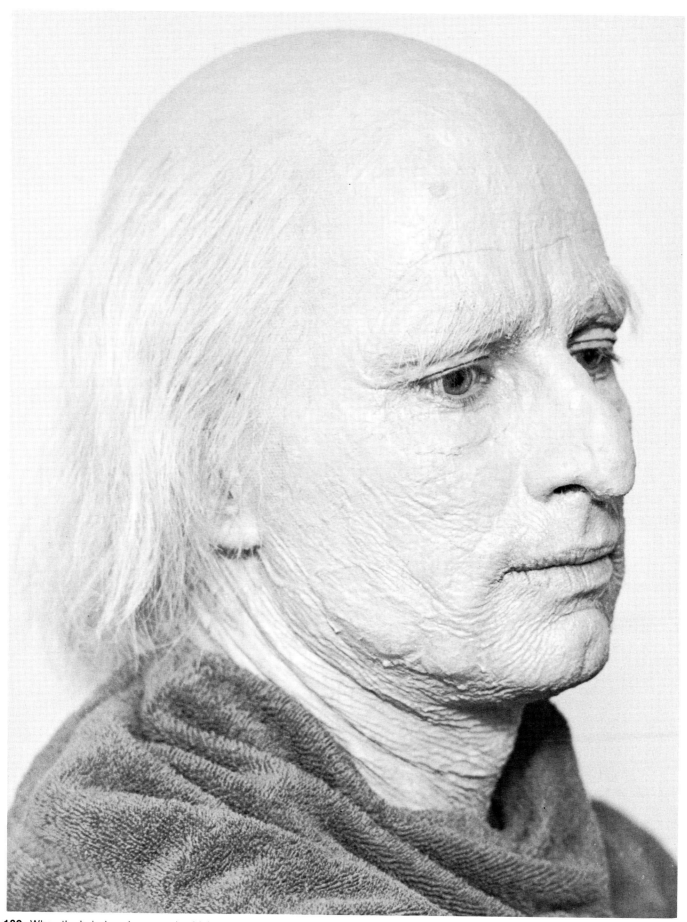

180. When the hairpiece is secured, add the eyebrows and the face work is completed.

RECIPE FOR SPECIAL GREASE BASE

When covering rubber with a makeup base, it is necessary to use a grease base that contains castor oil. To make a rubber grease base, just pour a small amount of castor oil into a dish, then rub, into another dish, a quantity of modified grease in the appropriate color. Pick up a small amount of the castor oil on your clean foam rubber sponge and then pick up some base color on the same sponge and apply them both directly to the model's face. If you wish, you may actually combine a quantity of base color and castor oil in a small jar. You can prepare rubber grease bases in a number of colors if you like. However, mixing the colors as you need them requires no extra effort, and you can get exactly the color you want without preparing in advance.

When you have applied the base over the entire face, you should stipple darker and lighter colors onto the face to accent the shadows and high points of the face. When the color satisfies you, apply a light touch of powder to remove the excessive shine produced by the castor oil.

AGING THE HANDS

Extreme age cannot be evident in the face without also being evident on parts of the body visible to the audience. All too often hands are either ignored altogether, or—at the other extreme—very elaborate rubber pieces are attached to the hands to create the effect of age. Actually, applying the cotton and latex to the hands is extremely fast, simple, and very effective. Simply follow the same procedures for the hands as described for the face. (See Figs. 181 to 186.)

MAINTENANCE

No extreme age makeup is totally completed in the makeup room. The face moves constantly, stretching and contracting, and this movement will create puckers and loosenings that will require constant regluing or touching up.

The greatest damage in the cotton-latex aging occurs around the mouth and on the fingertips. Talking or eating causes the thin application of cotton and latex to peel away in time, making it necessary to add touches of cotton or liquid latex to the mouth and to touch up the area with the correct base color. Handling anything damages the fragile, thin coat of cotton and latex on the fingertips, so be prepared to add or reglue bits or pieces here from time to time.

Body heat also alters the makeup. In most instances, the actor will be required to wear the makeup during the course of an entire day's shooting. Body heat causes the rubber pieces to loosen. It is possible to wedge a small opening at the juncture of the piece and to slip a cotton swab into this small slot so that you can dry up the perspiration and add new spirit gum to reglue the piece. When it is sufficiently glued, add a touch of liquid latex to cover the slit and then touch this up with the base color.

Any work you have applied can be repaired and maintained. So don't feel timid. This is to be expected as a normal part of the work.

Aside from the routine touching up and repairing necessary during a single day, you must expect that matching a makeup from day to day will be almost impossible, no matter how skillful the artist. Imperceptible differences are hard to discern if the matching is close. Don't be too perturbed if you find yourself touching up and repairing frequently and if the matching is not microscopically accurate.

Under some lights or in certain angles even the best makeup will appear obvious. If you notice this to be true, seek the assistance of the cameraman. A discreet shadow added by the cameraman can truly enhance your work in some cases. It is no secret that almost all makeup artists have needed this kind of assistance at times.

REMOVING COTTON AND LATEX MAKEUP

At the end of any day's work, it is part of your job to see that the performer's makeup is properly removed. Frequently, when the makeup is simple, the performers prefer to remove the makeup themselves. However, the cotton and latex makeup certainly does require removal by the makeup artist, and wigs and toupees should be removed by the makeup artist because they will require cleaning and possibly redressing for the next day's work.

First loosen the hairpiece by dabbing at the lace with a cotton swab saturated in acetone. When the corner of the piece at the sideburn is loose, lift it away and by continued dabbing at the spirit gum beneath the hair lace, slowly loosen and remove the hairpiece from the head. Put the hairpiece away for later cleaning.

To remove the cotton-latex, first wet a tissue or cloth with an oil base remover (any spirit gum remover from the Suppliers List will do) and dab around the ear at the juncture of the bald cap. (Don't use acetone for this operation because it is too harsh a solvent for the face in this particular case.) When the solvent has softened the joint sufficiently, lift the cap up as much as the softening will allow and insert a cotton swab which has been dipped in the spirit gum remover. Using the swab or a soft brush, dab on more and more of the solvent, lifting the edge of the cap or the makeup away from the face. The process will be a slow peeling-away of the makeup.

Continue this process: rewet the cotton swab or brush with the solvent and slowly apply it to more and more of the face as you ease away the makeup. Be particularly gentle around the eyes, and take care to avoid getting any of the solvent in the eyes. Although none of the liquid removers are harsh, you should avoid getting it into these sensitive areas. Continue this process slowly and steadily over the face until you have removed all the makeup and the bald cap. (See Figs. 188 to 192.)

Removing the makeup from the hands is easier. Pour the liquid remover into the performer's cupped hands and have him rub the solvent over the hands as if he were washing. Once the makeup is loosened, you may continue the process with the solvent, or actually soak the hands in warm water and slowly work the makeup off as the water saturates its way through.

When the makeup is completely removed, wash hands and face in warm water with a mild soap. After making sure that all the spirit gum is removed and the face is clean, splash the face with cold water or with a mild astringent, such as witch hazel or Sea Breeze, to close the pores.

A. Model with face clean, prepared for makeup.

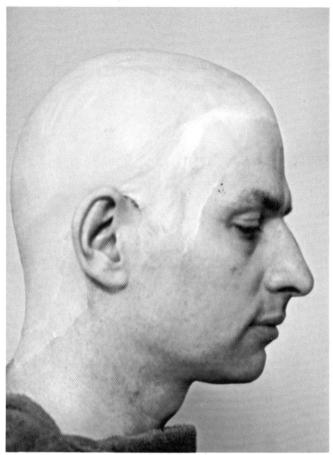

B. Bald cap fitted, cut, and glued. Profile view.

C. Bald cap, front view. Note that even without makeup the cap almost disappears into the forehead.

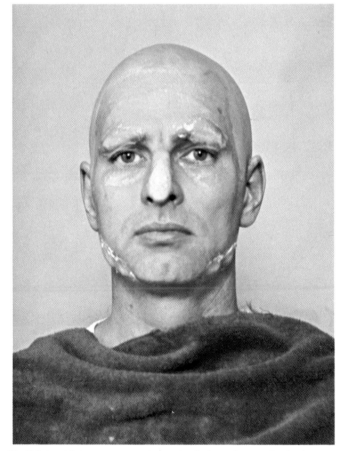

D. False rubber nose, eye pieces, jowls have been attached.

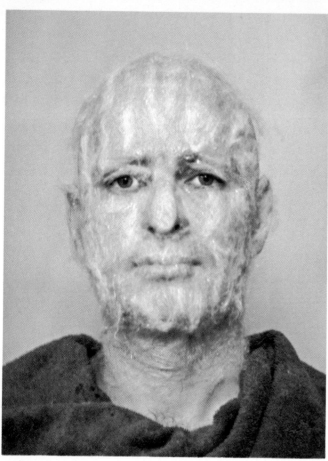

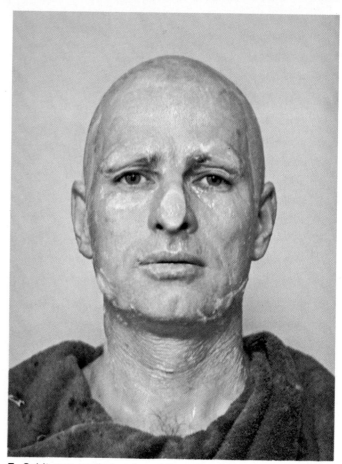

E. Absorbent cotton glued on top of the entire face and combed down to thin layer.

F. Spirit gum applied on top of the cotton layer.

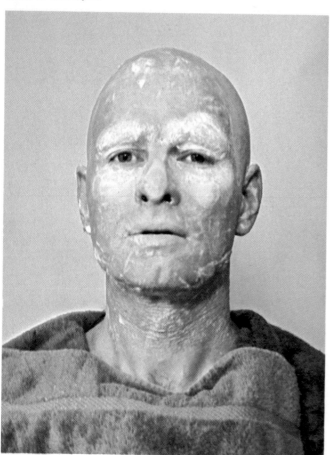

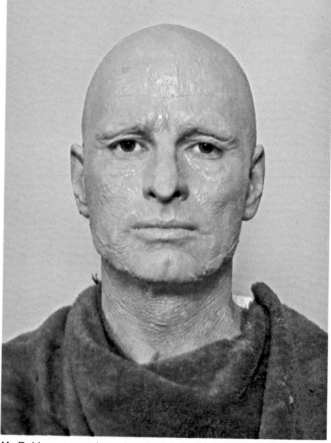

G. Liquid latex stippled on top of the dried spirit gum.

H. Rubber grease base (castor oil added to the base color), applied over the face.

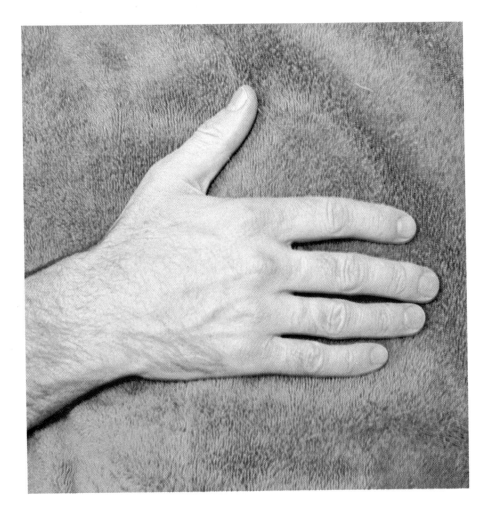

I. The hands are cleansed in preparation for makeup.

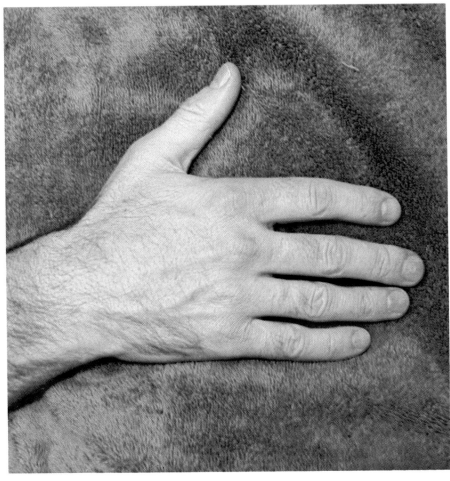

J. Base applied to hand, followed by same procedure as described for the face.

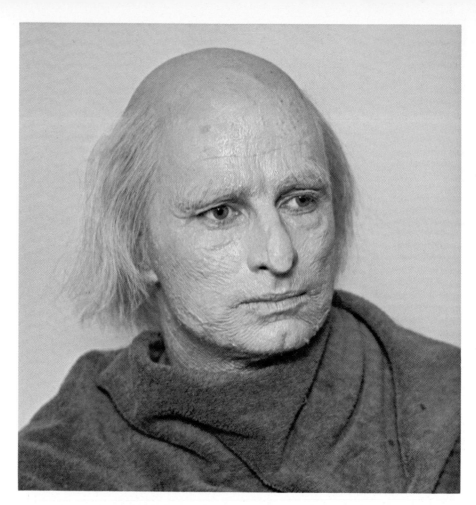

K. Three-quarter view. Note that the eye has been rimmed in red.

L. Hands completed, face hairpiece, eyebrows added.

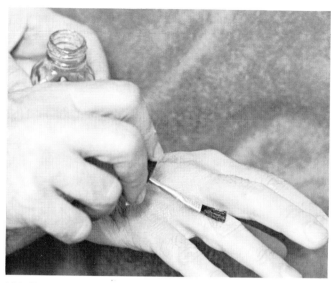

181. To age the hands, first apply spirit gum to the top of the hand.

182. Add the cotton segment to the top of the hand.

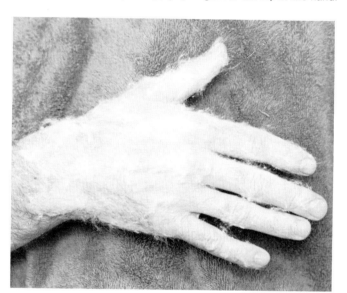

183. Comb away excess cotton, leaving a thin, even veil of cotton.

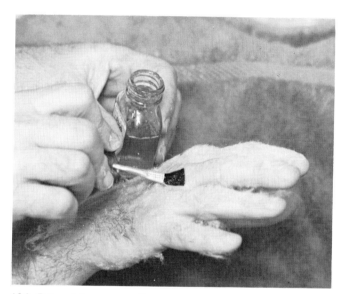

184. Dab spirit gum over the cotton.

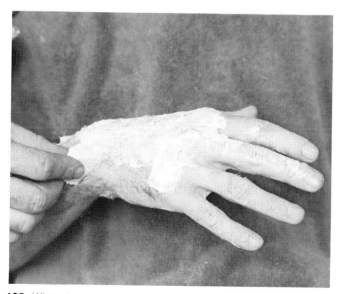

185. When the gum is dry, stipple on the liquid latex.

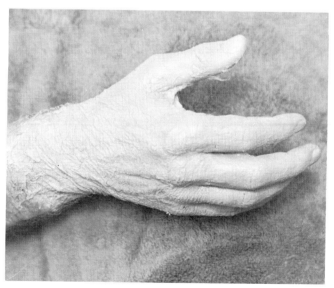

186. Powder the hand, to avoid parts sticking to each other, particularly the fingers, and add rubber grease paint and powder away excess shine.

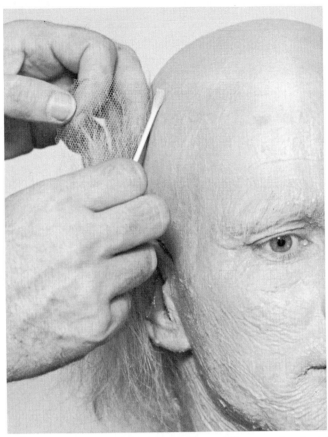

187. First remove the hairpiece, using spirit gum solvent and lifting the piece away gently.

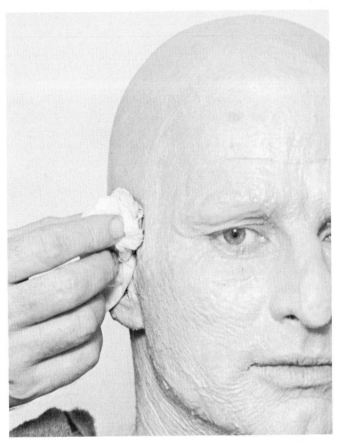

188. To remove the cotton latex, first wet a cloth with spirit gum solvent and dab around the ear at the juncture of the bald cap.

189. When the solvent has softened the paint sufficiently, lift the cap up with a cotton swab.

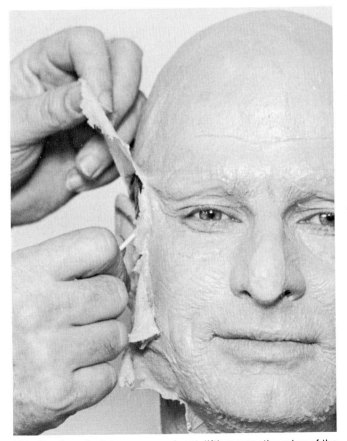

190. Continue to dab on more solvent, lifting away the edge of the cap.

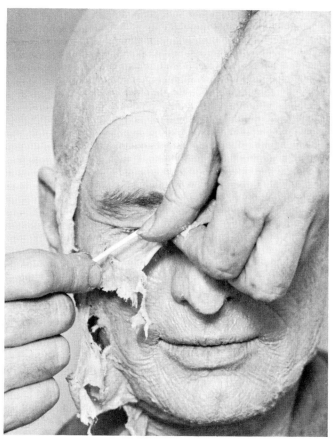

191. Be particularly careful around the eyes and avoid getting any solvent in the eyes.

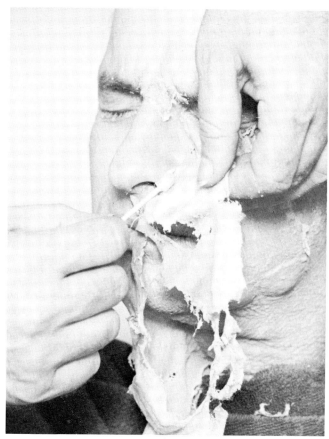

192. Continue to lift away the cotton latex until you have removed the entire layer of material.

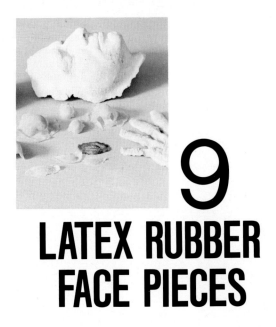

9
LATEX RUBBER FACE PIECES

As we have just seen, when it is necessary to age a performer beyond the limit of painted shadows, face pieces are called for. These pieces are made of flexible plastic, foam sponge rubber, or liquid latex rubber. The flexible plastic and sponge rubber are far too complex to make without setting up a laboratory including complex double molds, ovens, mixing machines, and great precision. For our needs, the raw latex rubber piece is quite suitable. It can be made with a minimum of equipment and in a comparatively short period of time.

To make a face piece, it will be first necessary to make a mask of the performer's face. Then the desired feature will be modeled onto that in clay, and then from this feature a mold will be made. In this mold you paint in the liquid latex in layers, and when it dries, you can pull out the rubber face piece. Each of these steps will be demonstrated here.

For this process you will need the following materials:

Petroleum jelly (Vaseline)

Plaster of Paris

Plaster of Paris bandage

Cold dental impression material

Towels

Modeling clay

Six rubber or plastic mixing bowls

Two rubber spatulas

Liquid latex rubber

Cotton swabs

Shears

Water

MAKING THE MOLD FOR THE MASK

The first step is to take an impression of the performer's face which will serve as the basis for all future work.

The impression is taken while the model is lying prone. Set up a comfortable place, a low flat couch, a reclining chair or, if necessary, the floor. The model's face must be kept still throughout the process, or this step will result in failure. The model must anticipate at least a half an hour for the entire process.

Drape towels around the model's face and neck, and if the impression is taken on a couch or bed, spread newspapers under and around the model to catch any splatter.

Set up a table to hold your materials and lay out the petroleum jelly, the impression material measured into six mixing bowls, spatulas, and ten plaster of Paris bandage pieces cut into 6″ and 12″ lengths. When you start, you must move quickly because the impression material and the plaster both set quickly. Be prepared to continue each step without pause until all phases are completed; otherwise, your work will be spoiled and you will have to start over.

APPLYING THE IMPRESSION MATERIAL

With your finger or brush, apply a small amount of Vaseline to the eyebrows, eyelashes, and to any exposed part of the hairline (Fig. 193). Clean your hands. Mix the first amount of the impression material with the prescribed amount of water at the proper temperature (Figs. 194 and 195). Colder water will set more slowly and will give you more time for application. You will be mixing the impression material as you work because it dries so rapidly. For this reason, I have suggested six mixing bowls. (In this demonstration I used D.P. Elastic Impression Cream manufactured by Teledyne-Getz, available from Becker-Parkin in New York. However, there are many other materials available that will do the job just as well.)

First, apply the impression material on one side of the forehead onto the temple, down the side of the face, and onto the eye socket. Continue making the mixture as needed, keep the thickness at about ½" to 1" in depth.

Try not to move the skin as you apply the material and spread it. The mixture should be soft enough to spread quickly, like a heavy batter. Use the spatula to keep it from dripping off the face and continue the applications. (Six is about the number of applications necessary. If this number is not sufficient, mix more until you have enough to cover the entire face.)

Make sure at all times to leave the nostrils clear. Do not impede breathing. If any of the impression material inadvertently gets into the nostrils, clean it out immediately and calm and reassure the model.

When each section sets enough to hold in place, mix the next batch and continue to apply in sections until the entire face is covered. Do not carry the material beyond the front of the ears, or behind the hairline at the temple and forehead. You can carry it below the jawline, but no further than the windpipe. Around the eyebrows apply the mixture in the direction of eyebrow growth. Around the eye socket be particularly careful to pour the mixture and use the spatula only when absolutely necessary. You want this area to remain as still as possible.

I repeat, place the mixture carefully around the nostrils. Be sure at all times that there are adequate breathing holes open. If breathing is affected in any way, the model will become unsettled and may panic, so be careful and constantly reassuring. (See Figs. 196 to 198.)

APPLYING PLASTER BANDAGES

After the impression material has been applied, we now move to the plaster of Paris bandages which have been precut. Don't wait for the impression material to set. Quickly wet one of the plaster of Paris bandages in the water. Squeeze out the excess water and lay it on the mask. Continue to apply other strips. Let the plaster of Paris bandages dry a period of roughly ten to twenty minutes. The plaster of Paris will heat up as the drying process starts. During this time, talk to the model and keep him or her reassured at all times. (See Figs. 199 to 204.)

COMPLETING THE MOLD

When the plaster of Paris outer bandages are firm to the touch, hold the mask with one hand and pull lightly at the skin around the edge of the mask to start the loosening process (Figs. 205 and 206). Be particularly careful to separate the hair at the temples or forehead from the mask. Ask the model to move his face under the mask (to loosen it), then ask him to sit up. Hold the mask in place all this time. As the model sits up and bends slightly forward, slip the mask off the face gently. Hold the mask below, at the plaster of Paris, keeping the inner mold of the impression material in place. (See Figs. 207 to 209.)

193. With the finger, brush, or cotton swab, apply Vaseline to the eyebrows, eyelashes, and entire hairline along the temples and forehead.

194. Measure out the impression material exactly, following precisely the manufacturer's instructions.

195. Measure out the precise amount of water. The proper measuring cups are supplied with this particular impression material. Then mix the material with your spatula.

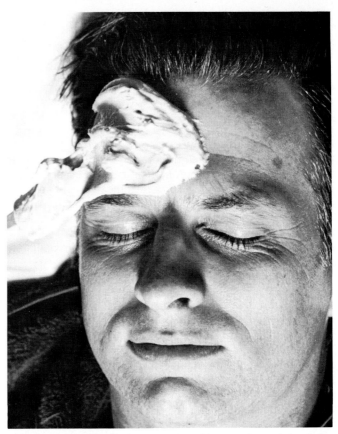

196. Apply the impression material with smooth strokes of the spatula, first on the forehead and down on to the cheeks.

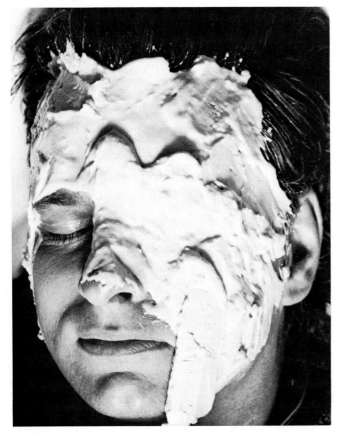

197. Carry the mixture down one side of the face and then across and down the other side.

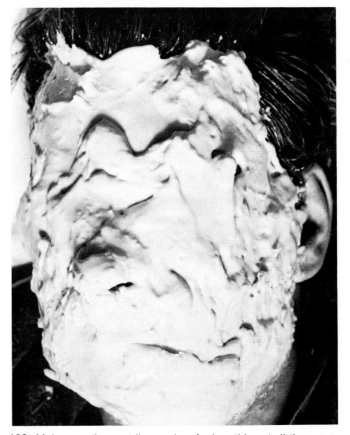

198. Make sure the nostrils are clear for breathing at all times.

199. The sections of plaster of Paris bandages should be pre-cut to 6″ and 12″ pieces.

200. Dip the bandage into a bowl of water set aside for this purpose only and squeeze out the excess water.

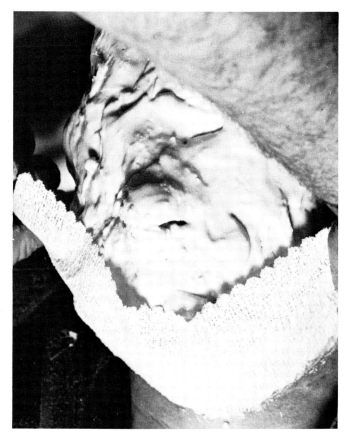

201. Apply the strips of wet bandage over the impression material to create a firm cradle.

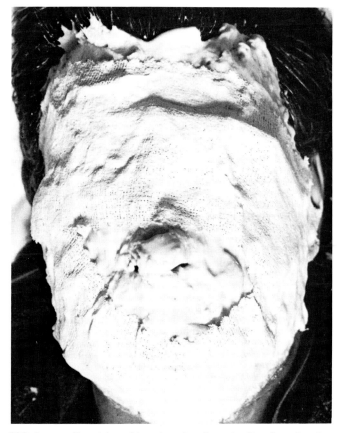

202. Lay on the strips of bandage in alternate directions to give them a stronger bond.

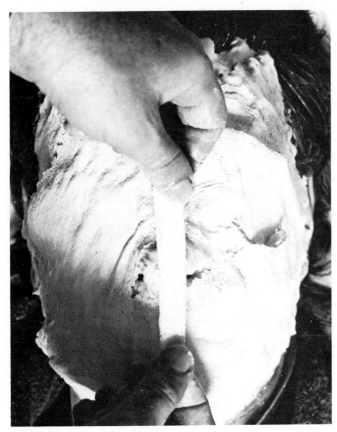

203. Be particularly careful to strengthen the nose, but to keep the nostrils clear at all times.

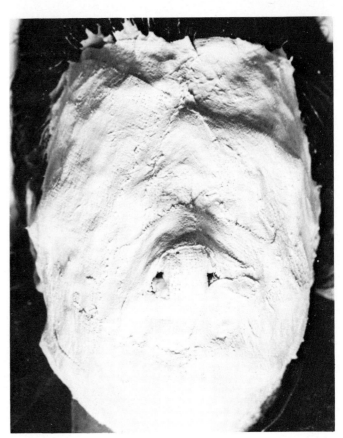

204. Let the plaster dry. When it is warm to the touch (about twenty minutes), you can start the removal process.

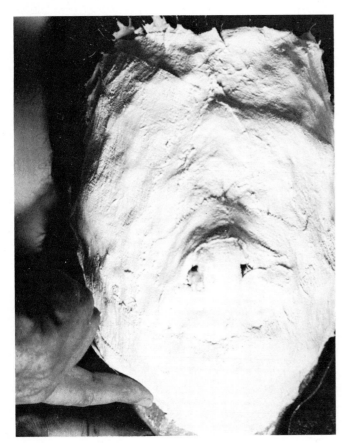

205. Gently pull at the skin around the edges.

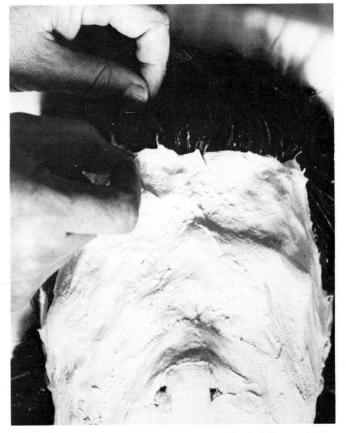

206. Carefully separate the mask all along the hairline and have the model move his face muscles to further the loosening.

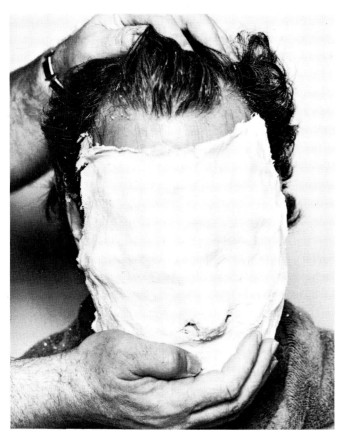

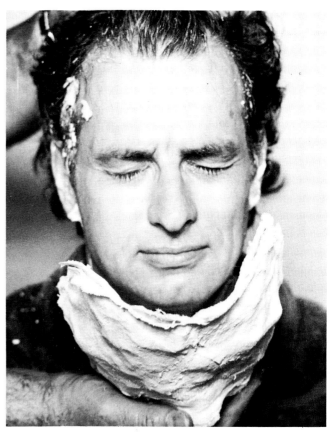

207. When the mask is loose, hold it in place with one hand and supporting the back of the head with the other, help the model to a sitting position.

208. Slide the mask down and off the face, cradling it in your hand.

209. The mold for the mask is completed. Notice the negative form of the face in the impression material.

MAKING THE MASK FROM THE MOLD

You now have your mold. From this you will make the positive mask, which will be made by pouring plaster of Paris into this mold. Look over the interior carefully for any bits of broken off impression material or plaster. Carefully remove them. Insert two plugs of clay into the nostrils, so that the plaster of Paris will not leak out (Fig. 210). Set the mold on a table, placing some bits of modeling clay under it to hold it steady, and position it on an even level so that the shell will retain the liquid material like a soup bowl.

Into a clean mixing bowl pour three cups of fresh plaster of Paris. Add water and mix. The mixture should have the consistency of pudding. If the mixture is too watery, add more plaster; if too thick, add water. Tap the bowl on the table to eliminate any air bubbles that may have formed.

After the plaster of Paris is thoroughly mixed, pour about a cup into the shell, then pick up the shell and swirl the plaster around so that it forms an initial inner coat on the interior of the shell, or spread the mixture with a spatula, depending on consistency and thickness. (See Figs. 212 and 213.)

When the interior is coated, set the shell level on the table and again spoon in more of the plaster of Paris mixture. Use your spatula to build up the thickness on all sides of the shell (Fig. 214). Add more plaster until you have at least 1" to 2" thickness throughout the mold.

You may fill the entire mold if you wish, but this is not really necessary.

The mold will harden in about one hour. When it is hard, pick it up, turn it over, and carefully separate the impression material and outer shell from the inner mold (Fig. 216). Examine the inner mask. If you have carefully followed these instructions, you should have a good reproduction of the face.

Now clean the mold of excess bits of plaster (Fig. 217). If you find some small air holes, you can fill them in with a touch of soft plaster of Paris. If there are some uneven lumps in the mold, you can easily scrape them away with a small knife. Scrape carefully, because the plaster of Paris mold is still comparatively soft and can be easily damaged by the knife. When you are satisfied, put the mold away to harden overnight.

If you wish to preserve your mask permanently, give it two successive coats of shellac or varnish after the plaster has dried. Let the first coat of shellac or varnish dry thoroughly before applying the second. When this is completed, you are ready to model the artificial feature.

This mask will now be used to make a mold for the rubber piece. Now you will model the shape of the features to be worn. Restraint is the key here. The initial urge is always to make many more features than are really necessary; each piece you build requires a separate mold-making process, which is time-consuming.

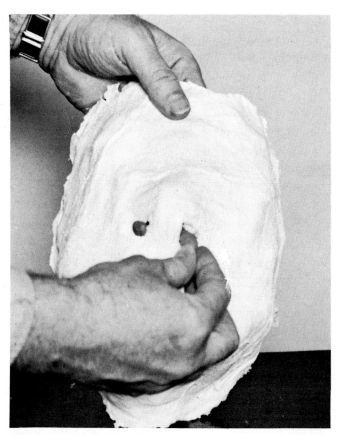

210. Insert dry plugs into the nostril openings of the mold. Set the mask on a level surface, supporting it where needed with lumps of clay.

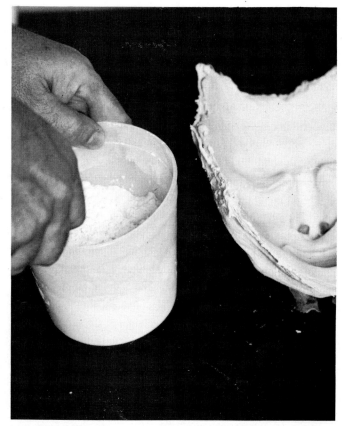

211. Pour plaster of Paris in a clean bowl, add water, and mix.

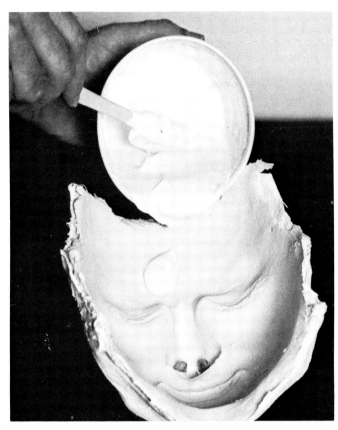

212. Pour in the first layer, spoon in enough to cover the entire surface of the mold.

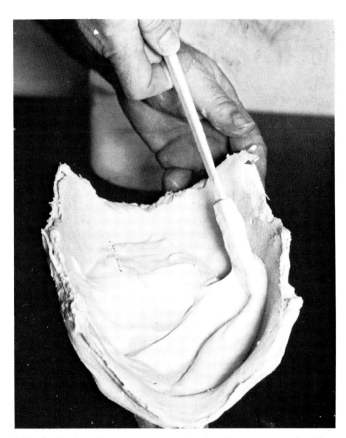

213. Swirl the plaster to cover the interior, or spread with a spatula, depending on density of plaster. Tap the sides to shake out bubbles.

214. Place the mold back on the clay supports and pour in more plaster of Paris.

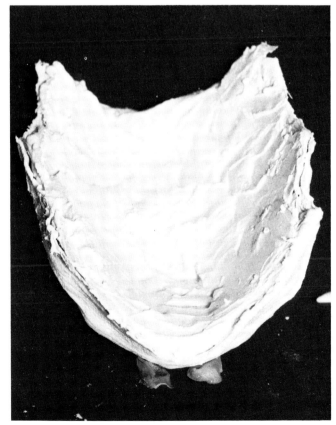

215. Spread the plaster to a uniform thickness of at least 1″ and let the plaster dry.

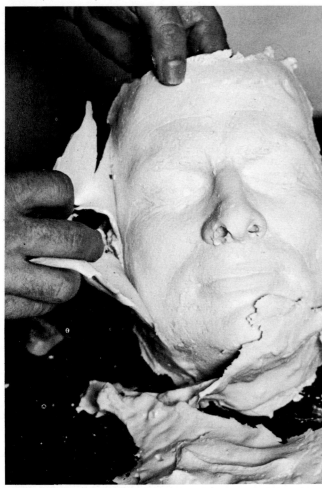

216. Once the plaster is dry, begin to peel away from the face impression, and be careful to avoid breaking any part of the impression.

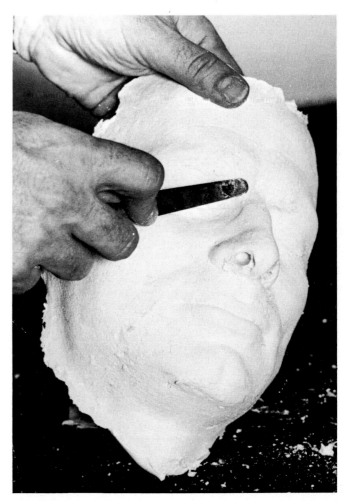

217. Scrape away any bumps or irregularities in the plaster and fill in any holes with fresh mixed plaster of Paris. Let the mask dry overnight.

MODELING THE FEATURE

Setting the face mold on a table, place a small quantity of modeling clay on the feature you are going to alter. Here we will mold a nose. Shape the clay on the nose to the shape you want (Fig. 218). Examine it carefully from all views, front, side, below. Avoid the urge to make the feature too large. The shape should fit naturally with the shape of the mask. Is this the shape of the feature desired? If not, alter it any way you please. Blend the edges into the mask.

Treat the clay very much as you would Derma-Wax. When you are satisfied that the built-up feature is what you want, create a pore texture by patting it with a piece of heavy red artificial sponge rubber, the type used by cashiers to moisten their fingers when handling money. (See Fig. 219.)

MAKING THE MOLD

The modeled feature will now be transformed into a mold from which you can make your rubber piece. Set the mask on the table and build a "well" around the feature with modeling clay. Shape the well so that its walls are even all around and are higher than the top of the feature itself. Using the fingertip, brush, or cotton swab, coat the interior of the well and the feature with a light layer of Vaseline. (See Figs. 220 to 222.)

Now prepare a mixing bowl with plaster of Paris as you did to make the mask. The amount needed for the mold will be less, about a cup or so of plaster of Paris. Add water and mix the plaster. Pour a small amount into the mold and swirl the plaster about so that all surfaces of the mold receive a thin coating of the plaster. When you are satisfied that all interior surfaces are covered, pour in additional plaster to within ¼" of the top of the mold. (Obviously, if the walls of your mold have not been constructed to an overall even height, the plaster will spill over the walls.) Drum on the table with your fists to work out some of the air bubbles in the plaster. (See Figs. 223 to 226.)

Now let the plaster dry. First it will heat up, then harden. When the plaster is quite hard, remove the clay walls of the well and carefully separate the mold from the mask. Now remove the clay nose from the interior of the mold (Figs. 227 to 231). Check immediately for any air bubbles and fill in, or chip away any parts that would impair your mold. Put it aside to dry and harden overnight.

218. Place a piece of modeling clay on the nose and shape the form you want. Blend the edges into the mask.

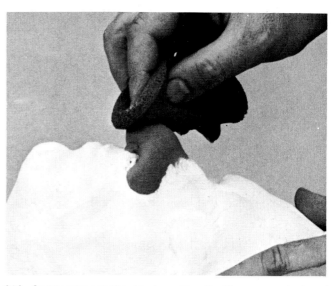

219. Create pores in the clay by patting it with a coarse-textured red sponge.

220. Begin to construct a well around the features with modeling clay.

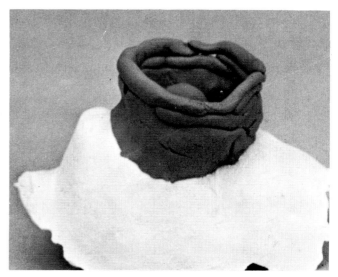

221. The walls should surround the feature and be higher than its topmost point.

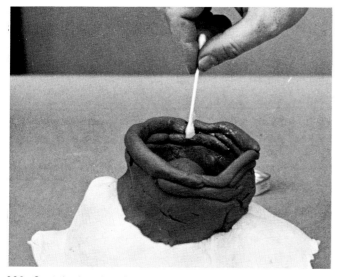

222. Coat the interior of the mold—all inside surfaces—with a thin coat of Vaseline.

223. Mix a fresh, smaller batch of plaster of Paris. Blend the plaster thoroughly, removing any air bubbles by gently tapping the side of the bowl.

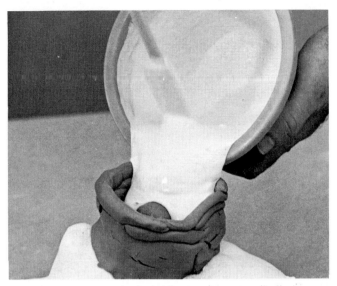

224. Pour in the plaster carefully to avoid capturing any air pockets in the mixture.

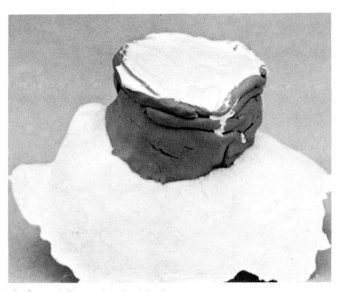

225. Pour in the rest of the plaster practically to the top of the walls of the mold.

226. Drum the table surface with your fists to get air bubbles in the plaster to the outside surface.

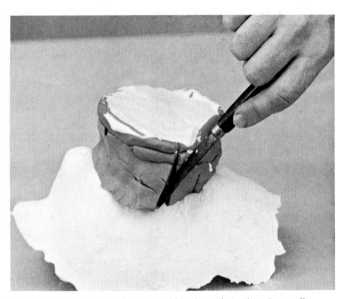

227. When the plaster is dry and hard, cut into the clay walls.

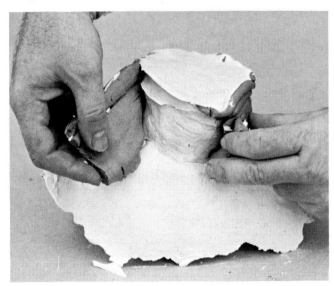

228. Peel away the clay carefully.

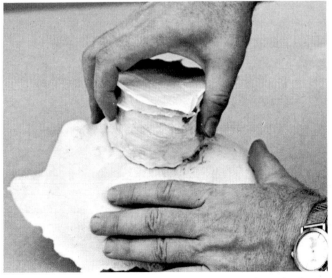

229. Holding the mask firmly, ease the mold away from the face.

230. The mold is separated from the mask.

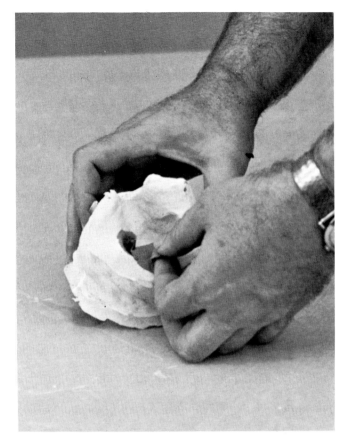

231. Now remove the clay from the mold. The Vaseline enables you to detach it easily.

MAKING THE RUBBER PIECE FROM THE MOLD

When the mold is dry, clean it of any residue Vaseline or bits of clay or plaster. Dry the mold with a towel or tissues. Open the bottle of liquid latex and, using a cotton swab, paint a very thin coat of the latex to the interior of the mold (Fig. 232). Carry this thin coating over the edge of the mold's interior, coating the top edge of the mold.

Allowing about ten minutes for the latex to dry between each application, apply additional coats of the latex to build up the piece so that it will hold its shape and have body. This process calls for a least ten to fifteen layers of the latex, but experience will help you determine how many layers you will need for the latex to hold its shape. Don't be disappointed if the first few pieces turn out badly. You cannot hurry the skills acquired with experience. It does require a high degree of skill, which comes from practice, to layer on a piece so that the outer edge will be so thin that it will blend easily into the skin when attached, yet firm enough to retain its shape.

Replace the cover or lid on the latex bottle when you are not actually using it. Exposure to air will cause the liquid to vulcanize and harden. In fact, if you store your latex for a long period of time without using it, you will note a progressive deterioration and hardening of the liquid. It should be a milky or off-white color and not much thicker than the consistency of cream. If it is cracked or thick, don't bother using it. Get a new supply if you want a good piece.

When you have applied enough layers of the latex to make the piece, set the mold aside for proper drying. When the milky white color of the latex has turned to a light tan,

the rubber has vulcanized. This process will take from two to six hours, depending on the number of layers of latex you have applied.

Once the latex has dried thoroughly, powder the interior of the mold with a powder puff (Fig. 233). Then carefully peel away the latex from the mold (Fig. 234), starting to lift the rubber away from the furthest, thinnest edges in toward the heavier center, powdering the exterior of the newly exposed rubber as you peel. (The powder prevents the rubber from adhering to another area of rubber.) When you have removed the rubber piece, check it carefully. Make sure the piece has been thoroughly powdered. Then brush off the excess powder and trim some of the excess edges down to the size of the piece you want. The mold is now permanent and you can make as many additional pieces with it as you may need.

For making up extreme age, you will require additional pieces: sagging top eyelids, bottom eye pouches, and jowls. Each of these pieces must be well-constructed, and a mold must be made for both sides of the face, to account for the irregular difference in the two sides of the performer's face.

For these additional molds or features, follow the procedure exactly in the same manner as that outlined for the nose piece. (See Figs. 237 to 239.)

Naturally, as you make more and more features and molds, you will begin to acquire a stock of molds whose pieces might be useful for other performers. The more you make and the greater stock of pieces available, the greater your ability to provide pieces quickly and efficiently.

232. After cleaning the mold of residue clay or Vaseline, paint a thin layer of latex rubber on the interior surfaces of the mold.

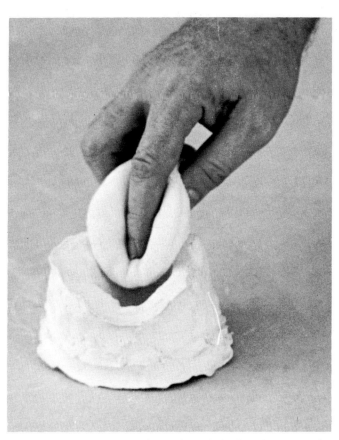

233. When enough layers of latex have built the piece up to the desired thickness, and it has vulcanized, powder the interior of the mold covering all of the rubber piece.

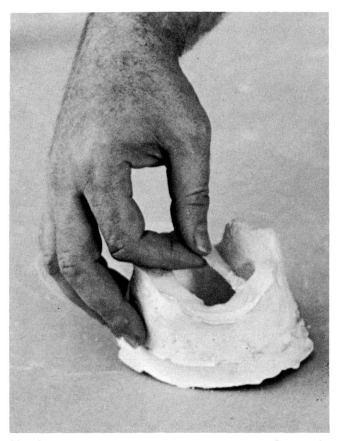

234. Carefully peel the piece away from the mold. Powder the exterior as you do this.

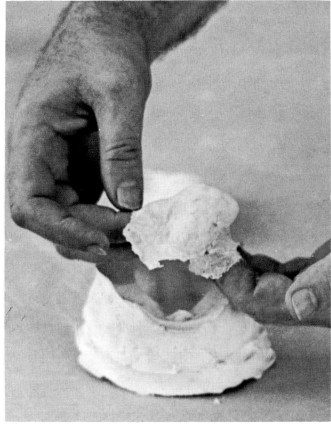

235. The piece removed from the mold.

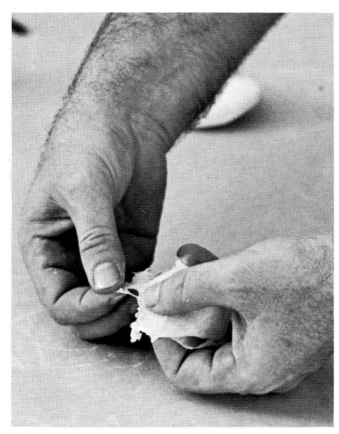

236. Peel off the excess edges.

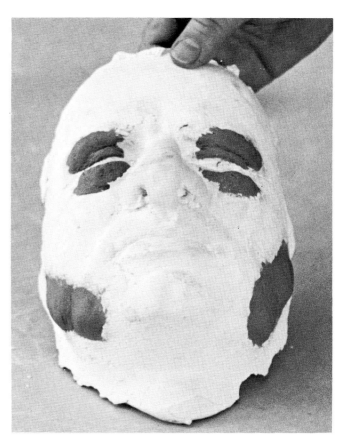

237. Top and bottom eye pieces and jowls have been modeled on the mask.

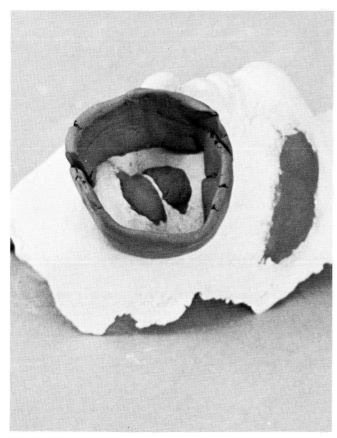

238. It will be necessary to construct a well and make a mold of each feature separately. Here one area is surrounded by a well.

239. Here a well is constructed around one jowl area. The piece is made following the same techniques.

10
WIGS

An essential means of depicting a character in makeup is by adding a wig. As we have seen, not all wigs add hair to the head; wigs include totally bald caps, bald fronts, full heads of hair, stylized formal law and court wigs. The one aspect all wigs have in common is that hair is attached to a base which is worn on the head. This base is made of netting or of a silk material which is cut and sewn to conform to the shape of the head. The hair is attached to the base and either knotted or sewn on to long strips—called *weft*—or knotted and tied on in very small clumps by hand, a process called *ventilating.*

All wigs suitable for films require a fine transparent net for the hairline. The hairs attached to this net first are tied in one at a time and must have the transparency of the natural hairline.

MEASURING THE WIG

To serve its purpose, the wig must fit properly. It must cover all existing hair (unless it is a toupee) without being too large (it may shift or not hold), nor too tight (which would cause serious discomfort). You must therefore know how to measure the head properly so that you can order the correct sized wig. There are five measurements that are necessary, and Figs. 240 to 245 will show how to get them accurately:

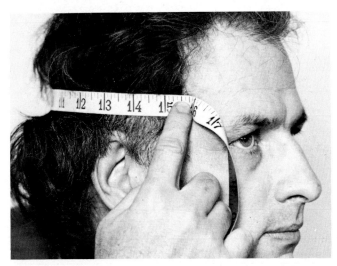

240. Using a cloth tape measure, first measure the area from the hairline at the temple around the back of the head to the temple on the other side. This is described, when ordering by mail, "from temple to temple."

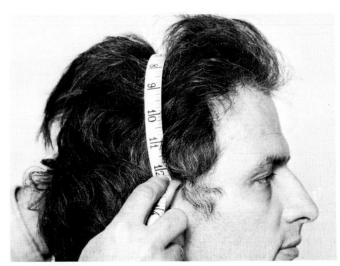

241. Start the tape from the point where the top of the ear joins the head. Measure up and across the top of the head to the same point at the other ear. This measurement is described as "from ear to ear over the head."

242. Start the tape at the hairline and carry it back over the head to the nape of the neck. Measurement is called "from hairline to nape of neck."

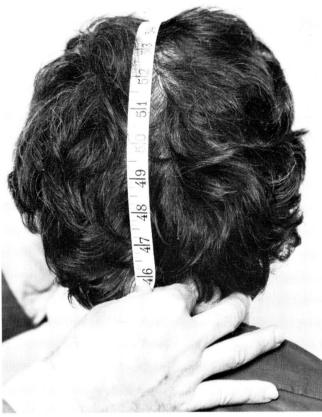

243. Back view of same measurement shown in Figure 242.

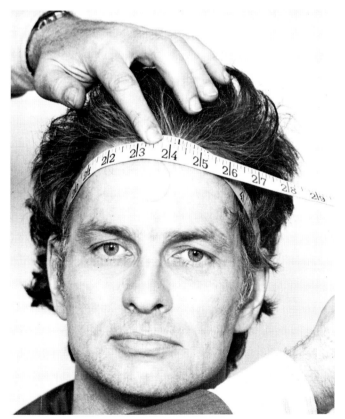

244. Measure from the front of the hairline around the temple and around the base of the head. Describe measurement as "around the head."

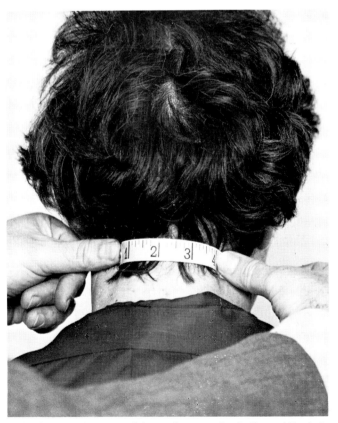

245. Measure the nape of the neck across the bottom of the hairline. Describe as "across nape of the neck."

POSITIONING THE TOUPEE

When a new hairline is needed, a toupee may be called for. To position the toupee, first comb the model's hair in the direction desired. Comb out the toupee as well. Hold the toupee by both outside edges of the lace front and ease it onto the head so that it covers the area for which it was made (Fig. 247). Carefully fit both sides of the toupee so that its hairline matches that of the model. Hold it firmly in place.

For a toupee adhesive, use Matte Lace Adhesive, a product of the Research Council of Makeup Artists, Inc. (available from Ira Senz Wigs—see Suppliers List). Make sure the bottle is open in advance. Pick up a small quantity of the adhesive on the brush, and still holding the toupee in place, glide the brush with the Matte Lace Adhesive over the lace netting (Fig. 248). Avoid getting any of the adhesive into the hair of the toupee, or onto the hair of the model. Hold the toupee in place during this time, until the adhesive dries, which will require about a minute. Touch the net lightly with the fingertip and if the toupee moves at all, or shows any gap or lift of the net from the forehead, apply another thin coat of the adhesive. This adhesive does not require pressing with a silk cloth as you would need to do with spirit gum. When you are sure the adhesive is dry, and if the toupee is large enough to require a double adhesive attachment at the back, apply this and press it to the crown of the head. Then carefully comb the hair of the toupee into the model's natural hair.

246. A toupee will be placed over this performer's head to form a new hairline.

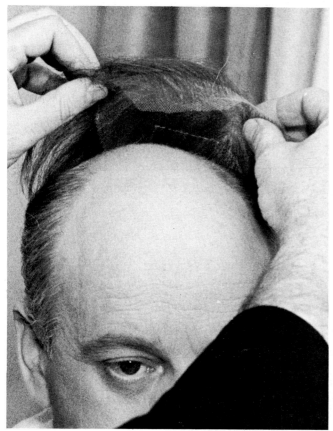

247. Hold the toupee by both outside edges and ease it onto the head to cover the entire area for which it was made.

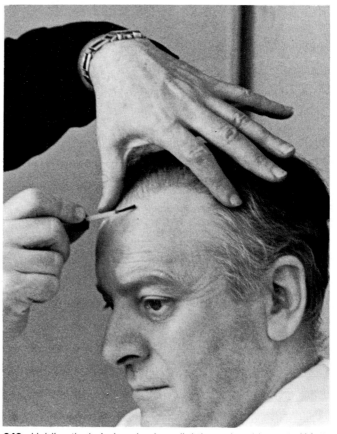

248. Holding the hairpiece in place, lightly apply a thin coat of Matte Lace Adhesive over the hair lace.

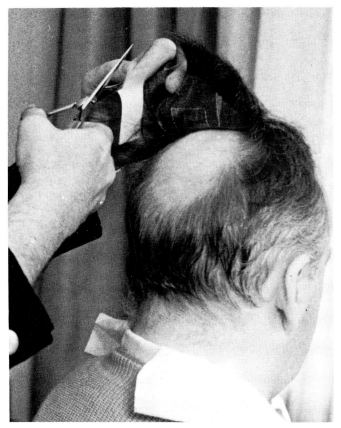

249. If baldness permits additional adhesion, attach a piece of double face tape to the underside of the hairpiece at the crown and press the piece into place.

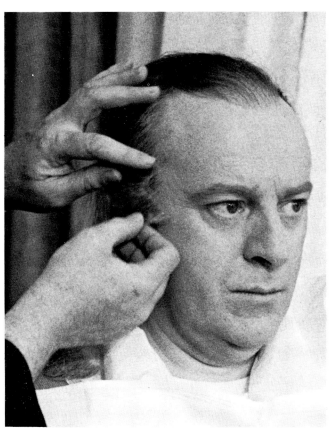

250. Fit sideburns into position in preparation for gluing with spirit gum.

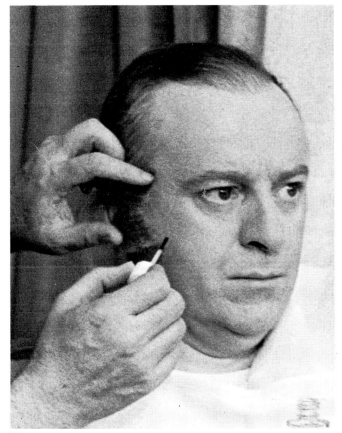

251. Holding sideburns in place, apply spirit gum to the lace and under the sideburn for good adhesion.

252. The mustache added and toupee combed into place.

POSITIONING THE FULL FRONT WIG

To cover the entire hairline, a full front wig may be called for. This procedure for positioning the full front wig is very similar to that for a toupee, except that a full head wig is a much larger piece. Hold the wig with its front facing you and held open at each side by the hands. Lift it up over the top of the model's head, ease it down so that the front of the lace touches the model's forehead an inch or so below the natural hairline, or at the place where the wig will sit. Have the model hold this point of lace net to the forehead and, opening the wig to its fullest, slide it onto the head.

Across the forehead it is possible to use the Undetectable adhesive if the fit is perfect. If not, use spirit gum (applied in the same manner and pressed firmly with a silk cloth). For a full front wig use spirit gum on the sides and along the temples and sideburns. As a stronger adhesive, spirit gum is preferable in these areas where the muscles and skin move constantly.

POSITIONING A FALL FOR A MAN

A fall may be needed for a male performer in a historical film. To position the fall, using a comb first, part the hair horizontally along the line where the fall is to be fitted. Lift up the hair above this line and keep it out of the way with hair clips (Fig. 253). Place the fall along this line to check the fit (Fig. 254). Separate a small clump of hair from the center of the hairline and wind this clump a number of turns around the open part of the clip attached to the center of the fall (Figs. 255 to 257). Position the lace behind the ear and hold it in place (Fig. 258). Apply the spirit gum under and over the lace (Fig. 259). Press down firmly with a silk cloth until the lace glues and dries to the skin (Fig. 260). Do the same on the other side of the head. The fall should fit securely, glued at both sides and clipped in the middle. Remove the hair clips and comb the hair over the edge of the fall so that it looks like a natural extension of the model's hair (Fig. 262).

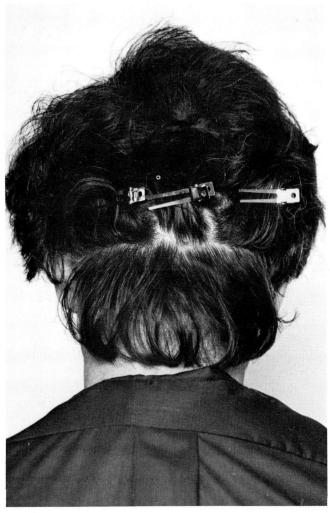

253. Part the hair where the fall is to be placed. Lift top hair out of the way and secure with hair clips.

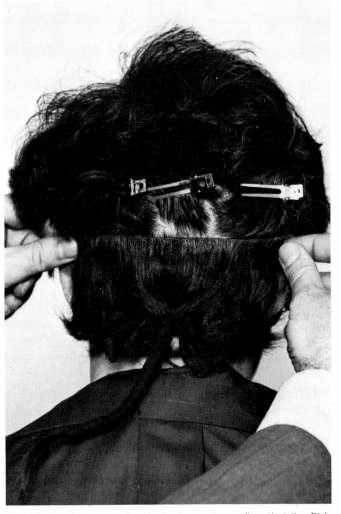

254. Fit the fall across the desired area to confirm that the fit is proper and that there is ample area for adhesion at both sides.

255. Separate the back of the hair from the center of the head to wrap around clasp attached to the fall.

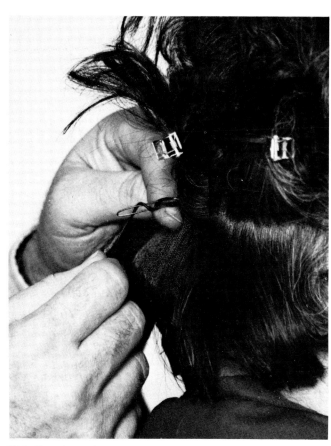

256. Turn the lock of hair around the outer half of the clasp three or four times.

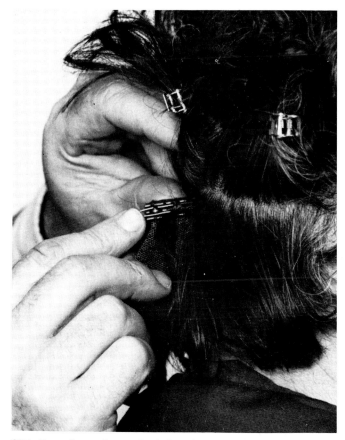

257. Snap the outer part of the clasp together to anchor the center part of the fall.

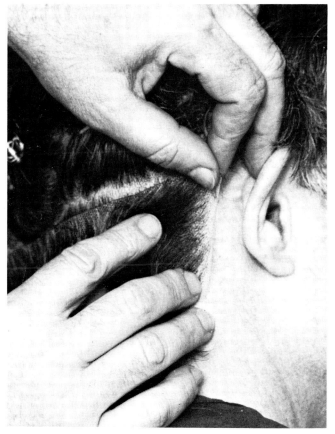

258. Comb the hair away from the back of the ear and position the net for gluing.

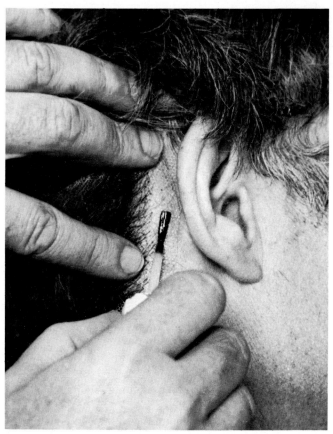

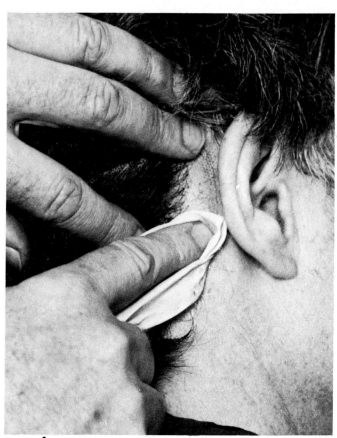

259. Apply adhesive under the lace if possible, and apply the adhesive above the hair as well, to insure firm adhesion.

260. Press the adhesive with a clean silk cloth to remove excess adhesive and to hasten drying.

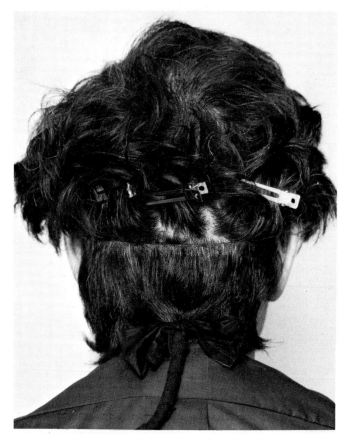

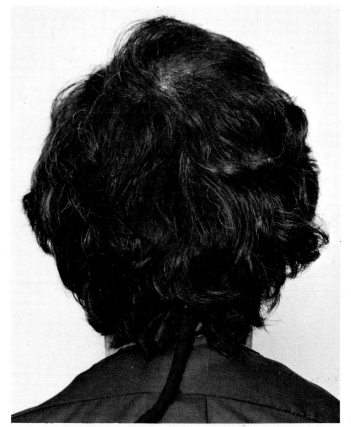

261. The fall is glued at both sides and anchored in the center.

262. The model's hair is carefully combed over the fall to blend in perfectly. Thus, we have created the pigtail pullback style of the American Revolutionary Period.

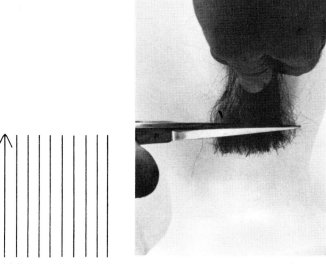

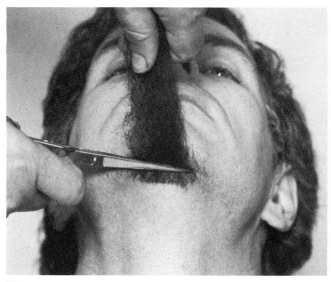

294. Underjaw, center: the hair is positioned under the jaw and is trimmed horizontally or straight across.

295. Underjaw, center: shown on the face.

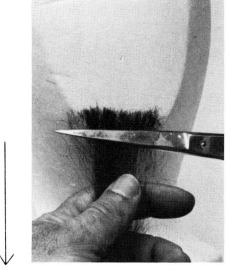

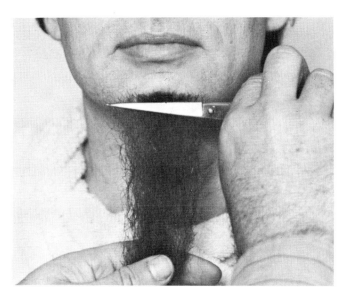

296. Above jaw, center: the hair is positioned above the chin in the center of the face and is trimmed horizontally.

297. Above jaw, center: shown on the face.

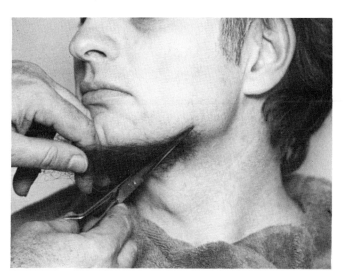

298. Side of face, underjaw: the hair is positioned to the underside of the jaw and is trimmed at a slight angle to the jawline.

299. Side of face, underjaw: shown on the face.

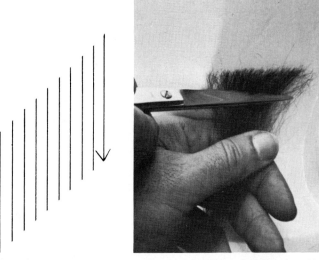

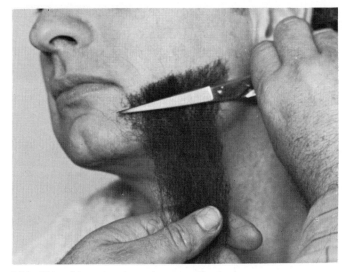

300. Side of face, top jaw: the hair is positioned above the chin and on the side of the cheek and is trimmed at a slight angle to the line of the jaw.

301. Side of face, top jaw: shown on the face.

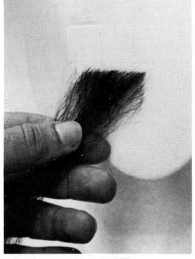

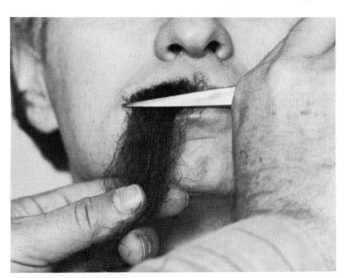

302. For the mustache, the hair is positioned above the lips and is cut at a slight angle, so that the hair grows away from the center of the face.

303. Mustache: shown on the face.

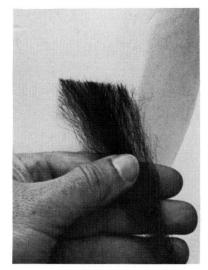

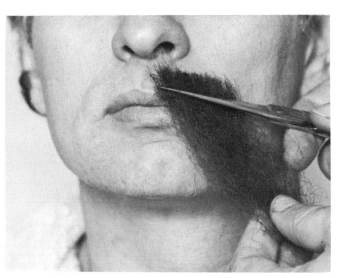

304. A different angle is used for the other side of the mustache.

305. Mustache: shown on the face.

STRAIGHTENING CREPE HAIR OR CREPE WOOL

Rarely does facial hair grow as straight as does the hair on top of the head; most facial hair has some curl. Since this is so, it is a common mistake to use absolutely straight hair, laid on the face for a beard. But the effect is false. So we use techniques to add curl to straightened hair before applying it to the face. It is possible to use a hot curling iron on straightened hair to give some indentation, a process called *crimping.* This is a slow, laborious, and usually dissatisfying technique. There is another process of curling hair: lengths of the hair are knitted to a braid, and then boiled in hot water to produce a tight kinkiness. The product of this process is called *crepe hair.*

When you are ready to use the hair, remove it from the braid, lay it out on an ironing board, and press the hair with a warm iron (preferably steam) to take out some of the kink. Hair prepared in this way is as close to perfect as possible for use in laying on a beard. Crepe hair can be obtained from wig makers, and in some instances from hair suppliers.

For practice purposes, crepe hair is too costly and inaccessible, and I recommend you substitute crepe wool instead. Crepe wool also requires straightening: first, remove the string around the braid; wet the braid with water; while it is still wet, stretch the braid to its normal length and fasten it in a fixed position until it is completely dry. The crepe wool may have to dry overnight. To hasten the drying process, you can lay the braid on or between some toweling. If you are in a great hurry for the wool to dry, you can press the heated iron to the wool. In fact, today's steam irons permit you to straighten crepe wool or hair without prior wetting. Place the wool on a board and run the steam iron back and forth over the braid until the wool has straightened sufficiently for usage. (If you use a regular iron, keep a cloth between the iron and wool to prevent scorching.) Stretch enough colors to allow you to mix the shade you will need.

PREPARING THE STRAIGHTENED CREPE HAIR OR WOOL

When the crepe hair or wool is dry and as straight as desired, release the hair or wool from the tight braid. While holding it with one hand, tug at the other end until a segment is loosened and pull this away from the hank. Repeat this process and add the newly pulled segments to the first. (See Figs. 306 and 307.) Use this technique to mix your colors. These segments should be 1″ to 2″ in width and about 6″ to 8″ long, or longer if you are after a very long beard.

These straightened segments will be applied to the face in a technique called *layering.* As the name implies, this technique means applying the hairs in layers and duplicating actual hair growth on the face.

306. To pull the straightened hair or wool from the braid, hold it in one hand and tug the other end of the segment.

307. Repeat the process until the segment is loosened and entirely free of the hank.

LAYERING THE BEARD

Layering can be done with straightened crepe wool, yak, crepe hair, or straight human hair. The technique with each of these materials is the same. Your fingers will have to make adjustments to the varying textures and strength of the type of hair used, but the procedures described here are identical. As I have already said, because of the prohibitive cost of yak or human hair, I suggest you practice this technique with straightened crepe wool.

To layer the beard, small segments of straightened wool or hair will be applied in layers so that each layer overlaps the preceding one. By this means, it will be possible to build up a blend, control its density, and lay the hair in precisely the correct direction of growth to create a remarkably natural beard.

To learn the physical coordination necessary in layering, practice without using the spirit gum to glue the wool or hair to the face. First, take a segment of the mixed straightened wool or hair in your left hand if you are right-handed (the reverse if you are left-handed). Hold the segment 1½" to 2" from the edge.

Turn the edge in the proper manner—a horizontal cut for laying in the center of the face and a right angle or a left angle cut for the respective sides of the face, as shown in Figs. 294 to 305.

Before attaching the beard, put aside at least a dozen segments of hair (so that you may add one segment after another with speed and rhythm). After you have used up this group of segments, set up another quantity of units. To glue the hair, apply the spirit gum to the area that will fit the clump in your hand (Fig. 308). (Do not apply wide swatches of spirit gum all over the face. Use it only where you intend the immediate gluing.) Carefully position and lay the hair or wool on the glued area. Pick up your shears and, using the flat part of the closed blades, press the shears against the hairs to secure adhesion (Fig. 309). Then slightly relax your hold on the hair, roll the shears off the hair, and gently, in order not to pull out any hairs, trim the length of the segment to approximately the length you want for the final beard. (See Figs. 310 to 312.) Do not cut the hair too short because you want to allow some length for the final trimming.

If the blades of your shears become tacky and covered with spirit gum, clean them with a rag dipped in acetone, and then go on to other segments until all the hair has been applied to the face. When you complete the area below the jaw, use a cloth for pressing the hair firmly against the face. Add more segments until the entire jaw area has been glued. Do the same for the upper center section of the face and for the sides. Keep on adding layers until the entire top beard area has had the hair laid on. The layers should be no more than ½" apart. Placing them closer creates a beard that is too bulky and layers farther apart tend to produce a thin, sparse, sketchy beard. Once the layers have been applied, firmly press both sides with the cloth and the beard area is complete. Add the mustache area and the laying on of hair is complete. (See Figs. 313 to 322.)

At first, your hands, shears, hair, and glue will seem to get in each other's way. Try to be patient. It will take time to master this technique and find continual use for it in your work.

TRIMMING THE BEARD

Trimming the beard is an art in itself. Using the barber shears properly demands practice, first in conceiving the mental image of the style you desire, and then in developing the skill to render that style effectively. For a variety of styles, refer to the gallery in Chapter Sixteen. Think carefully about what you intend to do before you actually begin to trim. Remember, once you have trimmed the beard, you cannot make it larger without starting over again. (In this demonstration, the hair was laid on deliberately long so that it would allow for a number of different beard shapes in the trimming.) Use your shears with restraint, and cut slowly and carefully (Fig. 323). When trimming around the mustache or mouth, use a finger as a guide or rest for your shears (Fig. 324).

After trimming, use the large teeth of your comb to remove odd loose bits of hair from the beard.

When you have trimmed the beard to your satisfaction, spray it lightly with a hair-set lacquer to keep its shape for a longer period of time.

REMOVING A LAYERED BEARD

To remove the wool or hair from the performer's face, simply pull the wool or hair away. The adhesive will not hold so firmly that it will hurt the skin. Moisten a cloth or tissue with any of the listed spirit gum removers and gently rub it over that part of the face where spirit gum had been applied. When using acetone be careful to avoid breathing the fumes. It is a strong solvent and should be used only in a well-ventilated room. When the spirit gum has been removed, cleanse the face with a pure cleansing cream and finish as usual with a mild astringent such as witch hazel or Sea Breeze.

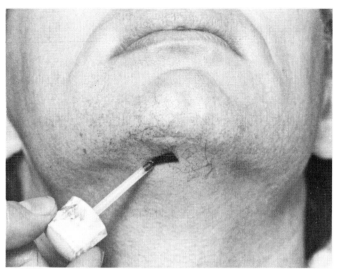

308. To begin layering the beard, first apply spirit gum to the center area under chin.

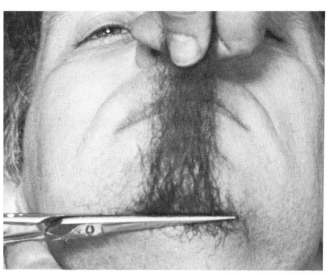

309. Lay the hair in place and press it onto the spirit gum with the flat edge of your shears.

310. With a dummy used for clarity, the method of holding the shears against the hair is clearly shown.

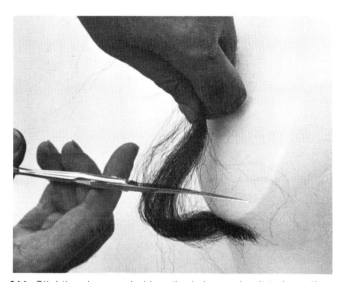

311. Slightly relax your hold on the hair, causing it to loop, then roll off the shears from the face and gently trim to the length you want for the final hair.

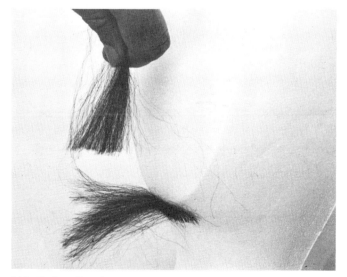

312. By bending the hair as shown, you avoid pulling the section off the face when it is cut.

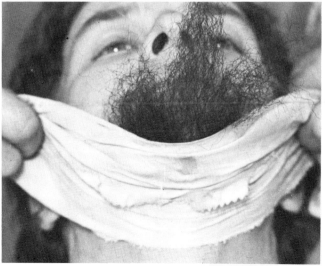

313. After laying on a number of sections, press the cloth against the chin for better adhesion.

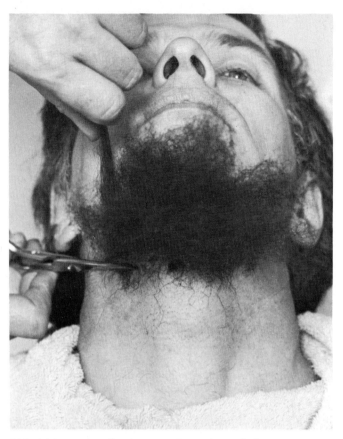

314. Add more sections to cover the entire underjaw area.

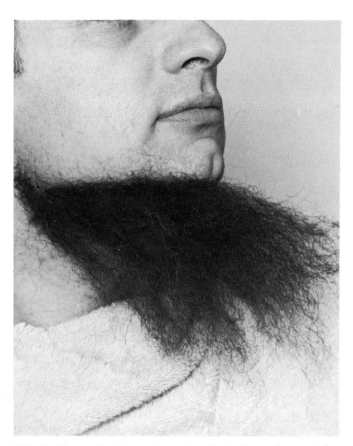

315. Sections of hair have been glued onto the entire underjaw area of the face.

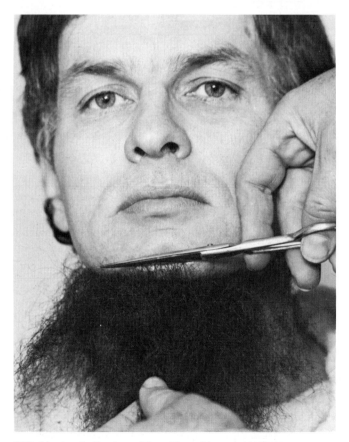

316. Moving to the top of the chin, add more sections.

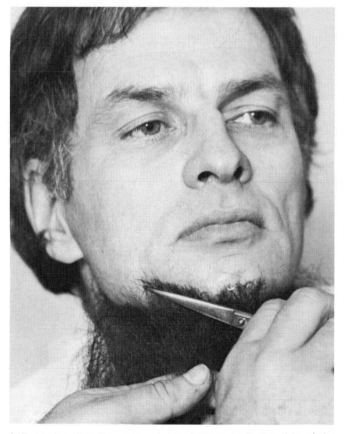

317. Notice that the angle of cut changes to fit the side of the chin.

318. The hair has been laid partially up one side of the face.

319. Sections have been added up the side of the face.

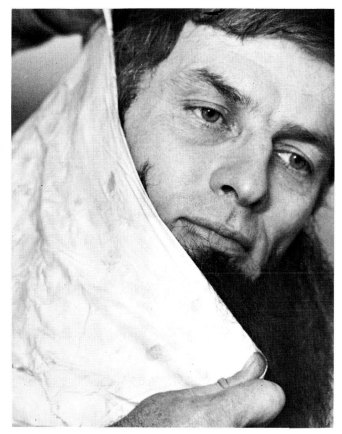

320. When the entire jaw area has been covered, use a cloth to press the hair firmly against the face. Repeat this process on the other side of the face.

321. The entire beard area is now complete.

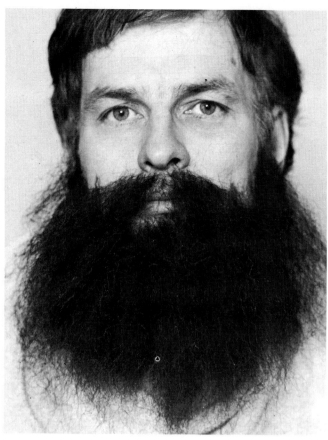

322. A mustache is added to the face in the same manner.

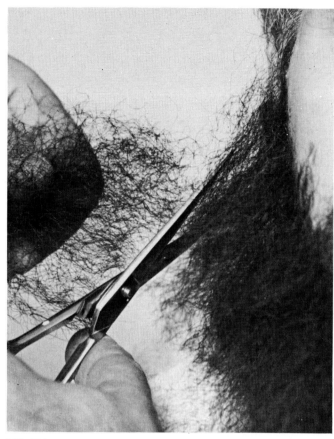

323. Trim the beard carefully, pulling away the hair as you cut.

324. In the mustache area use your finger to guide the shears as you trim.

325. A trimmed long beard.

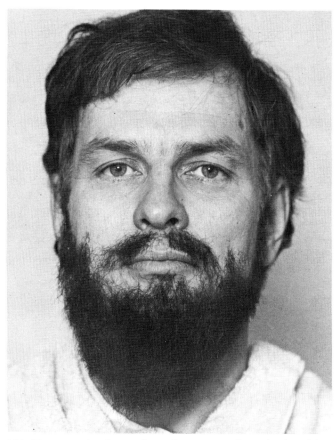

326. The beard has been trimmed even more for a shorter style.

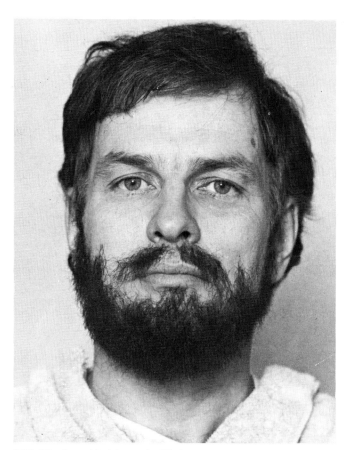

327. The beard is trimmed still shorter.

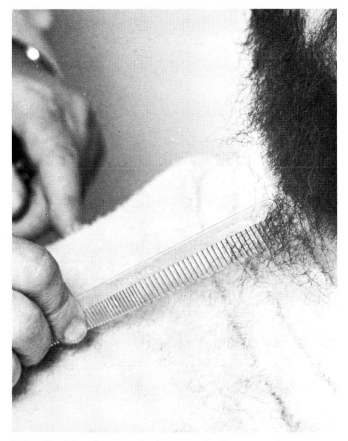

328. After trimming, use the large teeth of your comb to remove odd loose bits of hair from the beard.

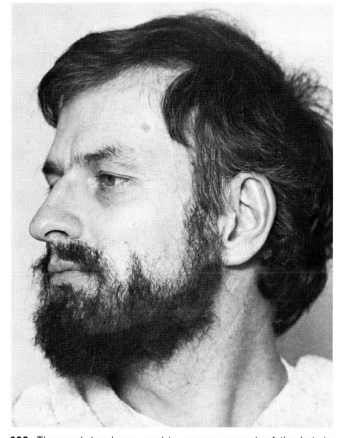

329. The comb has been used to remove enough of the hair to show the shape of the jaw. Trimmed even further, this would result in no more than a stubble of a beard.

FACIAL HAIRPIECES

There will be many occasions where it will be necessary to use the same beard or mustache for extended periods of days, or even weeks. In such an instance it is extremely impractical to apply a beard or mustache in the layering technique, since matching perfectly from one day to the next will require long and expensive periods of time. Facial hairpieces, designed to fit the performer, are invaluable in these cases. They are applied to the face in the same manner as you would handle a head hairpiece. Like the hairpiece for the head, the facial hairpiece is knotted by hand onto a fine lace backing which has been shaped to fit the performer for whom it has been designed. The net is fragile and must be handled with extreme care. Facial hairpieces range in style and use from sparse mustaches, to rakish sideburns, to beards of all shapes and sizes.

To apply the facial hairpiece, first fit it onto the face to confirm the shape and fit. You may trim excessive amounts of hair lace from the piece. Apply spirit gum to the area the beard will adhere to, position the piece carefully and press it onto the face. Use your cloth to press the piece against the face firmly (Fig. 330). If necessary, add dabs of spirit gum to any loose area (Fig. 331). Again firmly press it with your cloth (Fig. 332).

REMOVING AND CLEANING FACIAL HAIRPIECES

To remove the facial hairpiece, first moisten a cloth or cleansing tissue with acetone. Ask the performer to hold his breath so that he will not breathe in the fumes and dab at the hair lace with the acetone wet cloth to loosen the hold of the spirit gum. As soon as the piece is loose, simply peel it away from the skin. If any particular area adheres firmly, loosen it with a few dabs of the acetone wet cloth, or you may use other liquid cleansers, such as those made by Ben Nye or Mehron.

When the pieces are removed from the face, use a tissue wet with some spirit gum remover to dissolve the rest of the spirit gum from the face, then cleanse as prescribed. When using acetone, avoid breathing the fumes, and use it for as short a period as is possible. Keep the container capped, and make sure the room in which you are working is well-ventilated.

To clean the facial hairpiece, lay it lace side up on a clean towel, which in turn is on an enameled or wood surface clear of any shellac or varnish. (The acetone used to clean the lace will soak through the towel and dissolve any lacquered, varnished, or enameled surface.) Dip an eyebrow or hair dyeing brush with natural bristles and wooden handle into a shallow china dish containing acetone. (Plastic bristles or handles will dissolve in acetone.) Dab at the surface of the lace with the brush until all of the spirit gum is dissolved and caught in the towel below the piece (Fig. 338). When clean, dry the piece by gently waving it in the air, and then carefully put it away in a box large enough to hold it without crushing it.

With gentle care, even the most delicate lace piece can be maintained for use over a considerable number of performances. Conversely, carelessness can destroy the piece after one performance.

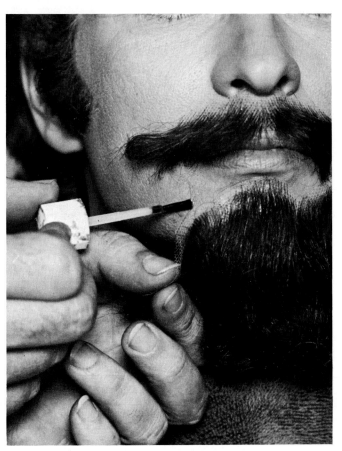

330. Glue the facial hairpiece in place and then press with a cloth.

331. Add dabs of spirit gum to loose spots.

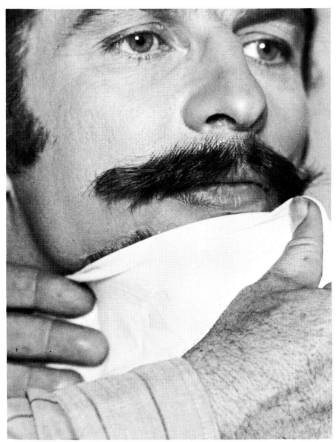

332. Press again for firm contact.

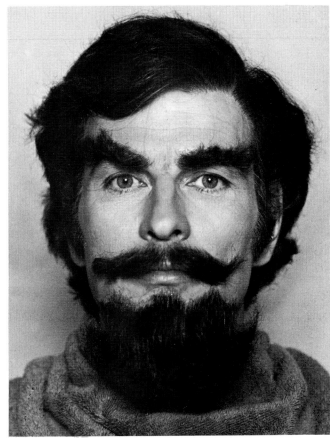

333. Lace beard, mustache, and eyebrows.

334. The face has been aged and facial pieces applied to complete the effect.

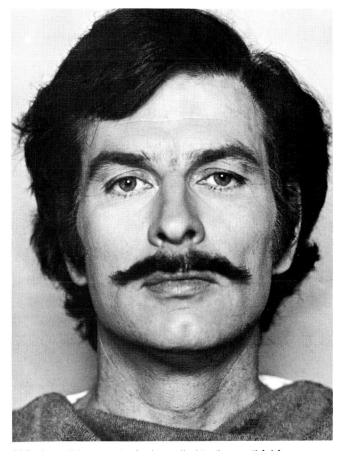

335. A small lace mustache is applied to the youthful face.

336. A larger lace mustache has been applied.

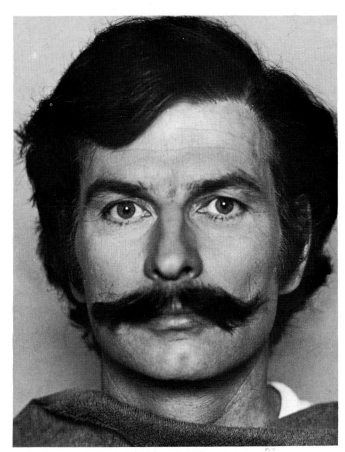

337. The variation of shapes is endless.

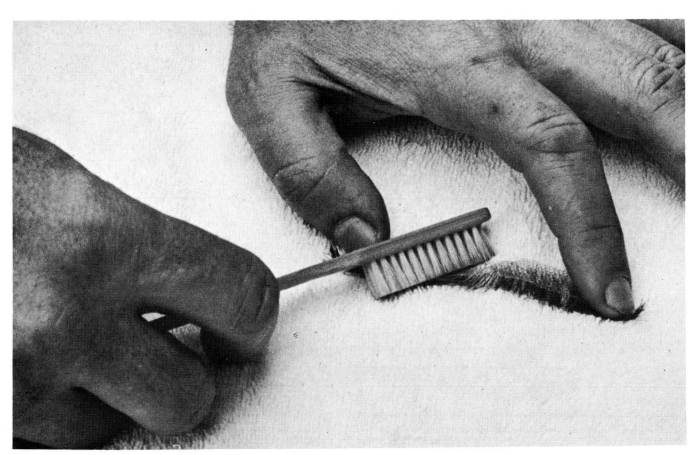

338. To clean a hairpiece, dip a brush in acetone, and brush the surface of the lace on a clean towel until you remove the spirit gum.

PREPARING CREPE WOOL FOR BEARD

In the beginning of this chapter I mentioned that crepe wool could be applied in sections to make beards suitable for performers seen from a distance, in mob scenes, for example. In layering the beard you apply straightened hair, a time-consuming process which produces astonishingly realistic results. Unlike the layering technique, crepe wool beards are applied rapidly, but should only be used as a last resort when facial hairpieces are unavailable and when a face will not be seen from close up.

Crepe wool is a soft wool-like fiber that comes braided in solid colors, usually red, black, brown, tan, gray, and white. In preparing crepe wool for a beard you must unravel the braid so that you can cut the sections of wool that will form the beard. First open the string which ties and holds the braid together (Fig. 339). Loosen or cut this string about half-way down the braid and pull the braid free (Fig. 340), then separate about half the length of wool. In its braided form the wool is curly and compacted and this braid must be opened. With the fingers, spread the wool and open it so that it is somewhat transparent (Fig. 341).

With the wool opened and separated, it becomes possible to remove a segment. Put the spread open wool on your thigh and hold down firmly with the palm of your hand (Fig. 342). Try not to cover or hold more than ½″ or 1″ of the spread wool. The wool will stretch and open considerably. Gently pull the braided part of the hank (Fig. 343) until a segment is separated from the braid (Fig. 344). Now go back to the rest of the braid and pull as many segments from the braid as you will need. (For example, you will need two segments for a Van Dyke beard, and six segments for a full beard.) Mix colors if you so desire. (See Fig. 345.) Try on each piece for the area of face it will cover, then pre-cut the edges to conform to the shape of that part of the face (Fig. 346). Cut the segments and put them aside until you are ready to apply the beard.

APPLYING CREPE WOOL BEARD AND MUSTACHE

Using the sections we have pulled, we will now make a full beard. To apply the crepe wool sections you will need spirit gum, barber's shears, and a clean section of cloth about the size of a man's handkerchief, which should be clean and lintless, either silk, rayon, or nylon.

Taking a section which has been shaped to fit the lower part of the face, apply spirit gum to the center of the bottom face (Fig. 347). Be sure that the beard area of the face is free of any makeup. When the gum has been applied, give it a moment to dry.

Take the first segment of wool and position it under the jaw, the trimmed edge touching the windpipe and the uncut edge projecting forward past the edge of the chin. Press the segment into place (Fig. 348), with your fingers remaining pressed against the face for a moment until you can feel that the wool has adhered slightly. Holding one end of your cloth in each hand, lay the cloth against the wool and press it against the wool firmly to facilitate adhesion of the wool (Fig. 349). Pull away the cloth carefully without removing particles of the wool at the same time. Check the segment for adhesion and placement. Now continue to apply additional segments as described in the illustrations, using the same procedure.

If you want to add a crepe wool mustache, pull a section of wool from the hank and comb through it so that you catch a quantity of wool in the teeth of the comb (Fig. 357). Hold down the combed section of wool with the palm of your hand as you lift the comb out of the section (Fig. 358), then trim off the rough wool edge to make the lip section (Fig. 359). To apply the mustache, follow the same procedure as you did for the beard: apply spirit gum, press the wool into position, use the cloth for final adhesion.

All styles of beard can be produced with this technique. Simply cut the sections to the style desired and apply as directed.

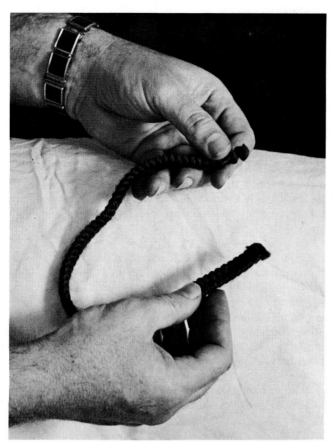

339. To open a braid of crepe wool, place the hank on your knee and open the string that ties the braid together.

340. Cut the string part way down the braid and begin to loosen the hank.

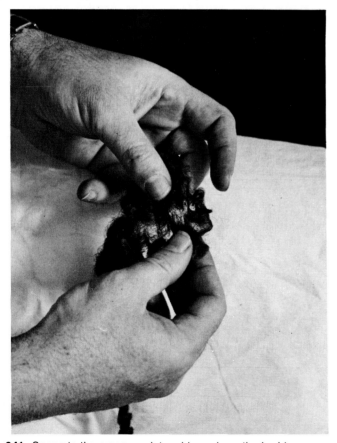

341. Separate the crepe wool, to midway down the braid.

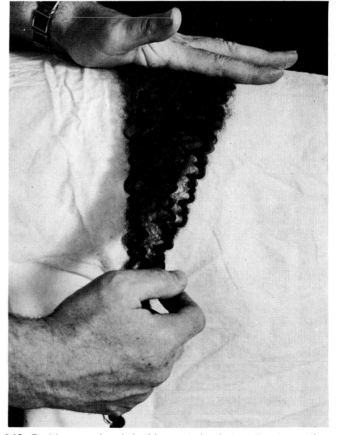

342. Position your hands in this way to begin to pull out a section.

343. Holding the palm of your hand firmly on your thigh, gently pull out a section with the other hand.

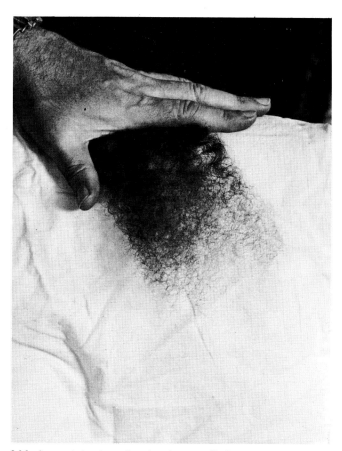

344. A good-sized section has been pulled.

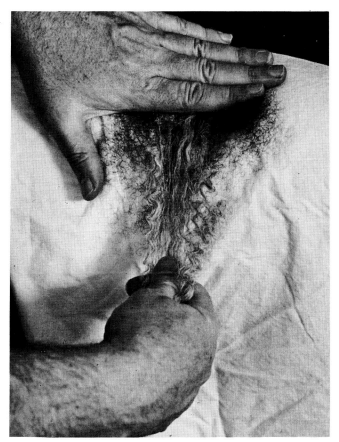

345. Add other colors if you want to mix shades in the beard.

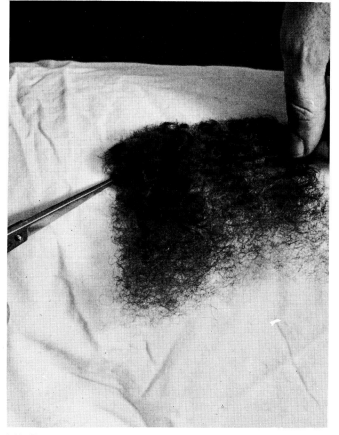

346. Trim the section with a straight edge for the bottom section of the beard.

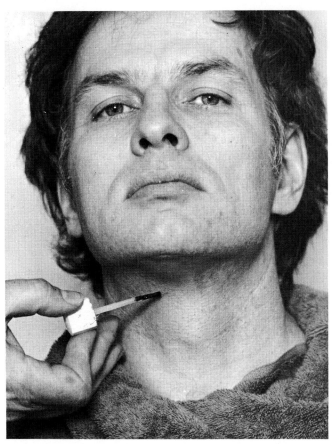

347. Apply spirit gum to the underjaw over a large enough area to take the section of crepe wool.

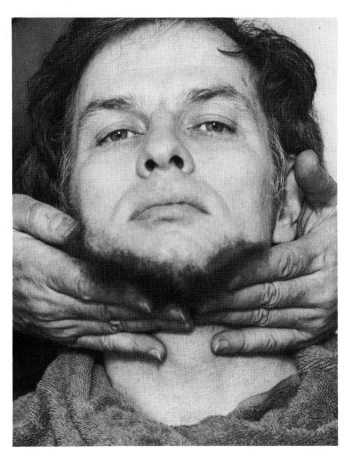

348. Position the bottom section of crepe wool and press it into place.

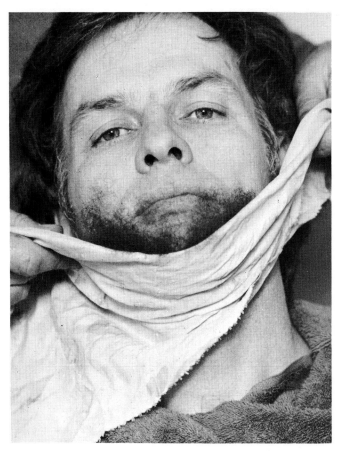

349. Using a silk cloth, press firmly to insure adhesion.

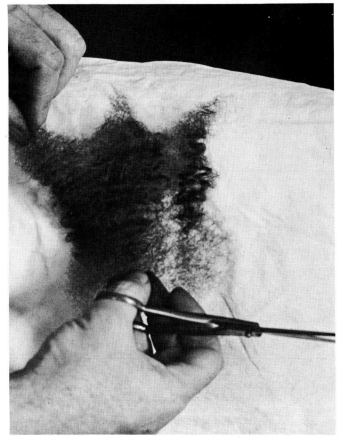

350. Cut a section of crepe wool for the top section of the beard.

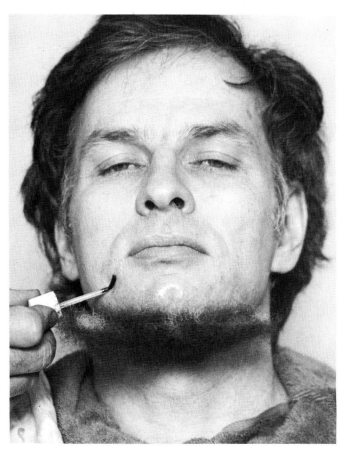

351. Apply spirit gum to the top of the jaw in the shape of the prepared section of wool.

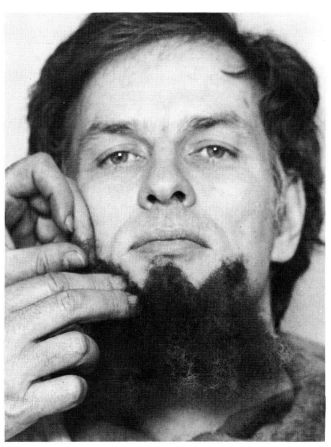

352. Place the crepe wool into position and press gently into place.

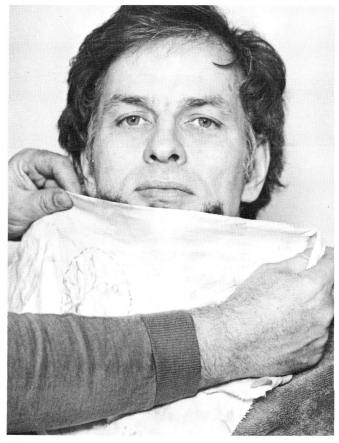

353. Use the silk cloth pressed against the face for full adhesion.

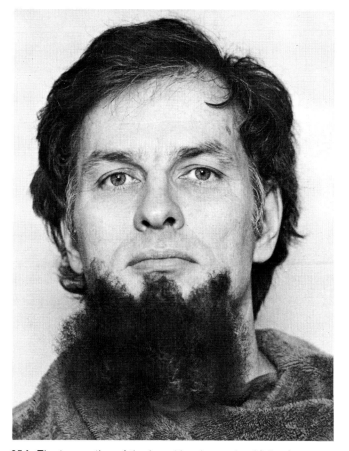

354. The top section of the beard has been glued into place.

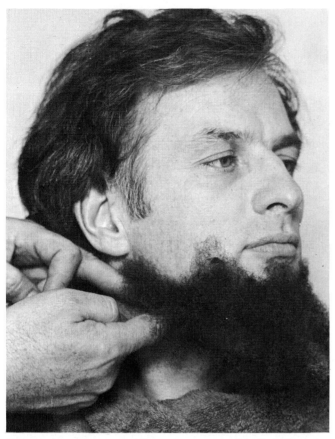

355. Apply spirit gum and then glue on a section that fits under the jaw and back to the ear.

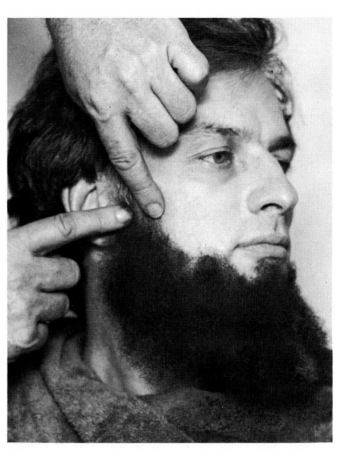

356. Glue and apply section that fits onto the cheek and into the sideburn. Complete the other side of the face in the same manner.

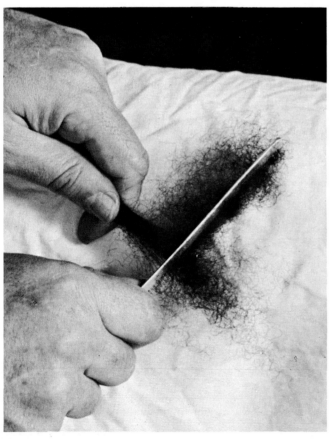

357. Pull the comb through the wool to gather a mustache section. Let the teeth of the comb catch the wool.

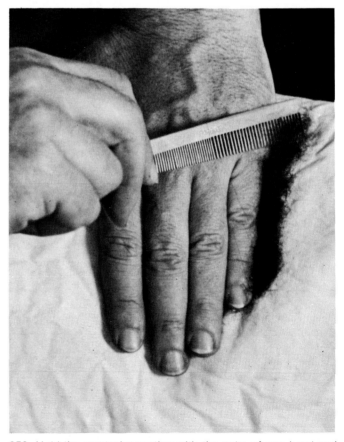

358. Hold the mustache section with the palm of one hand and lift out the comb.

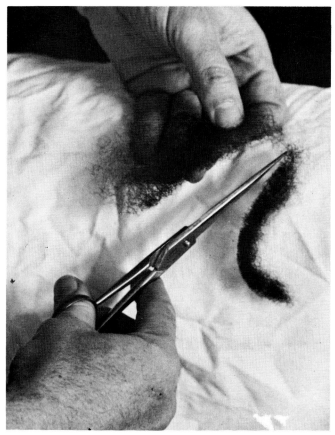

359. Trim the edge of the mustache section. It is now ready for use.

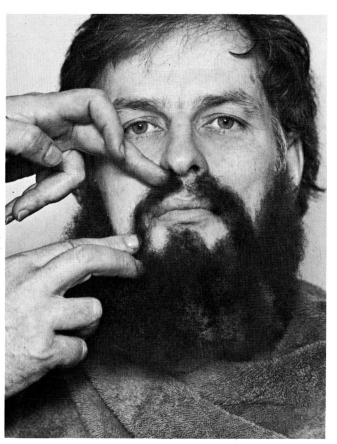

360. The mustache pieces are added to the face.

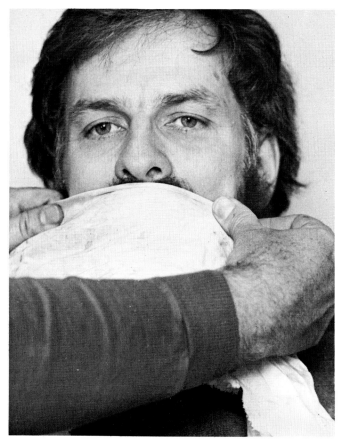

361. The mustache is adhered firmly with pressure from the silk cloth.

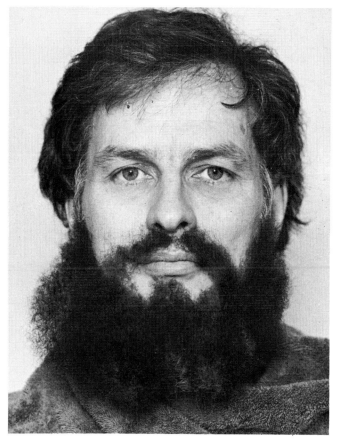

362. A full beard has been created with the crepe wool sections.

363. You may trim the wool into any beard shape you desire.

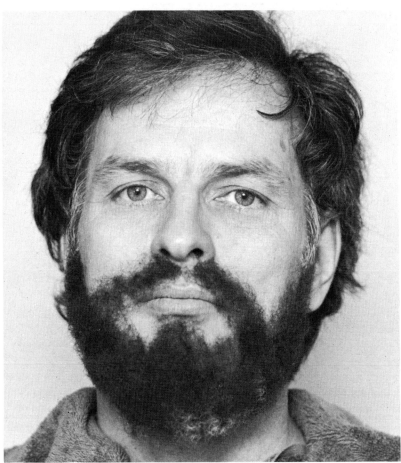

364. Here the beard has been trimmed for spade beard shape.

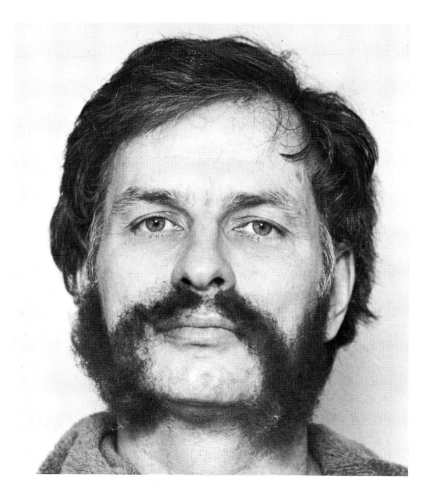

365. With the crepe wool, mutton chops have been created.

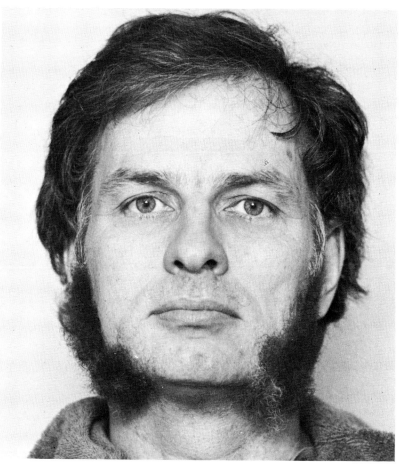

366. Without the mustache, we have chin whiskers.

143

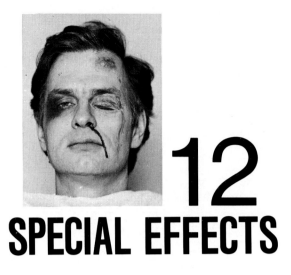

12
SPECIAL EFFECTS

Blood, sweat, tears, bruises, and scars are what can be called *special effects.* Creating special effects in makeup does not always require special preparation, but these effects are different enough from the norm to warrant a separate section. However, since these aspects of makeup *are* different from the norm, and are both dramatic and conspicuous, the temptation to overdo the effects is enormous. Restraint *must* be exercised in this aspect of makeup, particularly for work to be seen on a motion picture screen, for here the magnification will turn what seems to be a small wound into a bloody horror. So do be precise and careful. For TV the image on the screen will be *smaller* than life, so exaggeration may be called for, but be sure to ask for a rehearsal, an opportunity for you to look at the work on the monitor, especially important when the effect is to be viewed in a close-up.

Since the photos used to illustrate the work in this chapter are greatly reduced, I have exaggerated the effects to make them more visible to you. Bear this in mind when you practice. If I had softened the effects (as I would ordinarily do for work being projected on a big screen), It would not help you in learning the craft of makeup.

BLOOD

Two types of blood are important for our work, They are not A, B, or O, but panchromatic for black and white photography and technicolor for color photography. Originally blood used for black and white film had to be very dark in order to register. In view of the fine resolution of today's film—a great improvement over the past—a blood color that looks real to the eye will register satisfactorily in all types of film and in all media. Therefore, by following simple instructions, you can make blood that will be perfectly suitable for black and white motion pictures, or TV,

still photography, or color motion pictures.

For the blood mixture you will need a liquid to act as the base, either glycerin or Karo light corn syrup. Glycerin has two disadvantages: it may remove the makeup base it is applied over. This may present no problem, however, since the face may already be a mess for the scene. Furthermore, depending on its thickness, glycerin will also have varying degrees of viscosity, sometimes running too quickly or too slowly. In spite of these minor drawbacks, don't discount glycerin as a base for blood; these properties might be exactly what you need.

In the demonstration illustrated here in color, I use Karo syrup, for it is inexpensive, harmless, and readily available in all food markets. This recipe calls for one cup of blood. Diminish or expand the formula in proportion to your specific needs.

Take one cup of Karo syrup (or glycerin) and pour it into a clean plastic or glass container. Add one teaspoon of red vegetable coloring to this container and stir it in. Add one half teaspoon of yellow vegetable coloring to the container and stir it in. Then add one teaspoon of non-toxic, water soluble red poster paint (for opacity) to the container. This mixture should have a bright blood color, a good reflective sheen, and a nice syrupy viscosity. Take some and place it on your hand. It will dry in time, though not as quickly as glycerin, and if held in the mouth for a particularly bloody effect may be swallowed with no ill effects. (For this reason, the poster paint must be non-toxic and water soluble. The quantity of paint in the mixture is so minimal that it will cause no harm when swallowed.)

SWEAT

Sweat is an effect that must be used with great discretion. The slightest excess of sweat, when magnified on the screen, makes the performer look as if he had just walked through a Brazilian rain forest. Sweat can be used to point up any of a number of dramatic effects: heat, exertion, fear, or a combination of these. For this reason, it is most important to find out how much of an effect the director wants, and, after you have accomplished that, find out from the cameraman if the effect is registering in the camera, since the angle of the light can totally obliterate the effect of perspiration, in which case you may have to add more than the director originally wanted and vary that amount from scene to scene, or from camera angle to camera angle.

Naturally, water is the easiest thing to use for sweat. This can be applied with an atomizer and you can control the quantity from a mere suggestion to a virtual downpour (Fig. 367). Water, however, quickly runs off the face and dries very rapidly, so if the scene is long, water alone will not do. Water will hold longer on the face if there is some glycerin beneath the water. Apply some glycerin with a sponge to the part of the face that is to perspire and then atomize water onto the glycerin with your sprayer (Figs. 368 and 369). Or you may *mix* the water with glycerin, about one part glycerin to three parts water. Shake it up and use this mixture as a spray. Spray only on the area intended to appear sweaty; continued spraying will create larger droplets, and even more spraying will make the droplets run down the face. The water mixed with the glycerin will not dry too quickly, and when it does run, it will leave some effect of sweat rather than just disappear.

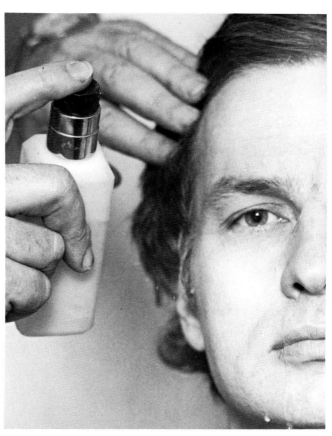

367. To create perspiration, you may simply spray water from an atomizer onto the face.

368. Water will hold longer on the face if there is some glycerin beneath the water. First dab on glycerin to the area you want to perspire.

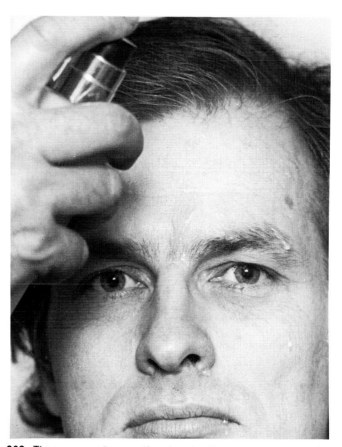

369. Then spray water over the glycerin. Or you can mix the water with glycerin before spraying it on.

TEARS

Although a seemingly simple effect, tears are difficult to illustrate with photographs. Tears are rarely visible except when in an extreme close-up shot, and tears usually arise in an emotional scene so that they become part of a much larger effect. If you have that rare performer who can create his own tears at will, be grateful and leave him alone. If tears must be induced, wait until everything else is ready in the scene, just before the camera is about to roll. Await the director's instructions before you proceed.

One way to induce real tears is by breaking an ampoule of spirits of ammonia. Have the performer breathe the fumes just before the scene. (See Fig. 370.) If this does not work, you can induce tears by using a Vicks menthol inhalator (the type used when you have a stuffy nose). Unscrew the inhalator out of its case, remove the small plastic plug at the back end of the inhalator, then place the point of the inhalator a few inches away from the tear

duct in the inside corner of the eye. Blow gently into the other end of the inhalator (Fig. 371). The fumes directed toward the tear duct should act as a mild irritant and stimulate the tear duct to create tears. As soon as the performer says he feels the effect of the fumes, move out of the camera range and let the scene take place.

If neither of these artificial stimulants achieves the results needed, you may have to fall back on the simple expedient of putting a drop or two of glycerin in the inside corner of the eye near the tear duct just before the camera rolls (Fig. 372), and let gravity and the viscosity of the glycerin create its own tear as it works its way down the cheek.

These effects described are used for films only. On a live TV show it may be impossible to use either the inhalator or the ammonia. The eye dropper and glycerin technique may be the only answer, and if the scene is not a close-up, even glycerin may not register. In this case, only the acting can carry the effect of tears.

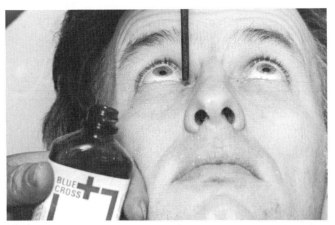

370. To stimulate tears, break an ampoule of spirits of ammonia and have the subject breathe in the fumes just before the scene takes place.

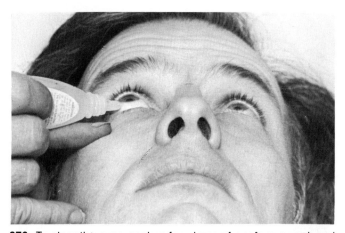

371. You may also stimulate tears by blowing the fumes through a menthol inhalator into the tear duct of the eye.

372. If these fail, add some drops of glycerin to the skin near the tear ducts.

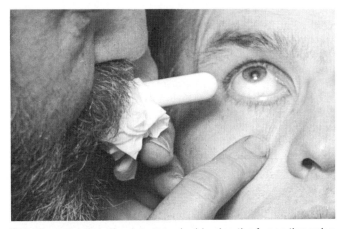

373. To clear the eyes, apply a few drops of a safe eye wash and wait until the medication shrinks the capillary blood vessels of the eye.

BRUISES

A bruise actually takes a period of time to become evident. If a bruise does not break the skin, it will show very little immediate effect on the skin, if it shows any at all. Physical damage is noticeable immediately after an accident only if

the surface of the skin has been broken, in which case the blood makes the wound very apparent. If there is damage to the muscle or bone structure beneath the skin, the area will swell and form a lump and in time the damaged blood vessels and capillaries will discolor the skin surface and create a bruise. The small bruise that simply turns into a small swelling is barely distinguishable from any distance. It is recognizable as a bruise only after it has discolored.

The illusion of a bruise can be created by using first a blue-gray lining color. Apply this, using the same illusion as illustrated diagramatically in Fig. 24, Chapter Two. This will give the effect of swelling to create a lump or roundness. Apply the blue-gray paint darkest in the center of the appointed bruise, blend it out in all directions to the size desired, and blend it to disappear into the base. When you have shaped the bruise to the desired size with the blue-gray, add a maroon lining color on top, heaviest in the center and blending out to simulate the purple discoloration of the bruise. Don't carry the maroon out as far as you did the blue-gray, and don't blend it evenly, because you want a splotchy effect, since discoloration is irregular. Once you get the full effect of swelling with the maroon, you may—in the instance of a black eye—add a touch of moist rouge to the inside of the eyelid to help add the effect of a bloodshot eye.

BURNS AND CHAPPING

In creating burns and chapping, you must give the illusion of a broken skin surface that is either in a raw or healing state. These effects can be obtained by using surgical adhesive or liquid latex (which are basically the same). Apply and spread the liquid rubber to the area to be chapped (the lips) or burned (the forehead). Let it dry, and then begin to pick at the adhesive, rubbing it with the fingertip to break its surface. Lift little bits of the adhesive away from the skin. This will give the effect of chapping. For burns, add maroon liner unevenly to the broken skin. You may also use maroon on the chapped lips, or if a more extreme effect is wanted, use an off-white grease color to accent the contrast. Apply both unevenly.

ABNORMAL EYE

Obviously, there are many types of damaged eyes, scarred and bloody, dislocated pupil, etc. A lifeless or dislocated pupil can be created very easily for film by using any of the enormous variety of contact lenses available today. Prior to the development of the contact lens, this was a difficult and often terribly painful effect to create, since a dislocated pupil meant applying a foreign material directly against the eyeball. Although the effects may have achieved the shocking results they were designed to achieve, the performer could suffer excruciating pain. Lon Chaney, for example, actually created a startling illusion of a blind eye in Road to Mandalay. Taking the white membrane from the inside of an egg, he inserted the thin film directly against his eyeball, though I can't imagine how he stood the pain! Happily, nothing like this is necessary today; contact lenses can easily create these illusions.

Making a scarred and bloody eye is also easy. First, make a latex rubber piece (as described in Chapter Nine) which will fit over the eye and will simulate the swollen, damaged effect you're after. Hold the piece next to the eye for a fitting. Glue the piece into place with spirit gum. Blend and seal the edge with liquid latex and, when this is dry, add a coat of sealer (as you would do in applying a bald cap). Then paint over this eye, blending the piece into the base color and shading it for the shape and degree of eye damage you want to show.

SCARS

A scar is a cut in the flesh. In the healing process the flesh frequently rejoins in an irregular shape. When healed, most scars show little more than a slight welt. The effect of this minor scar is easily obtained by applying a thin sketching of collodion along the line of the scar you wish to create. This effect is so subtle that I doubt you can see it at all.

A deep, heavy scar can be built up with liquid latex, mortician's wax, scar plastic, or collodion. Collodion is a plastic material which seals the skin and creates the natural welting of a healed scar. Latex and surgical adhesive are painted on in successive layers, building up the effect of scar tissue. Mortician's wax and scar plastic can be layered on in the required density and then modeled and carved to create these illusions.

Apply the material to be scarred. Shape it or carve it into the desired effect. Run the edge of an eyebrow tweezer down the length of the scar material to create the cut. Then cover the scar with base color and paint in the degree of scarring you desire—fresh, scabbed, or healing—using rouge, maroon, blue-gray liner, or add blood if you want a fresh scar. A heavy scar has been painted in the color demonstration.

Keep scar lines uneven and be very careful not to overdo them. Use restraint rather than gore.

UPS AND DOWNS

Roles that call for the physical disintegration or marked improvement of a performer are uncommon. The special effects required for showing obvious changes in a performer throughout a film are what I call "ups and downs." In two films I have worked on—Panic in Needle Park and Born to Win—the script called for the physical disintegration of the leading characters through use of drugs. In one script the time span involved months, and in the other only a few weeks. In terms of makeup, the effect of drugs—while ruinous to the health and appearance of the characters—was still basically subtle. To create the illusions that would express the disintegration of the characters and yet work with subtlety was the problem I had to resolve in both these films. I relied on a few basic illusions: a sickly pallor (created with lighter base color) and sinking eyes and cheek (created carefully with blue-gray shadow). Note the decline of the character in Panic in Needle Park, played by Kitty Winn (Figs. 375 and 376) and the character played by George Segal in Born to Win (Fig. 374).

374. George Segal in Born to Win played a character overcome by drugs. To suggest his decline with makeup, I used blue-gray shadow and a light base color. Photo Muky.

375. A natural, healthy color is given to Kitty Winn's face for *Panic in Needle Park.* Photo Adger Cowans.

376. For the role of a girl who has fallen into the world of drugs, the makeup must reflect her decline. A lighter base color and blue-gray shadow created pallor. Photo Adger Cowans.

TRACKS

"Tracks" is a name describing the scarred wound that results from successive injections of narcotics into a vein. The needle continually puncturing the vein and the narcotics entering the vessel ultimately infect the vein and cause it to collapse. The addict then enters other areas of the vein, seeking uninfected portions to receive the needle. Although any vein in any part of the body can be used, the addict generally makes use of the veins in the arm or hand. Rarely does this kind of wound actually break the skin surface. To create tracks in makeup you will create a seriously discolored scar.

Along the line of the vein, apply a thin coat of collodion (Fig. 377). Wait for the collodion to dry and crinkle. If necessary, apply a second coat. When the collodion is dry, carefully paint along the line of the scar with blue-gray liner. Make sure the application of paint is irregular, yet

blend it so that no paint spots are conspicuous. On top of the blue-gray add some maroon liner to give the proper purple tinge of a severe scar wound. (See Fig. 378.) When this is painted to your satisfaction, apply a thin coat of colorless nail polish over the scar, and feather the edges of this coating with your fingertip (Fig. 379). This coating will keep the colors of the scar secure; the performer can safely touch and even rub it lightly without fear of its coming off. Since addicts frequently use more than one vein, it is usually necessary to apply more than one track to the arm. The demonstration photographs shown here were taken by the film still photographer Muky while I applied tracks to Paula Prentiss for the film *Born to Win.* I have also included an additional Polaroid photograph of tracks from *Panic in Needle Park,* which I used as a record to maintain a consistent position from one scene to the next (Fig. 382).

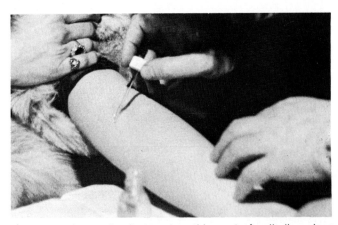

377. To create tracks, first apply a thin coat of collodion along the line of the vein. If necessary, a second coat. Photos Muky.

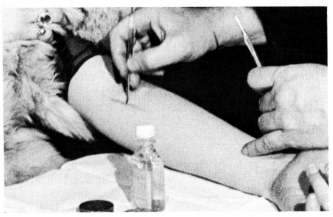

378. When the collodion is dry, carefully paint along the line of the scar with blue-gray liner. Add some maroon lines over this.

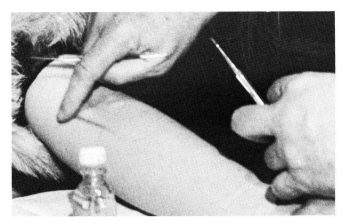

379. Apply colorless nail polish and pat it into the track with your fingertip. This will protect the tracks from smearing.

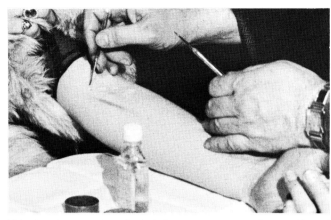

380. Another set of tracks is being started on another section of the arm.

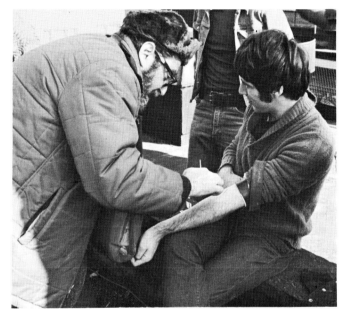

381. Tracks are being applied to Al Pacino on location for *Panic in Needle Park*. Photo Adger Cowans.

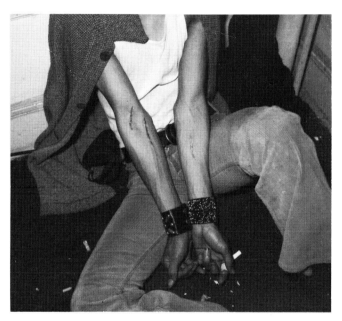

382. Polaroid photographs were used to record the accurate placement of tracks in the arms for *Panic in Needle Park*.

TATTOOS

As a special effect, tattoos may seem to be too simple a subject to warrant much space. As in all aspects of film making, however, they are unimportant until you need them; at that point they become the single most important factor in the film.

A tattoo is a picture or a design which has been pricked under the skin surface by needles. These needles force either a red or blue ink into the design which creates a permanent record that can only be removed by skin grafts or by acid. For a single day's shooting, creating a tattoo is simple. You just sketch the design onto the skin surface with blue and red pencils or pens. A tattoo becomes a problem when it must be repeated day after day. Sketching the same design from one day to the next would produce unacceptable inaccuracies.

This problem can be easily resolved. Have the design or picture made to the correct size and have a rubber stamp made of the design. (Only a few days are needed to make a rubber stamp.) Once you have the stamp only simple techniques are needed to repeat the tattoo for each day's shooting.

In a film I worked on recently, a tattoo was an important feature for the main character. When I was called about the film, I immediately told production to have a rubber stamp made with the design they required for the character. Evidently there were misgivings about using a stamp, so the company ordered decalcomanias to be made from the design. When applied to the skin, these decals proved unsatisfactory. Production agreed to order a rubber stamp. I asked for a blue ink pad but was given purple. This proved unsatisfactory. I finally succeeded in acquiring the blue ink pad—the material requested originally—and the problem was resolved.

Ink the stamp thoroughly and hold the area to which it will be applied so that it is steady. A small stamp may be applied directly, but a large one requires that you roll on the stamp from one side to another, maintaining even pressure. Then clean off any excess ink with a cotton wad dipped in acetone. Complete the tattoo by sharpening up the design where necessary with lining color or by adding any additional colors that may be called for in the tattoo.

The color demonstration shown here was taken by Muky as I applied a tattoo to George Segal in *Born to Win*.

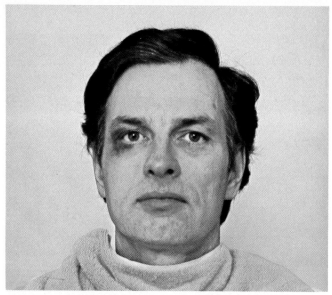

A. A bruise (in this case a black eye) begins with blue-gray liner painted on the area.

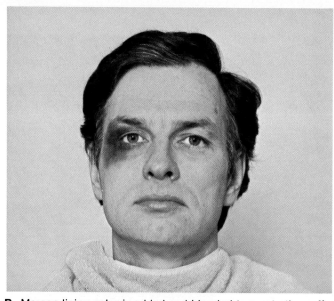

B. Maroon lining color is added and blended to create the puffy shape.

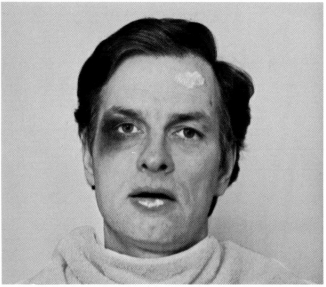

C. Liquid latex is painted on the lips (for chapping) and on the forehead for a burned effect.

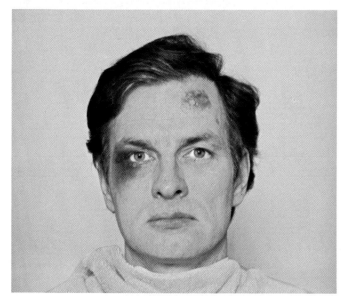

D. Maroon lining is added to both forehead and lips. Then the dried latex is carefully rubbed to break its surface.

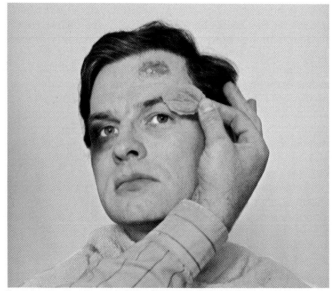

E. A rubber piece made to simulate a damaged eye is held next to the eye for proper fitting.

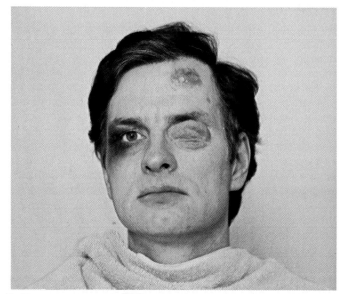

F. The eye piece is glued into place.

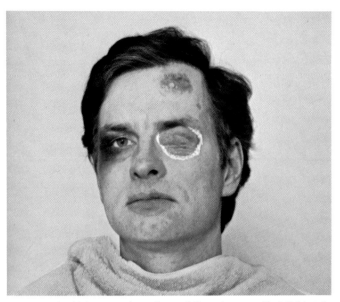

G. Apply liquid latex to the edges of the piece so that it blends into the skin.

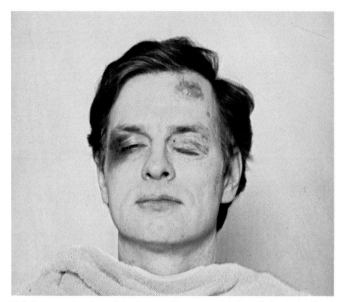

H. A base color is painted over the eye and the distorted effect is heightened with shading.

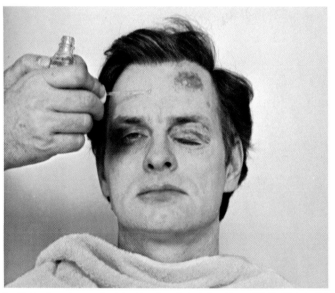

I. Collodion is applied to the forehead for the effect of an old healed scar.

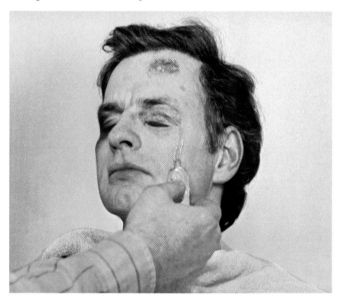

J. Scar plastic is applied to the cheek to start a recent scar.

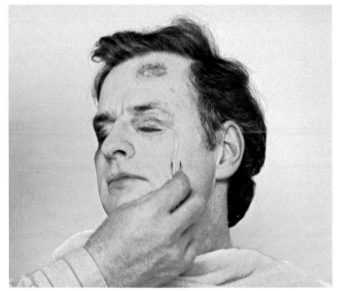

K. With the edge of an eyebrow tweezer, the scar shape is carved into the scar plastic.

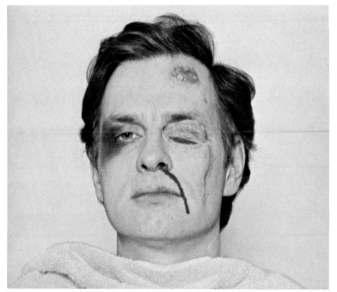

L. Base color is applied to the edge of the scar and it is painted to simulate a new healing scar. Add trickle of blood to the nose.

A. To make blood, first pour one cup of Karo Corn Syrup into a clean glass or plastic container.

B. Add one teaspoon of red vegetable coloring.

C. Add one-half teaspoon of yellow vegetable coloring.

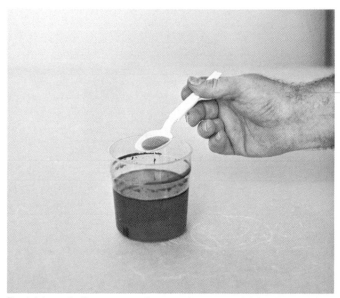

D. Add one-half teaspoon of non-toxic water soluble poster paint.

E. Mix the solution. The result has the opacity and consistency of blood.

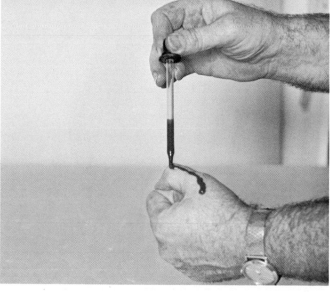

F. Here the blood is applied to the hand to show its holding and color qualities.

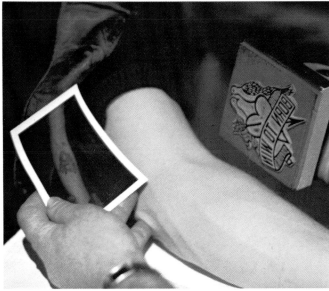

A. To make a tattoo, first position the area securely and ink the stamp fully. Check a record photograph for accurate placement.

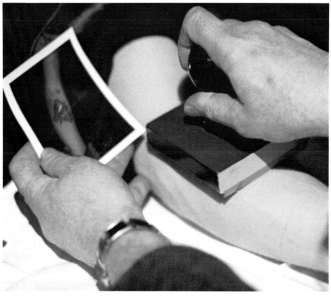

B. Roll the stamp firmly from one side to the other onto the tattooed area.

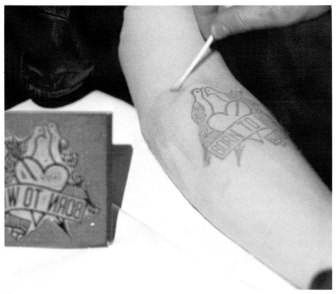

C. Clean off any excess ink with a cotton swab dipped in acetone.

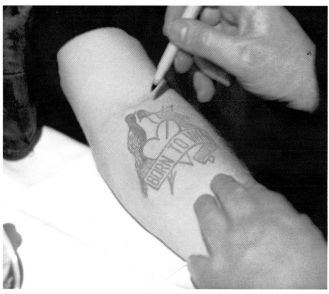

D. Sketch in the colors called for in the design.

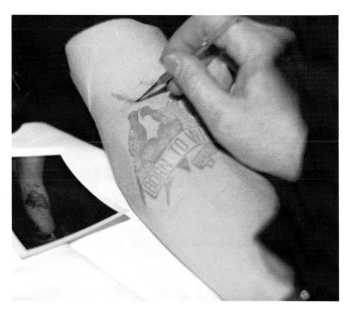

E. For this job, tracks were added to the arm.

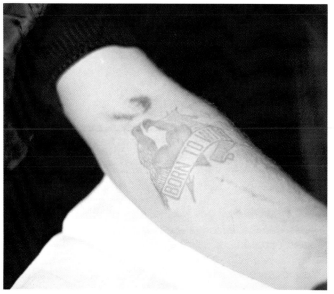

F. The arm is complete: tattoo, needle scars, and tracks.

13
BLACK PERFORMER

The black performer has for too many years been taken for granted in American theater. Stereotyped and caricatured unmercifully, some of the finest artists of our time have never had an opportunity to truly develop their talents, or to show the range of performance they were capable of. Ignorance of the proper use of makeup for the black artist has been one of the factors holding him back.

The most important contribution I can make to the black performer is to convince him that all of his makeup problems differ from those of the white performer in only two respects: (1) the black performer *may,* but will not always, require different shadow and base colors; and (2) the black performer may, on occasion—but not always—use his own skin color as a base color more successfully than is usually possible for the Caucasian. In every other respect—blending technique, use of optical illusions, and all other tools of makeup—the black performer uses exactly the same procedure as has been described throughout.

DETERMINING THE MAKEUP COLORS

Just as has been seen for the white performer, the black performer must determine the skin color desired for projection to the audience. Is it his or her own skin color, or is a darker, or a lighter color more effective?

It must be clear to you by now that skin tones may be realistically altered a few shades darker or lighter than the subject's own skin tone. A change of *more* than a few shades can be accomplished, but this runs the risk of looking unnatural, a risk that exists for Caucasian as well as for black performers.

As a general rule, it is advisable to darken the skin tones of most Caucasian performers (to stress the quality of tanned health). As a general rule, conversely, it is advisable to *lighten* black performers a few shades because of the

way in which black skin tones register on film. (See Fig. 383.) In black and white and in color film, dark skin tones tend to register with less definition than when the skin tone is a bit lighter. Even in scenes where black performers are filmed together, when extreme variations in skin tones are not a problem and the scene can be lit specifically to allow for a darker skin tone, the registration of skin colors will be improved if tones are lightened.

As in all aspects of film or TV makeup, the color variance must be performed with moderation. Excessive, or extreme changes are always proportionately more difficult; the danger of failure increases in proportion to the amount of change attempted.

Once the base color has been determined, the shadow tones must be effective when applied to this base color: darker base color calls for darker shadow tones, lighter base color calls for lighter shadows.

While the black performer has great latitude in choice of skin tone, difficulties can and do occur. The greatest problem for a black performer whose skin is very dark is in using makeup for a skin tone that is *considerably* lighter than his natural color. A very dark skin tone tends to "bleed" through the base, producing a chalky effect.

Yet there is a solution to this problem. It was my very good fortune to have done makeup for the renowned actor Canada Lee when he appeared in *The Duchess of Malfi* on Broadway in New York City. It was the first time that a black performer had an opportunity to play a Caucasian role. Lee's skin coloring was very dark, and it did bleed through the grease paints normally available. I explored and discovered a remarkable cosmetic called Lydia O'Leary's "Covermark," a makeup intended to cover birthmarks and severe skin discolorations. It is completely opaque. Using this cosmetic, I determined the base color, shadow mixture, highlight, and rouge.

I applied a nose, wig, mustache, and beard, details that were pertinent to the role. The makeup was so successful that Mr. Lee passed by his own brother backstage and went unrecognized. This material was successful on stage, but in my opinion it is too thick for film—it does not project as a normal skin tone on the screen. Because of the substantial reduction on a television screen, however, I do believe Covermark would be suitable for TV makeup.

Covering a dark skin tone with a light one was resolved in a similar manner for Godfrey Cambridge, a very fine black actor appearing in *Watermelon Man* in a role where a white man is turned into a black. For the portion of the film where he plays the white, Cambridge was made up with Caucasian skin coloring, with the addition of a full head wig. The effect was successful, and I have included a photograph from the film in the Gallery, Chapter Sixteen.

BLACK MALE PERFORMER: YOUTH, AGE, SPECIAL EFFECTS

To develop your skills in applying makeup accurately and successfully, you must follow the step-by-step development of the techniques as they have been outlined in this book. Techniques of painting and shading remain the same for all skin colors; the only variations are in the selection of the base and shading colors. For a listing of base colors applying to various skin tones see Chapter Two.

In the color demonstration in this chapter, study the techniques of making the performer more youthful and for aging him. For a youthful role, we will lighten his skin tone

383. In black and white the registration of skin tones is improved with a black performer if tones are lightened. Dark tones tend to register with less definition.

slightly, soften the beard tone, and attempt minor corrections. A modified grease is used for the base (in this case I have used pancake). For additional coloring, to give the face a healthy, youthful look, a slight tint of dry rouge—such as brown coral rouge tones—was added to the mouth. The eyes have been accented very slightly with pencil as well, and the ultimate result is very subtle.

I would certainly say that the change created here would be suitable for some roles, but by no means for all. There are many parts in which this fine performer would be more successful with no makeup at all. As I have said many times earlier, makeup is a tool to be used when it serves a purpose. If there is no advantage to changing a performer's appearance, do not attempt to do so. Be content with a good thing when you have it.

The first eight color frames (A to H) of this demonstration illustrate the use of makeup with a base. The balance of the color frames illustrate methods of creating illusions with no base at all. Here the performer, with only minor work, is transformed into a middle-aged character. First, dark brown shadow is applied around the inner socket of the eyeball. This is blended down to the eyelid. A highlight is applied to the lid itself and blended. More brown shadow is then applied around the socket of the eyeball and blended into the inner corner of the eye and shaped around the bone under the brows. Apply brown shadow around and under the eyeball and blend this up toward the eye. Next, shape the paint from the inner corner of the eye around the pouch and blend this shadow down toward the cheek. Brown shadow is applied just underneath the temple bone ridge and blended toward the hairline. A nose wrinkle is drawn with the flat sable brush and a shadow is applied at the hollow between the cheek and jawbone. A beard tone is applied, a red line drawn on the inside of the eyelid, and the effect of middle age is complete.

To this work I have added a bruise. First, apply blue-gray shadow intensely in the center and blend it out to grade into the skin color. Then add maroon to the center of the bruise area and grade the color unevenly. I have also added a scar, using the same methods described in Chapter Twelve.

Please remember that all of the color illustrations are the result of work deliberately made stronger than could ever be allowed on a motion picture screen. If they had been as subtle as the screen demands, the illusions would have barely been evident on these reduced images.

BLACK FEMALE PERFORMER

Color that looks natural to the eye will look equally good in both black and white and color. To demonstrate this, I have included both black and white and color pictures of the demonstration involving the black female performer.

For all female makeup, I like to shape the cheeks and eyes before applying base color. You may, if you wish, omit these early stages or shape on top of the base if you wish. Make sure the subject's face is clean of any soot or makeup before beginning the application. See to it that the hair is out of the way, and tissues or a towel are set around the neck and shoulders to protect the clothing. Proceed, using approximately the same techniques described in Chapter Four. Only the base color, shadow, and highlights are different.

384. Prepare subject for makeup—cleanse the face and add tissues or towel around the neck to protect clothing.

385. Under-eyeliner and shadow have been added. Base color has been applied.

386. Rouge is added to cheeks, forehead, nose, and chin, and eyeliner intensified by adding mascara line to top and bottom of eye.

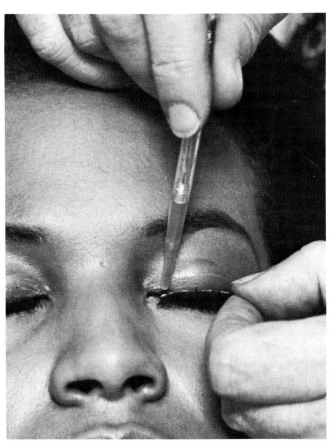

387. Add a thin film of latex adhesive to the edge of the eyelashes and gently position this along the eye.

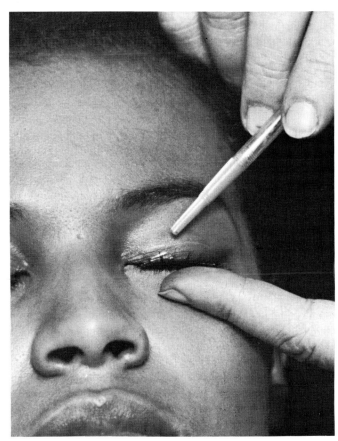

388. Holding the lash in place, gently prod the false lashes into place with the back of a clean brush.

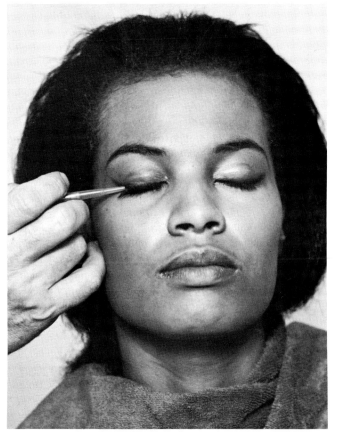

389. When the false eyelashes are set, go over the line with a touch of mascara.

390. Makeup complete with false eyelashes.

391. Lipstick color has been changed from a natural tone to a lighter, more "madeup" color.

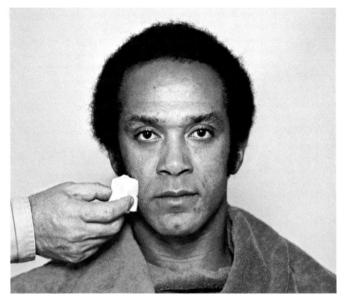

A. Jay Fletcher's beard tone is covered with a modified grease slightly lighter than the skin tone.

B. Apply a base color in modified grease or pancake.

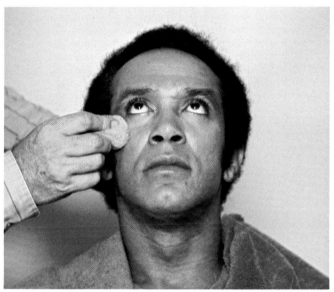

C. Add a highlight under the eyes to minimize eye bags or discoloration.

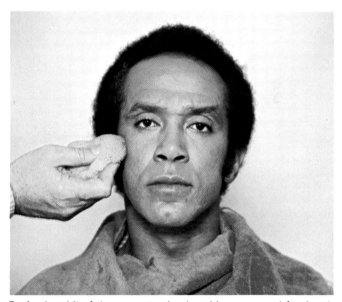

D. Apply a bit of dry rouge to cheeks, chin, nose, and forehead with silk sponge.

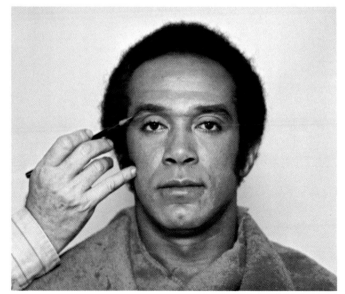

E. With a soft graphite lead pencil, shape the eyebrows.

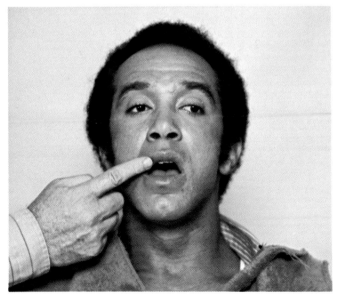

F. A slight tint of brown-coral lip tone is patted onto the lips to define the mouth.

159

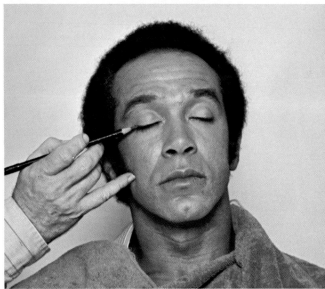

G. Draw a faint pencil line along the lashes with black eyebrow pencil to accent the eyes.

H. A youthful, glowing skin quality is produced with moderate application of makeup. Compare to the first frame.

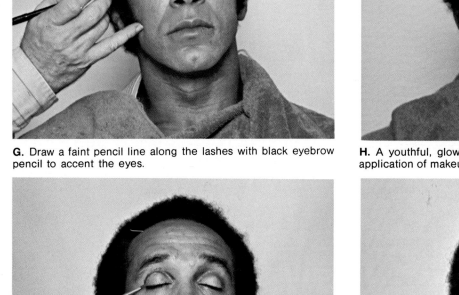

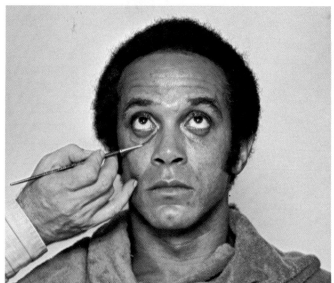

A. With no makeup base at all, the upper portion of the eye is painted to suggest moderate age.

B. The lower portion of the eye is now painted, and a slight pouch is suggested.

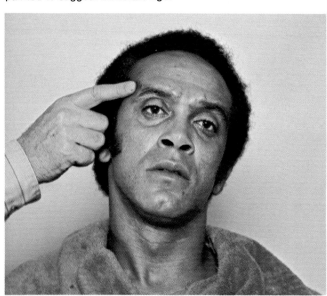

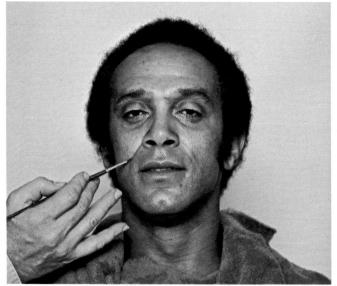

C. With the fingertip, apply brown shadow below the temple bone and blend toward the hairline.

D. Using the flat sable brush, paint the nose wrinkle and blend this color onto the cheeks.

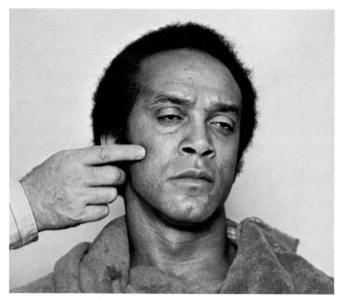

E. With the fingertip, apply shadow at the hollow between the cheek and jawbone and blend the color.

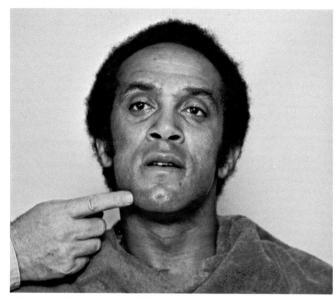

F. With the fingertip, apply blue-gray shadow to the entire beard area to create the effect of three days' beard growth.

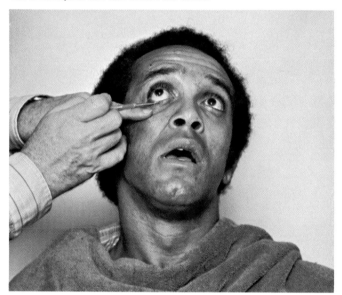

G. Using a fine brush, add a touch of pink and red to the inside of the eyelid to create bloodshot eyes.

H. Middle age has been created with minimum work and no make-up base.

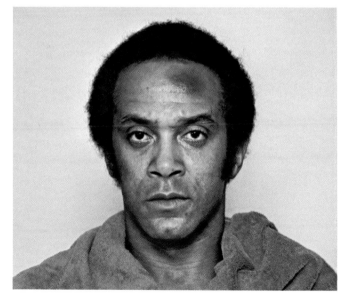

I. The bruise has been added with blue-gray shadow and maroon.

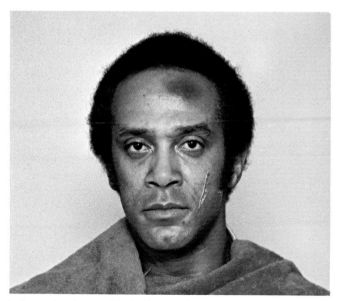

J. A scar has been added with scar plastic. The effect is complete.

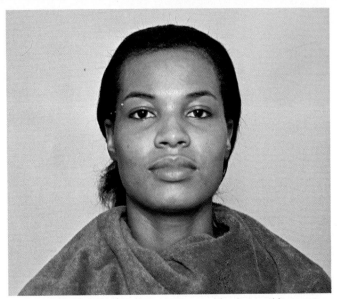

A. The subject, Julie Woodson, is thoroughly cleansed in preparation for makeup.

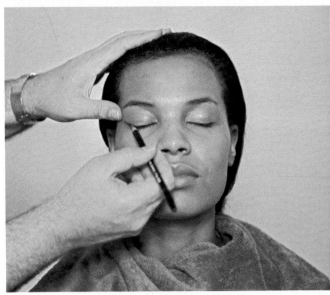

B. Pencil in the line along the eyelash from the inside to the outside corner and a bit toward the brow.

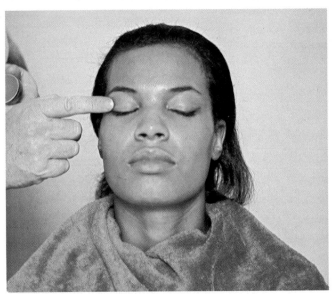

C. Apply shadow along this new lash line and blend up toward the brow and toward the temple.

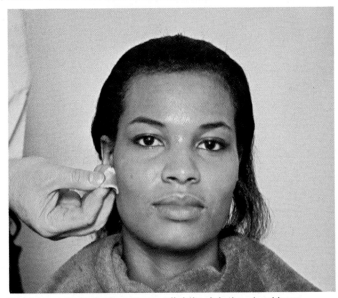

D. Using a dark shadow rouge, slightly sink the cheekbone.

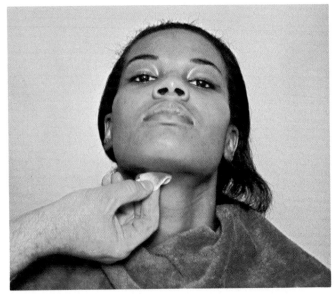

E. Shade under the jaw with the same dark shadow rouge.

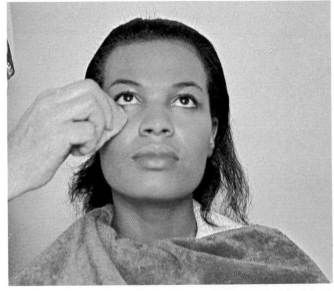

F. With a damp silk sponge, apply pancake base. Add highlight with corner of sponge to underside of the eye.

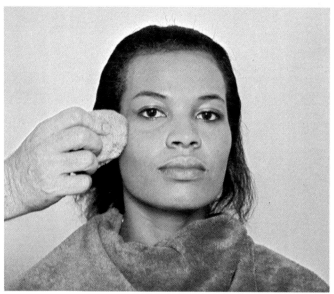

G. Apply a light blush of rouge to the cheeks with a damp sponge.

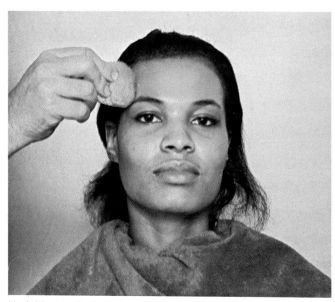

H. Add a touch of rouge to the forehead, nose, and chin.

I. Now the base color and shading have been established.

J. Touch up and intensify the eyeline, following the already-shaped line with a fine brush and mascara.

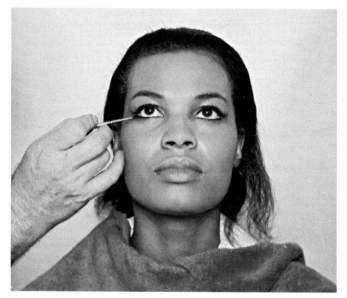

K. Carefully sketch in the shape of the lower portion of the eye with a faint application of mascara. Soften and blend with finger.

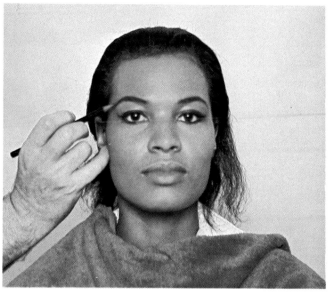

L. Sketch in the eyebrow, using a soft graphite pencil.

163

M. A touch of coral lipstick added to the natural shape of the lips completed this natural makeup.

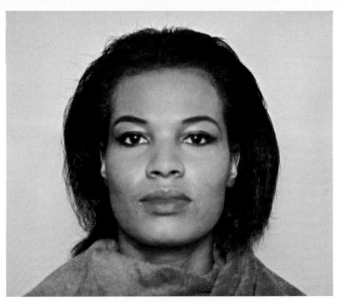

N. The hair is combed out a bit to create a soft frame for the face.

O. Brush a thin coat of latex adhesive along the adge of the lashes and carefully fit false eyelashes into place.

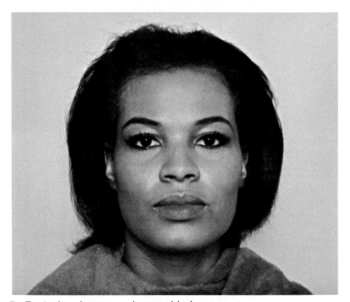

P. Eyelashes have now been added.

Q. A lighter lipstick produces a slightly more theatrical makeup effect.

SELECTING APPROPRIATE MAKEUP COLORS

As a general rule, always remember the following: (1) a base color that comes closest to the performer's natural skin tone is best; (2) you may go a few shades lighter or a few shades darker with impunity; (3) going much lighter or much darker than the natural skin tones becomes dangerous; (4) using the base colors listed in Chapter Two, and if necessary mixing them, will provide you with just about any desired skin color on earth; (5) a base color is only part of a total makeup.

For shading the eyes beneath the base, I prefer a sky-blue grease liner. This allows me to indicate the shading, which—when covered with the base color—emerges very softly from beneath the base.

For shading with rouge, sinking cheekbones, or minimizing the flesh under the chin, I like Dark Technicolor dry rouge. I have used this effectively on all types of skin colors.

For highlighting rouge, cheeks, forehead, chin, and nose, to create a fresh flow of health, I prefer Ben Nye's Coral, and I have used this very successfully on many different types of skin tones.

For giving the mouth a slight tint of color, I prefer a touch of brown-coral moist rouge for men. This color will frequently work for women as well, but if it seems too dark, any soft coral lipstick color, touched lightly to the lips with a fingertip, should produce a live and natural color.

Lipsticks, however, are another matter. Personal tastes and fashions change so rapidly that any color satisfying the performer and the dictates of fashion is acceptable. Skill and cleanliness of application are always called for.

As you can see, a comparatively small quantity of cosmetic colors are needed to successfully cover most of the skin color problems you will ever encounter. Naturally, there are always rare instances which may require more experimentation than usual. Intelligence, practice, and skill will solve these problems if and when they arise.

14 MAKEUP FOR TELEVISION

Makeup for television, both black and white and color, is seemingly so similar to makeup for film that you may wonder why I have devoted an entire chapter to it. Basically, because there are differences between film and television, not so much in technique as in approach. Three things make television different for the makeup artist: (1) Where the motion picture projection *magnifies* the image, the television image is *reduced.* In film every minute imperfection is exaggerated with magnification. Except in the case of extreme close-ups, the TV image is below lifesize and is not as critical in what it registers. (2) Due to atmospheric interference and the distance sets are viewed from the transmitter, the TV image is somewhat distorted, and needle-sharp reception is extremely rare. Only cable TV provides really sharp reception. (3) Most television studios are designed to use primarily overhead flat lighting which often creates shadows or produces a flat dimension to the face, which is very difficult to remedy.

PROBLEMS YOU WILL ENCOUNTER

In view of these realities, it should be obvious that creative makeup for television should allow for heavier statements in its use of illusions. This may seem obvious, but it is not the case unfortunately. When the TV director views the image, he is seeing the results from a control room which has a direct line from the camera to his viewing monitor, and the director receives an image without distortion or interference. So his observations are directed at an image that is rarely seen by the TV viewer.

The same is true of commercials filmed for television. The account executives from the agency in a projection room always view the commercial where the image is magnified many times more than it will ever be seen by the TV viewer. The critical judgments made are usually di-

rected at images that are very different from those that sell the product, or relate to the actor's image as it will actually be projected in the home on a television screen. I have always felt that all TV images should be evaluated in terms of their final form of presentation. Viewed under these conditions, it would be possible to determine if the makeup succeeds in its function or if more work needs to be done to create the effects desired.

LIGHTING PROBLEMS

TV studios are designed for speed and efficiency. Their designers were more concerned with the mechanics of moving a TV camera than with the amount and type of lighting that would be best for the performer. Overhead lighting is the dominant light source, with unnecessary shadows plaguing the performer's face. Flat overhead lighting may serve its purpose as a time-saver, and obviously floor lights and their cables do get in the way of a TV camera and its own cables. I don't presume to know the solution to these problems, but I don't understand why they cannot attach a light to the camera itself, a light that could so easily minimize the shadows cast into the eyes. Particularly on the close-up camera such a light could be of great value. But studios continue to be built with overhead lighting creating a constant problem to the makeup artist.

APPROACH TO TELEVISION MAKEUP

For television the real challenge is in making up the performer in a way that appears natural for the close-up shots and yet will project effectively in the scenes where the actor's face is reduced on the screen to only a few inches. The success of any makeup is how well it projects the appearance of the performer to the audience. All of the principles and techniques of film makeup are applicable to TV except that you may work with a good deal more emphasis in television than in film to achieve the best results.

A SPECIFIC ASSIGNMENT

Sometime ago I worked on a television commercial that I think illustrates and confirms my contentions. The campaign was created by Oglivy and Mather Advertising Agency for Shell Oil Company, directed by Mike Cuesta, and produced by Stan Lang Production Services of New York City. For this campaign five famous fictional characters from books were to talk to the audience: Dr. Watson (from *Sherlock Holmes*), the Cowardly Lion (from *The Wizard of Oz*), Long John Silver (from *Treasure Island*), Robinson Crusoe, and the Mad Hatter (from *Alice in Wonderland*).

I first met with the director Mike Cuesta, who told me in detail how he wanted the characters to appear. Since most of the fictional characters had appeared on screen or in plays, there was already a preconceived idea of how these characters should look, a danger we wanted to avoid. Mike Cuesta wanted a look that would capture the character in the books, yet would not copy in any way the concepts that had already been done on the screen or stage. For example, he wanted a cowardly lion from the *Wizard of Oz* that would not look like Bert Lahr when he played the role in the film. He did not want Dr. Watson to look like Nigel Bruce, or Long John Silver to look like Robert Newton, or Robinson Crusoe to look like Dan Herlihy.

These problems took considerable thought. I had to draw on my long experience with faces and historic periods before I could arrive at concepts that would describe the characters as the authors had originally written them and yet avoid the dangers Mike Cuesta had pointed out. There was less than a week from the time I had been consulted on the job to the two days of actual shooting.

As soon as the actors were cast for the parts, I took them to Ira Senz Wigs (very probably the best wigmaker in the world) where I told Robert Kushner what was required. He went through the stock and we selected the most suitable hairpieces. In the few days remaining, Mr. Kushner revamped the pieces, making the necessary changes in fit and styling. During these same few days, since time and finances did not permit custom-made pieces, I made a quantity of rubber noses from some molds I had accumulated from films I had worked on some time ago. On the first morning of shooting, I arrived early, set up my makeup materials, opened the wig boxes, and set up the hairpieces.

Dr. Watson was first. I seated the actor, put tissues around his collar to protect the clothing, and cleansed his face. I positioned the toupee. (Photographs from this demonstration were used in Chapter Ten, Figs. 246 to 252.) I added the mustache, and then the performer put on his costume. Dr. Watson was ready to go.

The actor playing Long John Silver had been asked not to shave for a few days prior to the shooting. Only a swarthy base color and a darkened beard tone were required. I also added some shading around the eyes and darkened the eyebrows. (See Figs. 394 and 395.)

Robinson Crusoe required a dark tanned color. I applied this dark base over the entire face (Figs. 396 and 397). The hair lace beard was then glued on (Fig. 398). For an adhesive I used a matte spirit gum to diminish the shine generally produced by regular spirit gum. Yet the matte has greater adhesion, and I felt this was necessary for this shooting. The mustache and costume completed the characterization of Crusoe. (See Fig. 399.) This makeup work had to be sustained during the entire day's shooting; I touched it up after lunch and whenever repairing was needed.

The next day began with the Cowardly Lion from the *Wizard of Oz*. I fitted on one of the rubber noses I had prepared, sealed the edges with liquid latex, and applied base color when this had dried. (See Figs. 400 and 401.) To cover the nose I used a base mixed with a bit of castor oil. The specially-prepared head piece was attached and the eyebrows glued on (Fig. 402). Then I added the mustache and some wrinkles around the eyes and face. We achieved a unique Cowardly Lion. (See Fig. 403.)

The last character of the series was the Mad Hatter from *Alice in Wonderland*. I positioned the rubber nose, applied glue, and then latex to the edges (Fig. 404). I shaded the nose, after the base was applied (Fig. 405). (Again, I mixed castor oil with the base to cover the nose.) I painted in eye pouches, and accented the nose wrinkle and the chin wrinkle (Fig. 406). I shaped the temples and glued on the wig lightly. Since the character was to wear a hat throughout the scene, I did not feel it was necessary to glue on the wig firmly. The hat was added and then the costume to complete the Mad Hatter. (See Fig. 409.)

This series was extremely interesting. It was quite a departure from the usual correctional work that is asked for in television work, and demanded imagination and professional skills.

The degree of broadness you have seen illustrated in these characters would have been much too strong for use in motion pictures, with the possible exception of the work done on Dr. Watson. The base colors and effects created on the other characters would have to be far more subtle for motion pictures. For television the work was successful.

392. The performer, Leo Leyden, is ready to be made up for Dr. Watson.

393. Dr. Watson with hairpieces and costume. (For step-by-step demonstration see Figs. 246 to 252 in Chapter Ten.)

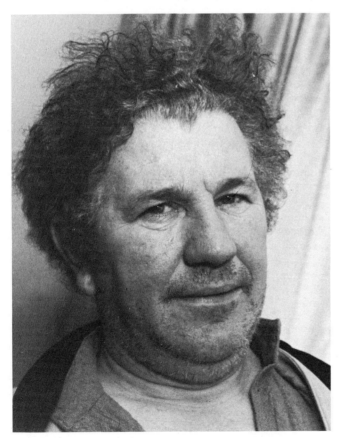

394. Having pregrown a beard stubble, Tom Clancy required very little makeup for characterization as Long John Silver.

395. A swarthy base color and beard tone were added. Some shading was accomplished around the eyes, and the brows were darkened.

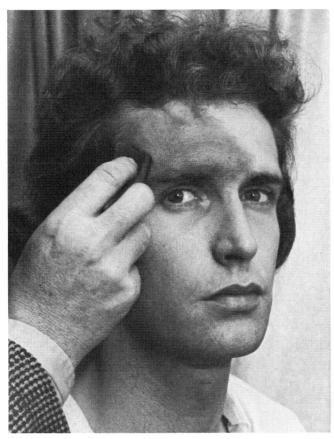

396. For Robinson Crusoe, a deep base was applied to Doug Jeffers to simulate a tanned complexion.

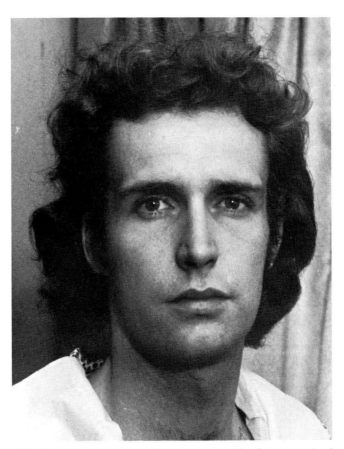

397. The dark base was applied evenly over the face, ears, back of ears, and exposed part of the neck.

398. The beard was fitted, then glued into place with matte spirit gum.

399. Robinson Crusoe, complete with facial hairpiece and costume.

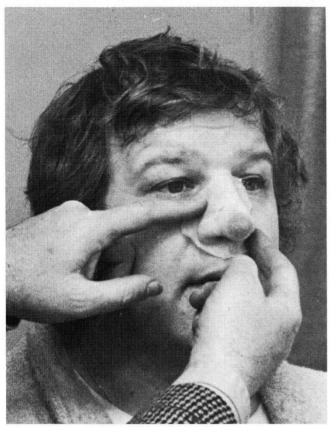

400. To begin the Cowardly Lion, the rubber nose is fitted onto Bill McIntyre. It is then trimmed of excess rubber and glued on.

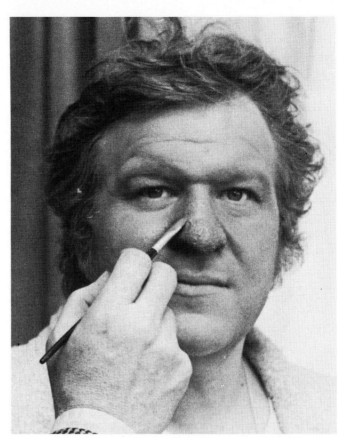

401. After the nose is glued on, the edges are sealed with liquid latex. Then a base containing castor oil is applied over the rubber nose. Regular modified grease base covers the rest of the face.

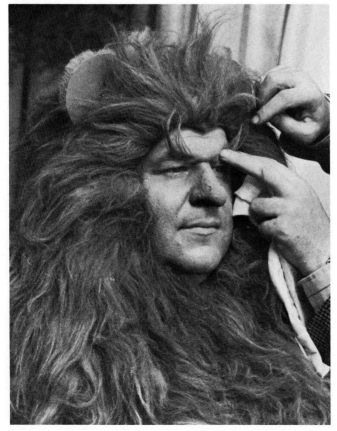

402. The costume headpiece slides over the head. Once this is in position, the eyebrows are glued on.

403. The mustache is glued into place. Painted eye and nose wrinkles complete the makeup of the Cowardly Lion.

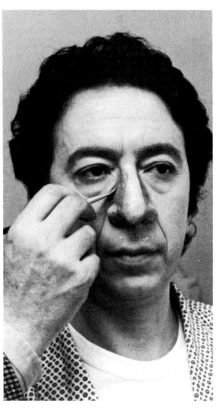

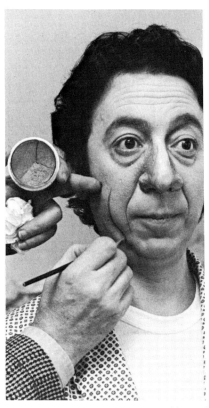

404. To begin the Mad Hatter (played by Eugene Troobnick), the rubber nose is positioned, trimmed, and glued. Liquid latex is painted around the edges to join and seal the edges onto the face.

405. Base color is applied. Then the nose is shaded.

406. Eye bags are painted, and chin and cheek wrinkles are accented.

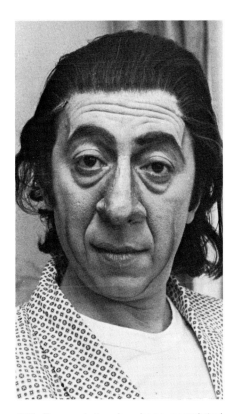

407. Face painting has been completed, and the wig is placed and glued on lightly.

408. The hat is fitted and wig hair shaped for character.

409. With costuming the Mad Hatter is complete.

ANOTHER TELEVISION ASSIGNMENT

It wasn't long before another TV commercial came up that presented an interesting challenge. The commercial was designed for Basset Furniture Co., conceived by VanSant Dugdale Advertising Agency of Baltimore, directed by Ray Baker, and produced by Stan Lang Production Services. The concept was to carry a couple through their married years, in four stages: as newlyweds, as parents of young children, as parents of older children, and as grandparents.

I met with the director Ray Baker and with Doug Tillet, a V.P. from the agency. The presented their concepts and we attended the casting sessions to select the performers. The concept demanded that we select performers whose faces could be aged with a minimum of makeup, a gradual change from the twenties to the sixties that could be accomplished with the greatest amount of effect in a minimum amount of time. The four changes required were to be accomplished in two days, with each change also requiring a physical move of equipment and locale for each shooting.

Once the performers were selected, I brought them to Ira Senz wigmakers to fit them for wigs and hairpieces. I described what was required to the manager—Robert Kushner—and we went through their stock to select appropriate pieces.

The location of the sets meant that the actual shooting could not follow the progression of aging in sequence. We were forced to go from the mature stage to the oldest to the youngest and to middle age in that sequence. For purposes of demonstration, however, I have chosen to show the photographs in the sequence ultimately seen on the screen.

For the youthful female, I applied a soft corrective makeup, seeking a natural look similar to the one demonstrated in Chapter Four. A young, buoyant hair style was created for this stage (Fig. 414). The youthful aspects of the make-

up were minimized and only the faintest suggestion of shadows were added around the eyes. A hair-bang piece suggested a more mature look (Fig. 416). For the third stage of aging, I used shading with discretion and a stylish, matronly wig (Fig. 418). Finally, a gray wig was substituted and painted aging was carried as far as was considered reasonable (Fig. 420).

The same progressive stages were followed with the male performer. Here his partial baldness gave me latitude. His sideburns were cut short and a false pair was made. For his youthful stage he wore these sideburns and a toupee (Fig. 413). For the second stage sideburns and full toupee were removed and replaced by a thinning toupee to show the passage of some years (Fig. 415). For middle age, an even sparser hairpiece was added, plus a mustache. I also accented the bone structure with paint (Fig. 417). For the final stage, grayed side pieces were added along with a sparse gray top piece and a clipped gray mustache. I painted as much aging as was possible (Fig. 419).

The point worth emphasizing here is that much of the alteration was accomplished by changes in hair, its quantity, styling, and color. It should be very apparent by now that facial makeup is never an entity in and of itself, but is part of a total concept, including hair and wardrobe as well. The concept determines the goal and this is executed in makeup, hairstyling, and costume. It is up to the actor to make the concept work.

When you consider makeup work for television, bear in mind the qualitative difference between television and motion pictures. However, if at any time you question whether or not too much makeup is being used, play safe and soften your work. You are always better off using too *little* makeup than using too *much*. Only experience and practice will help you develop the judgment to critically appraise and evaluate the needs of the job, and the skill to perform this work artistically.

410. Man and wife as newlyweds.

A. Dr. Watson: toupee and mustache applied.

B. Costume completes Dr. Watson.

A. The performer ready for makeup for Long John Silver.

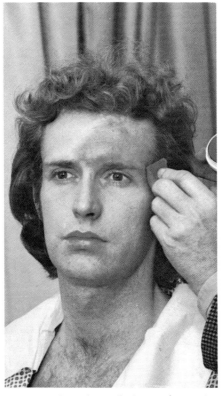

B. Only slight makeup was needed to complete the effect, since the performer had already grown stubble.

A. A deep base is applied to performer to achieve dark tan of Robinson Crusoe.

B. Elaborate facial hairpieces are applied for final effect of Crusoe.

173

A. Rubber grease base is applied over nose piece made for Cowardly Lion.

B. Facial hairpieces are attached to performer.

C. The Cowardly Lion is complete.

A. A rubber nose is applied to performer for the Mad Hatter.

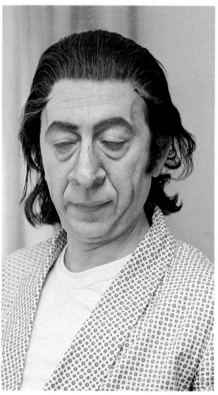

B. The face has been heavily painted for character effect. Wig is added.

C. Costuming completes the Mad Hatter.

A. A healthy young male skin color, plus a full toupee produces the youngest effect.

B. A healthy young female skin tone, with slight corrective make-up is applied. A youthful hair style also heightens the look.

C. The skin color has been lightened and a transparent balding toupee applied, plus eyeglasses for the earliest stage of aging.

D. A faint suggestion of painted age, plus a change in hair style, begin the aging process.

E. A very thin, partial hairpiece and mustache, with slight age painting completes the next stage.

F. To create middle age, I added an appropriate wig and painted in the signs of age very softly.

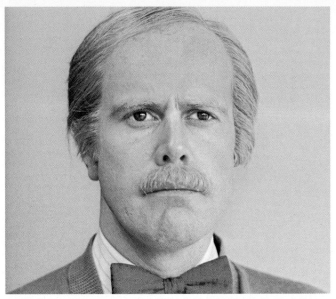

G. Gray-temple pieces, thin top hairpiece, and mustache placed over a pale skin tone age the character even further.

H. For the next stage, a gray three-quarter wig was placed on the performer, her hairline colored to match the wig.

I. Our performers as they appeared as newlyweds.

J. The final effect: the performers as grandparents.

411. The performer, Ken Kimmins, is seen free of any makeup.

412. The performer, Phoebe Dorin, is shown with no makeup. Her face has been thoroughly cleansed.

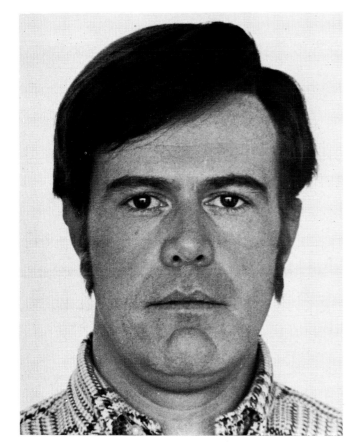

413. A full toupee has been added in addition to a corrective makeup designed to enhance the youthful look.

414. Natural corrective makeup has been added, hair styled to create a youthful appearance.

415. A more transparent toupee has been substituted and youthful makeup softened. Glasses suggest weakening vision.

416. A hairpiece has been added to create bangs and the makeup has been modified with the faintest suggestion of aging.

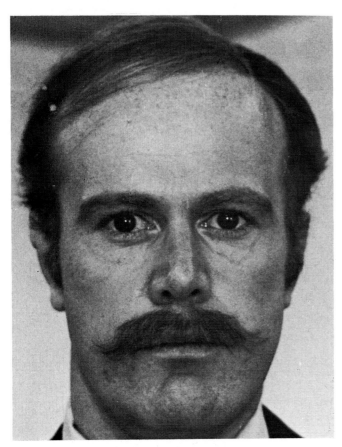

417. An even thinner hairpiece is substituted and a mustache added. The facial structure has been accented to suggest maturity.

418. A stylish wig has been substituted and a touch more age suggested by painting.

419. Gray side pieces and thin hairpiece, clipped mustache, and additional age painting strengthen the feeling of age.

420. Finally, a gray wig has been substituted and a heavier application of age completes the effect.

421. Man and wife as grandparents.

15
COURSE OF STUDY

To learn the necessary skills involved in makeup, the student must follow a progression of work. Recommending a practical progression is not at all simple. It is necessary to develop skills of analysis, knowledge of facial structure, handling of paints and tools, and a course of study must also account for the varying needs of the student.

Do not expect miracles! Progress will be, and should be, slow. Each work session should last between one and two hours. Less time than that will not allow for much accomplishment and cannot be productively sustained for more than two hours.

Before attempting any work in the course of study, read the book through at least twice. Familiarize yourself with the materials and the basic principles involved. For the following work sessions, always set out your materials and tools and prepare your subject as you would for professional makeup. Space your practice sessions. Time is needed to absorb the material and the work, so don't attempt to progress day after day. Working twice a week at most is best.

1. Analyze the face shape of the subject. Work out on paper the areas to be altered. Apply black pencil eyeliner, check, and correct. Apply undercoat of eye shadow, check, and correct. Apply base color, using appropriate modified grease. Check, correct, and remove carefully. Repeat the above, then cleanse.

2. If using a new model, analyze the face and chart corrections necessary. Apply black pencil eyeliner, check, and correct. Apply undercoat eye shadow, check, and correct. Apply shadowing rouge to cheek hollow and then to underpart of jaw; check and correct. Apply base color, using modified grease; check and correct. Remove properly and repeat same procedure.

3. Repeat all of the above. Powder the modified grease base. Apply thin application of appropriate pancake base over all. Apply highlight rouge. Cleanse carefully and repeat.

4. Repeat all of the above. Check every phase of work critically. Apply corrective shading where needed. Apply corrective highlights where needed. Cleanse and repeat.

5. Repeat all of the above. Carefully reshape top eyeline, then shadow the top of the eye. Carefully outline bottom of eye. Shape in new eyebrows. Cleanse and repeat.

6. Repeat all of the above. Carefully apply mascara to the eyelashes. Paint on a natural mouth. Cleanse and repeat.

7. Repeat all of the above. Paint on a shaped mouth. Cleanse and repeat.

8. Repeat all the above procedures with a subject who has a different face shape and/or skin tone from the model you have been using.

9. Repeat the above with a subject who has a different face shape and/or skin tone.

10. Repeat the above with a subject who has a different face shape and/or skin tone.

11. Repeat the above with a black female subject.

12. Repeat the above with an Oriental female subject.

13. Now concentrate on the male subject. Apply modified grease to minimize beard tone. Powder. Complete makeup with application of pancake base, with the addition of rouge highlighting, eyebrow, and mouth accents. Cleanse and repeat.

14. Repeat above with a black male subject.

15. Apply a toupee to male model. Complete makeup. Cleanse and repeat.

16. Apply makeup to a male subject. Add toupee and lace sideburns and mustache. Remove hairpieces. Cleanse face and pieces and repeat.

17. Male or female subject: Apply modified grease base. Sink temples and cheeks for aging. Check and correct. Apply sinking and aging to top and bottom of both eyes. Check and correct. Remove makeup and repeat.

18. Repeat all of the above. Apply painted nose wrinkle. Apply shading for forehead structure. Cleanse entire make-up and repeat.

19. Repeat all of the above. Complete painted aging techniques. Gray the hair. Add any facial hairpieces. Cleanse and, if there is time, repeat.

20. Repeat all of the above, using a female subject if you have first used a male, or vice versa. Cleanse.

21. Repeat all of the above, using a black subject. Cleanse.

22. Repeat all of the above. Apply a bruise. Check and correct. Apply a burn. Check and correct. Apply a scar. Check and correct. Cleanse.

23. Male subject: Lay on a crepe hair beard. (You may practice with straightened crepe wool.) If you complete this in time, trim and shape. Cleanse.

24. Repeat laying on a beard and mustache. Cleanse.

25. Repeat laying on a beard and mustache. Cleanse.

26. Repeat laying on a beard and mustache. Trim to completion. Cleanse.

27. Apply complete male age makeup. Complete with beard and mustache, layered on. Cleanse.

28. Apply bald cap. Apply base color and age. Cleanse.

29. Apply bald cap. Apply aging makeup. Lay on crepe beard and mustache. Cleanse.

30. Apply latex nose. Apply base color. Apply aging. Cleanse.

31. Apply cotton and spirit gum. Aging technique. Cleanse.

32. Repeat above and cleanse.

33. Apply bald cap, latex face pieces, and cotton and spirit gum aging technique. Cleanse.

34. Select historic character and apply total makeup to suit. Cleanse.

35. Repeat the above.

36. Repeat the above.

37. Apply youthful makeup. Cleanse. Apply aged makeup. Cleanse. Apply more advanced age makeup. Cleanse.

38. Repeat the above with a subject of the opposite sex.

39. Repeat the above with black subject.

40. Now begin practicing in earnest.

16
GALLERY
OF GREAT MAKEUP
ACHIEVEMENTS

I have attempted to show in detail the methods of achieving basic makeup effects for film. In concluding this book, I would be remiss if I did not try to show you how these effects have been used by the great artists to achieve their characterizations, and to serve this purpose I have selected still photographs to illustrate the great concepts of makeup used in motion pictures. Obviously, it would have been impossible to include every example of fine makeup work seen throughout the years. Such a task would have demanded a book in itself! But I have attempted to locate what I consider to be among the finest examples of imagination and creativity used in the craft of makeup.

Performers seem to fall into two categories: those whose appearance remains constant from one film to the next, and those whose characterization radically differs in each film. The first category contains performers who deviated very little from their image. Many fine actors and actresses, such as Clark Gable, Humphrey Bogart, and Barbara Stanwyck, have performed successfully in this category and I have included some pages to these. Here makeup has been used simply to enhance particular features already present. I have continually repeated that it is not always necessary to use a great deal of makeup to create the small alterations needed to communicate characterization.

Performers seem to fall into two categories: those whose ap-

pearance remains constant from one film to the next, and those whose characterization radically differs in each film. The first category contains performers who deviated very little from their image. Many fine actors and actresses, such as Clark Gable, Humphrey Bogart, and Barbara Stanwyck, have performed successfully in this category and I have devoted some pages to these. Here makeup has been used simply to enhance particular features already present. I have continually repeated that it is not always necessary to use a great deal of makeup to create the small alterations needed to communicate characterization.

The second category of performer includes actors and actresses whose faces and features constitute a base upon which characterization is structured. It is in this group that the great makeup feats have been accomplished. (I find it significant that this second group consistently includes performers who have had extensive theatrical training and experience.) Sir Laurence Olivier and Sir Alec Guinness were capable of superb characterization using minimal makeup, or they could use large makeup effects brilliantly. Lon Chaney was the master of grotesque effects. Unique star personalities like Dustin Hoffman, Ben Kingsley, and Cicely Tyson—while justifiably famous for their performances in leading roles—also reveal their theatrical roots by the range and quality of the character roles they perform with brilliance.

Laurence Olivier in *Wuthering Heights*. (retouched) Olivier's capacity for physical change originated from his strong theatrical background. For youthful roles in film, where little change could be expected in the face, he used hair changes to good effect. United Artists

Laurence Olivier in *That Hamilton Woman*. (retouched) For this role a formal, tie-back wig was appropriate to create the desired alteration. United Artists

Laurence Olivier in *Pride and Prejudice*. (retouched) Once again the hair comb of the period significantly changes the appearance of this performer. Metro-Goldwyn-Mayer

Laurence Olivier in *Fire Over England*. (retouched) Although the hair is changed very slightly in this role, the youthful beard and mustache accomplish a sufficient alteration. United Artists

Laurence Olivier in *Henry V*. (retouched) Youthful Shakesperian roles may not allow for great changes in makeup. Once more hair is used as a means of creating this alteration. United Artists

Laurence Olivier in *Hamlet*. (retouched) A change in hair color can be enormously effective in creating greater impact than one would imagine possible. Universal

Laurence Olivier in *Richard III*. (retouched) No great change in age has been accomplished here, but notice the effect created by the elongated nose. Also note the difference created with abundant eyebrows. Lopert

Laurence Olivier in *Othello*. (retouched) This production of *Othello* was actually a filmed stage performance. Therefore, the makeup was modified for the film, yet was not originally designed for film. Note, for example, the outlining of the mouth: useful on stage, but rather obvious for film. Warner Bros. Seven Arts

Laurence Olivier in *The Prince and the Showgirl.* (retouched) Natural hair is used for good effect here: a flat, smoothly combed style with gray temples was sufficient. Warner Bros. Seven Arts

Laurence Olivier in *Oh! What a Lovely War.* (retouched) The hair styling here also creates the maximum effect: center part, grayed hair, and mustache. Paramount

Laurence Olivier in *The Devil's Disciple.* (retouched) A white, pull-back wig was part of the officer's uniform. Makeup application was minimal. United Artists

Laurence Olivier in *Khartoum.* (retouched) This is more than a simple change in skin tone. Notice the expression created by the new shape of the eyebrows and by the altered mouth. United Artists

185

Alec Guinness in *Cromwell*. (retouched) Paintings of King Charles were used as reference to create this characterization. An effective wig was used, but the mustache and beard created the greatest alteration. Courtesy Columbia Pictures

Alec Guinness in *Fall of the Roman Empire*. (retouched) Statuary was the only guide used for Marcus Aurelius. The design of the wig and beard is flawless. Paramount

Alec Guinness in *The Mudlark*. (retouched) Photographs of Disraeli were used for reference here. Notice the effect created with use of the bald pate and beard styling. Courtesy 20th Century Fox. © 1951 20th Century Fox Corporation. All rights reserved.

Alec Guinness in *A Majority of One*. (retouched) To create this effect Oriental rubber eyelids and a specially designed wig were used. Furthermore, a skin color change was accomplished with an appropriate base. Warner Bros. Seven Arts

Alec Guinness in *The Swan*. (retouched) Guinness in another brilliant characterization. Here an artful toupee and small mustache accomplish the necessary alterations. Metro-Goldwyn-Mayer

Alec Guinness in *The Horse's Mouth*. (retouched) The amusing character was created with graying hair and a beard stubble. United Artists

Alec Guiness in *Oliver Twist*. (retouched) To create the character of Fagin was no small feat. A nose piece was added, eye pouches, age stipple, wig, beard, and mustache. The effect is stupendous. United Artists

Alec Guinness in *Lawrence of Arabia*. (retouched) Aside from the necessary change in skin color, the design and shape of the beard and mustache are vital. Courtesy Columbia Pictures

Lon Chaney in *Mr. Wu.* (retouched) A bald cap, blocked-out and lifted eyebrows, painted wrinkles, and modified hairpieces created this characterization. For its time this was brilliant work. Metro-Goldwyn-Mayer

Lon Chaney in *Mr. Wu.* (retouched) The painted aging is carried further very effectively. Notice how skillfully he uses the cowl to create the illusion of emaciation. Metro-Goldwyn-Mayer

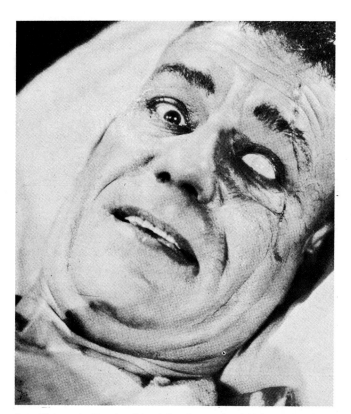

Lon Chaney in *Road to Mandalay.* (retouched) This extraordinary effect was achieved by using the thin white membrane from the inside of chicken eggs. This membrane was placed over the eyes so that it actually touched the eyeball. Metro-Goldwyn-Mayer

Lon Chaney in *The Unholy Three.* (retouched) Playing the part of an elderly woman was one of Chaney's most effective performances. Yet this required comparatively little work; a wig and skillful painting. Metro-Goldwyn-Mayer

Lon Chaney in *Tell It to the Marines*. (retouched) This characterization came as close to Chaney's normal appearance as any photo easily available would suggest. Use this as a gauge to determine the extent of the remarkable effects he achieved. Metro-Goldwyn-Mayer

Lon Chaney in *The Hunchback of Notre Dame*. (retouched) Using stage techniques in his makeup, Chaney achieved wonders. Here he used a putty nose, putty cheeks, frightful wig, and glass eye. He achieved superb results with primitive tools. Universal

Lon Chaney in *Phantom of the Opera*. (retouched) Here Chaney distended his nose by lifting it with tape, carrying the tape onto his forehead and gluing it under the bald cap wig. Then he added a putty nose, cheeks, and effective painting. Capped teeth complete the effect. Universal

Lon Chaney in *London After Midnight*. (retouched) In this film Chaney actually pulled his bottom eyelids down and glued them in this position. False teeth and painting create the rest of this grotesque effect. Metro-Goldwyn-Mayer

John Barrymore in *Dr. Jekyll and Mr. Hyde.* (retouched) Mishaped wig, false nose, and capped teeth; Barrymore used them all very well. Paramount

John Barrymore in *Svengali.* (retouched) Barrymore revealed his fine stage training by his use of wig, nose, brows, and beard. Warner Bros.

John Barrymore in *Rasputin.* (retouched) Known for his elegant profile, Barrymore used it effectively in his film work. Metro-Goldwyn-Mayer

John Barrymore in *Twentieth Century.* (retouched) Although not much makeup was necessary in this film, Barrymore made good use of his hair for effect. Courtesy Columbia Pictures

Charles Laughton in *White Woman*. (retouched) Notice how much change can be accomplished by simply curling the hair. The mustache is also splendid. Paramount

Charles Laughton in *The Private Life of Henry VIII*. (retouched) Hair color change and a red beard transform this performer into a Holbein painting. United Artists

Charles Laughton in *Rembrandt*. (retouched) Using Rembrandt's self-portraits for reference, a dramatic change was accomplished with a suitable hair style and mustache. United Artists

Charles Laughton in *Salome*. (retouched) A simple change in hair comb and the addition of a small beard create the necessary alterations. Courtesy Columbia Pictures

N. Cherkasov in *Ivan the Terrible, Part I.* (retouched) The nose has been straightened and the mouth strongly shaped. Cherkasov used classical theatrical techniques.

N. Cherkasov in *Ivan the Terrible, Part II.* (retouched) The straight, young nose becomes hawk-shaped. Eyelid pieces and brows add to the menace of the old Ivan.

N. Cherkasov in *Don Quixote.* (retouched) Eyelid pieces sagging downward with eyebrows following the form create the characteristic "woeful look." The hawk nose and design of the beard are classic techniques used to create the lean image.

N. Cherkasov in *Boris Godounov.* (retouched) This is a perfectly classic reconstruction of the round stout face needed to create the character of Varlaam. Notice that the nose, cheeks, eyes, and design of the beard emphasize the horizontal.

N. Cherkasov in *Peter I.* (retouched) The forehead has been lifted with a bald cap and a dramatic wig used to create the character of the young Tsarevich Alexei.

N. Cherkasov in *Peter I.* (retouched) As the character aged in the film, the forehead retained its prominence and a change in wigs created the necessary effect for a character who had become the Tsar.

N. Cherkasov in *Inspector General.* (retouched) A transformation in the eyebrow structure and a broad nose produced a totally new dimension to this performer's face.

N. Cherkasov in *Moussorgsky.* (retouched) A large nose has been added and a superb beard used to effect this change.

Fredric March in *Dr. Jekyll and Mr. Hyde.* (retouched) Extraordinary distortion of the face was achieved with the use of a wig, nose piece, capped teeth, and enormous eye pouches. Metro-Goldwyn-Mayer

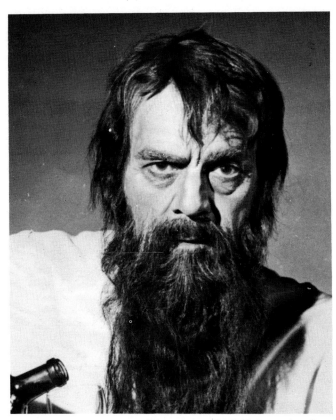

Fredric March in *Les Miserables.* (retouched) Eye pouches have been added again, but with paint this time. A beautiful beard and wig complete the effect. Courtesy 20th Century Fox. © 1935 20th Century Fox Film Corporation. All rights reserved.

Fredric March in *Inherit the Wind.* (retouched) An excellent bald cap has been applied, with the addition of a wig. Notice the perspiration applied to the brow, probably with the addition of glycerin to the water. United Artists

Fredric March in *A Christmas Carol.* (retouched) A bald pate has been applied, and hair from the wig combed forward. A huge nose was added and age painted with subtlety. Courtesy CBS Television

Paul Muni in *Juarez*. (retouched) Mexican Indian skin tone was applied in addition to a new nose, fine wig, and eyebrows that cover part of the eyelids. The result is superb. Warner Bros.

Paul Muni in *Pasteur*. (retouched) Muni always used makeup, even when it is not easily apparent. Notice the eye pieces used here. A wig and beard also accomplished a dramatic change. Warner Bros.

Paul Muni in *Emile Zola*. (retouched) The hairline recedes with the application of a full front wig. Eyebrows and carefully styled beard and mustache have been grayed. Warner Bros.

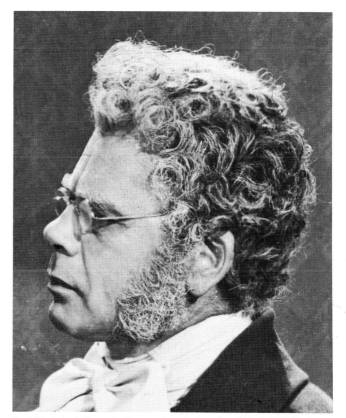

Paul Muni in *A Song to Remember*. (retouched) Very little makeup has been applied to the performer. Age is suggested with graying sideburns, hair, and glasses. Courtesy Columbia Pictures

Sam Jaffe in *I Can Get It for You Wholesale.* (retouched) There is very little evidence of makeup here. Compare this photograph to the other three on this page. Courtesy 20th Century Fox. © 1951 20th Century Fox Film Corporation. All rights reserved.

Sam Jaffe in *Gunga Din.* (retouched) To create the effect of an Indian character, a dark skin stain was applied to the performer. The turban meant that there were no alterations in hair quality or styling. R.K.O. Radio

Sam Jaffe in *Ben Hur.* (retouched) For the character of Simonides notice the age stipple applied to the skin. Notice also the fine wig and beard used to create the effect of age. Metro-Goldwyn-Mayer

Sam Jaffe in *Lost Horizon.* (retouched) This is one of the most outstanding aging effects created in its time. The application of wig and eyebrows emphasize the aging techniques used on the skin. Courtesy Columbia Pictures

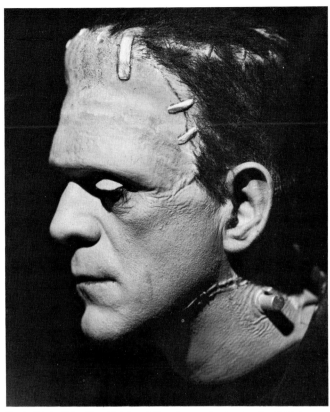

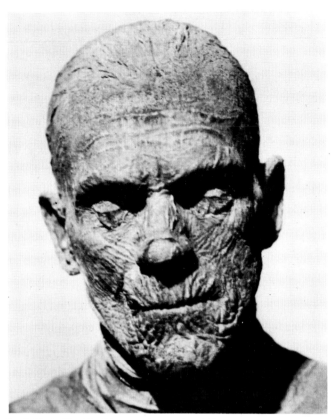

Boris Karloff in *The Bride of Frankenstein.* (retouched) This was the greatest of all monster concepts. With the additional pieces added to the eyelids, throat, and head you can understand why this makeup took hours to apply. Universal

Boris Karloff in *The Mummy.* (retouched) Using excessive applications of cotton and latex (see Chapter Eight), this grotesque effect was accomplished. Universal

Boris Karloff in *The Mask of Fu Manchu.* (retouched) More cartoon than real, this theatrical concept is nevertheless effective. The techniques are exaggerated. Universal

Boris Karloff in *The Tower of London.* (retouched) This menacing effect was created with excellent use of the bald cap, nose piece, and eyebrows. Universal

Marlon Brando in *Julius Caesar.* (retouched) Little makeup was needed for this characterization of Marc Antony. Only a simple combed-forward hairstyle, combined with the magnetism of the performer, was needed. Metro-Goldwyn-Mayer

Marlon Brando in *Teahouse of the August Moon.* (retouched) Oriental eye pieces were placed around the eyes and a slick black wig applied to the head. Appropriate base was added to simulate an Oriental skin tone. Metro-Goldwyn-Mayer

Marlon Brando in *Viva Zapata.* (retouched) A dark skin tone and appropriate mustache transformed this actor into a Mexican. Courtesy 20th Century Fox. © 1952 20th Century Fox Film Corporation. All rights reserved.

Marlon Brando in *Burn!* (retouched) Playing a British agent who foments a revolution on a tropical isle meant giving the character a healthy coloring. A wig provided the abundant hair. United Artists

Bette Davis in *The Little Foxes.* (retouched) The unique quality of the Davis personality projects itself in spite of the conventional Hollywood makeup. R.K.O. Radio

Bette Davis in *Juarez.* (retouched) The only alteration in the performer's appearance here is the application of the dark wig. Otherwise, the makeup is unchanged: painted lips for the period are inaccurate. Warner Bros.

Bette Davis in *The Private Life of Elizabeth and Essex.* (retouched) By using a beautiful bald pate and blocking out the natural eyebrows, an excellent effect is created. Warner Bros.

Bette Davis in *The Virgin Queen.* (retouched) Here the bald pate produces an even higher hairline and the eyebrows disappear altogether. The result is even better. Courtesy 20th Century Fox.

Their Individual Looks Became Their Trademark

Vivien Leigh

Jane Wyatt. Courtesy Columbia Pictures

Barbara Stanwyck. Courtesy Columbia Pictures

Bette Davis

Ingrid Bergman

Katharine Hepburn

Elizabeth Taylor. Courtesy 20th Century Fox

Claudette Colbert. Courtesy Columbia Pictures

Merle Oberon. Courtesy Columbia Pictures

Joan Crawford

Greta Garbo

Dolores Del Rio

Grace Kelly

Marilyn Monroe

Carole Lombard. Courtesy Columbia Pictures

Jean Harlow

203

Their Individual Looks Became Their Trademark

Marlene Dietrich

Rita Hayworth. Courtesy Columbia Pictures

Clark Gable. Courtesy Columbia Pictures

Ronald Colman. Courtesy Columbia Pictures

Stewart Granger. Courtesy Columbia Pictures

Cornel Wilde. Courtesy Columbia Pictures

Robert Taylor

John Garfield

Paul Newman with Joanne Woodward

William Holden

Gary Cooper

Burt Lancaster

James Cagney

Humphrey Bogart

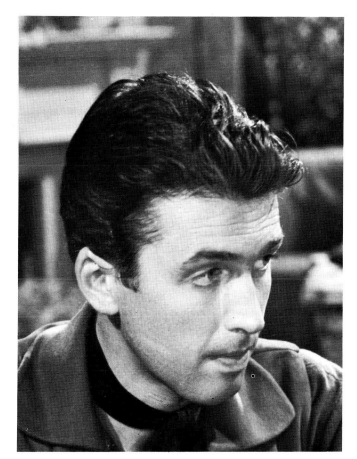

James Stewart

Rex Harrison. Courtesy 20th Century Fox

David Niven

Cary Grant

Spencer Tracy

Leslie Howard

Louise Rainer in *The Good Earth*. (retouched) To create the effect of an Oriental character appropriate base color was applied as well as eye pieces and wig. Metro-Goldwyn-Mayer

Katharine Hepburn in *Dragon Seed*. (retouched) A deeper base color has been applied here. Also notice the eye pieces attached for an Oriental effect. Metro-Goldwyn-Mayer

Agnes Moorehead in *Dragon Seed*. (retouched) In addition to the eye pieces, notice the nose piece and heavier painting used to create an Oriental face. Metro-Goldwyn-Mayer

Anna Demetrio in *Dragon Seed*. (retouched) Heavy work has been done on the face to achieve an aging Oriental appearance: bald pate, eye pieces, jowls, eye bags, nose piece, and lip pieces. The work is excellent. Metro-Goldwyn-Mayer

Nils Asther in *Bitter Tea of Gen Yen.* (retouched) The theatrical structure of the eyes and bald pate illustrate the concepts used in the early days of film. Courtesy Columbia Pictures

Paul Muni in *The Good Earth.* (retouched) A modern concept of achieving Oriental effects: eyelids, false nose, and bald pate. Edges are softened. Metro-Goldwyn-Mayer

Henry Travers in *Dragon Seed.* (retouched) For an aging Oriental male character, a wispy beard and mustache have been added along with the eye pieces, eyebrows, and nose. Metro-Goldwyn-Mayer

Paul E. Burns in *Dragon Seed.* (retouched) In addition to the eyelids, bald pate wig, mustache, and brows, age stipple was applied to create wrinkling. Metro-Goldwyn-Mayer

Greer Garson in *Valley of Decision.* (retouched) Eye, cheek, and jowl pieces are the foundations for a much greater attempt at creating age than is usual for films, especially with female characters. Metro-Goldwyn-Mayer

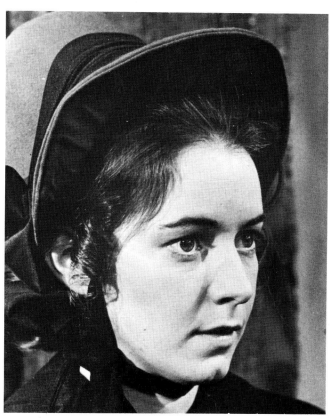

Kitty Winn in *Harriet.* (retouched) A simple corrective makeup is applied for the youngest stage of aging in this story of Harriet Beecher Stowe. Photo Luigi Pelletieri. Courtesy WNET Television

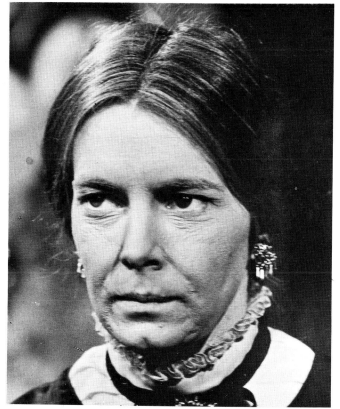

Kitty Winn in *Harriet.* (retouched) Latex jowls, eye pouches, and nose wrinkle carry the role to middle age. Photo Luigi Pelletieri. Courtesy WNET Television

Kitty Winn in *Harriet.* (retouched) Chin pieces carrying up to and on to the lower and upper lips, age stipple, and white wig complete this final transformation of the character. Photo Luigi Pelletieri. Courtesy WNET Television

Robert Donat in *Good-bye, Mr. Chips.* (retouched) The youth of Mr. Chips is accentuated by abundant hair, full mustache, and soft makeup. Metro-Goldwyn-Mayer

Robert Donat in *Good-bye, Mr. Chips.* (retouched) The age of the character is accomplished simply. Notice how the wig and mustache suggest so much of the aging. The shading is subtle and skillfully done. Metro-Goldwyn-Mayer

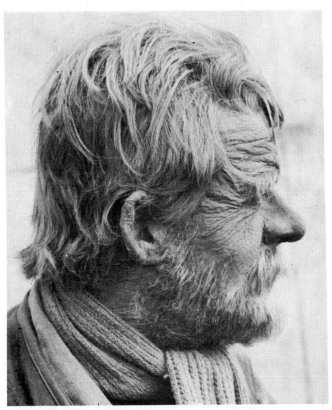

Hal Holbrook. (unretouched) Cotton and latex stipple was used here, along with a rubber nose. The beard and mustache, both hairpieces, were used to accentuate the aging.

Hal Holbrook. (unretouched) Here is the same performer shown in full face. The hair was bleached and then dyed to this gray color.

Jean Marais in *Beauty and the Beast*. (retouched) Although an early attempt at this makeup problem, this is one of the best of the man-beast concepts. Lopert

Jean Marais in *Beauty and the Beast*. (retouched) The beauty kisses the beast and she restores him to his original loveliness. Notice the exaggerated methods used of suggesting a youthful, handsome male. Lopert

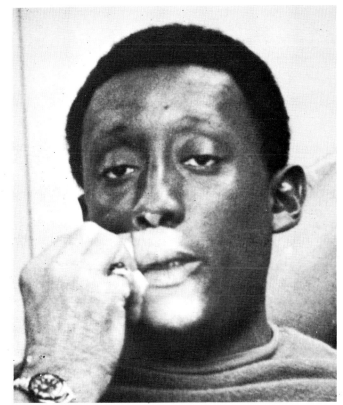

Godfrey Cambridge preparing for *Watermelon Man*. (unretouched) It is unusual for a black performer to have the opportunity to play a character role, let alone play a Caucasian. Here the makeup artist is beginning to apply the appropriate base. Courtesy Columbia Pictures

Godfrey Cambridge in *Watermelon Man*. (retouched) The performer's skin color has been totally changed. The wig and eyebrows and discreet shading produce a commendable effect. Courtesy Columbia Pictures

Henry Croach in *The Incident*. (unretouched) A rather unwholesome character was created with a bruise, stubble beard, and painted age. Courtesy 20th Century Fox. © 1967 20th Century Fox Film Corporation. All rights reserved.

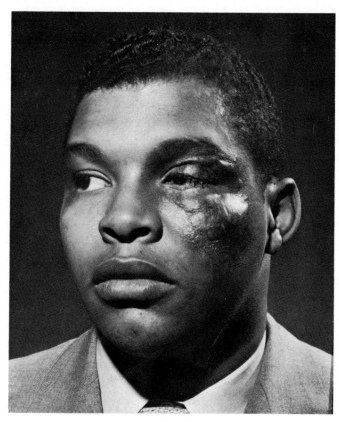

Coley Wallace in *The Joe Louis Story*. (unretouched) The area around the eye was built up with nose putty so that it appeared to be swollen. The performer wore this for a long hot day of shooting. United Artists

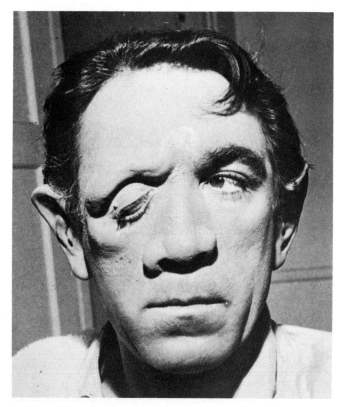

Anthony Quinn in *The Hunchback of Notre Dame*. (retouched) Face pieces were applied around the eye and nose to produce extreme distortion of these areas. The work is obvious, yet suitable for the purpose of this film. Allied Artists

Ben Piazza in *World in White*. (unretouched) By using the methods described in Chapter Twelve, dirt, bruises, and blood are easily created. Produced by CBS Television

Bela Lugosi in *Ape Man*. (retouched) Reversing Darwin's process, Man is transformed into an ape with wig and beard. Monogram

Lon Chaney, Jr. in *Wolf Man*. (retouched) A somewhat more elaborate feat is accomplished with the addition of artificial nose and teeth and eye pouches as well as the wig and beard. Universal

Roddy McDowall in *Beneath the Planet of the Apes*. (retouched) A very contemporary chimpanzee is created with superb rubber mask pieces, wig, and beard. Courtesy 20th Century Fox. © 1969 Apjac Productions, Inc. and 20th Century Fox Corp.

Maurice Evans in *Beneath the Planet of the Apes*. (retouched) Another brilliant use of face pieces, here to match the appearance of an orangutan. Courtesy 20th Century Fox. © 1969 Apjac Productions, Inc. and 20th Century Fox Corp.

Frank Morgan in *The Wizard of Oz.* (retouched) Very brilliant work was performed in the makeup for *The Wizard of Oz.* Look carefully and you will see the wig, eyebrows, rubber nose, cheek, and chin pieces used to create the character of the Wizard himself. Metro-Goldwyn-Mayer

Jack Haley in *The Wizard of Oz.* (retouched) It was an artistic feat to create a tin man without losing or concealing the identity of the actor. Metro-Goldwyn-Mayer

Ray Bolger in *The Wizard of Oz.* (retouched) In the remarkable creation of the Scarecrow, burlap fabric was carried up the neck onto the cheeks. The actor's personality is still retained. Metro-Goldwyn-Mayer

Bert Lahr in *The Wizard of Oz.* (retouched) Lahr's personality emerges from the forehead piece, eye piece, eye bags, nose, jowls, and wig. Metro-Goldwyn-Mayer

Brian Aherne in *Juarez*. (retouched) The beard captures the classic simplicity of an elegant period. It is truly aristocratic. Warner Bros.

Bela Lugosi in *Evil of Frankenstein*. (retouched) The shaggy wig and beard are used to good effect in this film. Universal

Raymond Edward Johnson in *Mr. Bell*. (unretouched) Another superb full wig, beard, and mustache used to age the character within the style of the period.

Akim Tamiroff in *The Buccaneer*. (retouched) A simple stubble and sweeping mustache suit the incomparable Tamiroff face perfectly. Paramount

In *Married to the Mob* Michelle Pfeiffer made a total character change through simple use of a full wig of another color. © Orion Pictures Corp. All Rights Reserved.

To create a realistic Willy Loman, Dustin Hoffman shaved his hair, added a thin hair piece, and used stippling for aging the skin. Permission courtesy of Dustin Hoffman.

Morgan Freeman used simple aging effects for his character in *Driving Miss Daisy*. © 1989 Warner Bros. Inc. All Rights Reserved.

Ben Kingsley's portrayal of the title character in *Gandhi* is one of the most successful transformations an actor has made into the actual historical personage. © 1982 Columbia Pictures, Inc. All Rights Reserved.

Cicely Tyson at her second stage of transformation, having aged from a young woman to a middle-aged matron, in *The Autobiography of Miss Jane Pittman*. T.E. Acquisition Co., Inc. All Rights Reserved.

For Tyson's final stage of transformation, she used a full wig and extensive stippling as well as foam latex pieces. The effect is superb. T.E. Acquisition Co., Inc. All Rights Reserved.

The very effective scarring of Tom Berenger in *Platoon* added enormously to the villainous nature of the character he created. © 1986 Helmdale Films. All Rights Reserved. Photo: Ricky Francisco.

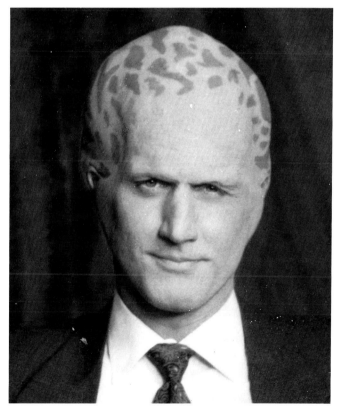

Eric Pierpoint in the TV show *Alien Nation* demonstrates the enormous results that can be accomplished by the skillful use of a dramatic bald cap. © 1989 Twentieth Century Fox Film Corp. All Rights Reserved. Photo: Brian Davis.

LIST OF SUPPLIERS

Ben Nye Company, Inc.
11571 Santa Monica Blvd.
Los Angeles, CA 90025
(213) 477-0443
Manufactures a complete line of theatrical makeup, including a large color range in foundation bases, rouges, highlights and shadows, eyeshadows, and lipsticks for all skin tones. Also makes a series of special effects products. Catalog and price list on request.

Mehron Inc.
45E Route 303
Valley Cottage, NY 10989
(914) 268-4106
Produces a complete line of theatrical makeup, including a large color range in foundation bases, rouges, highlights and shadows, eyeshadows, and lipsticks for all skin tones. Other products include spirit gum, crepe hair, latex, and cleansers for film, TV, and stage. Catalog and price list on request.

Cinema Secrets
4400 Riverside Dr.
Burbank, CA 91505
(818) 846-0579
Manufactures bald caps, prosthetic face pieces and noses, eye bags, etc. Supplies liquid cap material, adhesive remover, blood, blood gel. (Bald caps are made from John Chambers' original formula and set on Chambers' custom-made blocks).

Max Factor & Co.
12100 Wilshire Blvd.
Los Angeles, CA 90025
(213) 442-2000
Produces pancakes and pansticks. Materials are available from the above address or from drug stores and cosmetic counters.

Ira Senz Wigs
13 East 47th St.
New York, NY 10017
(212) 752-6800
Makes wigs, toupees, and hair pieces. Rents wigs and hairpieces. Supplies theatrical and motion picture makeup. Materials available at above address.

Wig Creations Ltd.
12 Old Burlington St.
London W1X2PX, England
Supplies wigs and hairpieces for hire or purchase; facial hair; theatrical and private wear; hair to pattern or in bulk.

Clairol
345 Park Ave.
New York, NY 10154
(212) 546-3289
Manufactures a portable makeup mirror, hair care appliances and products, and a complete range of hair colors. Produces the skin astringent Sea Breeze. Materials available at most drug stores, cosmetic outlets, and from the above address.

Blistex Inc.
1800 Swift Dr.
Oak Brook, IL 60521
(708) 571-2870
Manufactures Blistex creams for chapped lips and cold sores. Available at drug stores, cosmetic counters, and at the above address.

Johnson & Johnson
One Johnson & Johnson Plaza
New Brunswick, NJ 08933
(201) 524-0400
Makes fast setting bandages, gauze bandages, and surgical adhesive. Available at drug stores.

Becker-Parkin Dental Supply Co.
245 7th Ave.
New York, NY 10001
(212) 243-6696
Supplies impression material for use in creating molds, including D.P. Elastic Impression Cream by Teledyne-Getz and the dust-free alginate Jeltrate Plus by L.D. Caulk.

Utricht Manufaturing Corp.
33 35th St.
Brooklyn, NY 11232
(718) 768-2525
Manufactures artists brushes. Available at artists' supply shops, or from the above address. (EAST COAST)

Daniel Smith
4130 First Ave. South
Seattle, WA 98134
(206) 223-9599
Supplies artists' brushes. (WEST COAST)

INDEX

Edited by Susan E. Meyer
Designed by James Craig and Bob Fillie
Demonstration photographs by Susan E. Meyer
Composed in nine point Helvetica by University Graphics, Inc.
Printed and bound in Japan by Toppan Printing Company Ltd.